CONTENTS

POPULAR MUSIC

What is popular music?

Popular music is an expression of youth culture, the crucial ingredient in an advertising mix, life's ecstasies and agonies distilled into song, unforgettable tunes that capture moments in time – and these are only some of the features of the phenomenon. This broad and eclectic category has grown to embrace many different interpretations, including blues, ragtime, jazz, rock 'n' roll, soul, hip hop, dub, jungle and acid, all of which have happily developed alongside mainstream ballads and show songs. Often using simple tunes and lyrics, yet capable of emotional and technical complexity, popular music is perhaps the most difficult aspect of music to define, while continuing to be a major force in our society.

There is a myriad of styles, influences and subcultures surrounding popular music today, but the key characteristics are:

1 It is created for profit, adulation, and often both;
2 The melody is memorable and/or the rhythm is danceable;
3 The content is immediately relevant and attractive to the target listener;
4 It is capable of performance by an amateur.

TASK

- Test the validity of this statement by matching these four points to the current five bestselling singles on a checklist or grid.

Popular music, commonly in the form of a song with accompaniment, is designed for easy listening by the majority culture and was initially communicated and developed through oral tradition. One of the effects of the Industrial Revolution was to create a large middle class with disposable income, and popular music – providing both amusement and escape – became a potent social diversion.

Judged solely by popularity, its success was monitored first by the sales of sheet music then by record, cassette and CD. Unlike serious music it is mostly geared towards entertainment, although several movements in the early part of this century and in the 1960s, for example, sought to use it for political or social comment.

At the turn of the twentieth century two major musical forces were to determine the tradition: the influence of Afro-American music and Tin Pan Alley. Black music evolved from older folk music and challenged white cultural domination. One style, which contains distinctive black music elements and maintains a strong influence on musicians today, is the blues.

The blues

Originally taken from the sixteenth-century expression 'blue devils', this term refers to music originating mainly in the deep south of the USA. The sentiments describe the unique experience of black Americans of suffering, loneliness and poverty. The blues flourished after the Civil War, developing from work songs sung by slaves in the cotton plantations to relieve appalling monotony and harsh conditions. The melody was contained within twelve bars, made up of three four-bar phrases. Lyrics were normally constructed in three-line stanzas with the second line repeating the first, often in iambic pentameter. The classic song 'St Louis Blues', written by W.C. Handy in 1914, demonstrates the mood and structure:

I hate to see de ev'nin' sun go down
Hate to see de ev'nin' sun go down
Cause my baby, he done lef dis town.

Feelin' tomorrow lak ah feel today
Feelin' tomorrow lak ah feel today
I'll pack my trunk make me get away . . .

Instrumentation was simple at first, perhaps with acoustic guitar, banjo or harmonica or whatever was portable and accessible. As the style developed other characteristics became evident, for example blue notes which are the flattened third, seventh and fifth of the diatonic scale, syncopation (emphasising the off beat), instrumental breaks and improvisation. These elements were to influence all of popu-

Figure 1.1 *Big Bill Broonzy*

lar music, but jazz in particular. Singers of the blues from the past include Ma Rainey, Bessie Smith, Robert Johnson and Billie Holiday. Today great names include Muddy Waters, John Lee Hooker and B.B. King.

Another black music style which developed simultaneously with blues was ragtime. Originating as dance music (ragging) in the late nineteenth century, it was replaced by jazz in the 1920s. Ragtime is identified mainly with piano music, and involved highly-syncopated right-hand melodies contrasting with a steady but leaping left hand. Ragtime pieces are normally in 2/2 or 4/4 time with chromatic musical lines, which challenge the perfomer considerably. The most famous composer of ragtime music was Scott Joplin, whose music was popularised in the film *The Sting*, starring Robert Redford and Paul Newman. The theme music from *The Sting* is Joplin's 'The Entertainer'.

TIN PAN ALLEY

The other crucial influence on the tradition of popular music at the turn of the nineteenth century was Tin Pan Alley. The expression was derived from the racket created by hard-pressed New York commercial songwriters who were second-rate pianists. The noise was described by a musician walking through West 28th Street as sounding like 'tin pans'.

Music publishers employed professional songwriters to compose songs on West 28th Street and rush them down to the demonstration rooms for potential buyers. There were three main aims for this new commercial music. The songs had to be fashionable in style, have an element of social awareness and appeal to the public's emotions. Typically these songs had only two verses and a long 32-bar chorus. The verses functioned as recitative in opera – to move the narrative along and, importantly, the chorus contained a memorable melodic hook. The chorus was often in AABA form, with each section of eight bars in length.

This format set the pattern for many popular songs, and examples around this time include 'Alexander's Ragtime Band' by Irving Berlin and 'My Blue Heaven' by Walter Donaldson.

TASK

- Assess the influence of Tin Pan Alley and the blues on three different styles of popular music.

Jazz

Meanwhile in New Orleans a melting pot of styles including blues, ragtime, marching bands, black folk work songs and spirituals was bubbling over. Jazz music was on its way.

Characterised by improvisation, unique instrumental tone, riffs, breaks, polyrhythms and other effects, this style has influenced much of popular and serious music.

TRAD JAZZ

First came Dixieland or New Orleans jazz, which later became known as trad (traditional) jazz to distinguish it from the more modern forms (swing, bebop and the cool school). Often based on the form and harmony of marching tunes, this style was greatly improvised incorporating blue notes, a fast driving beat and considerable syncopation.

At this point simple instrumentation included:

1 a rhythm section consisting of either a string bass or tuba together with guitar or banjo
2 a brass section, which played the melody or harmony, of cornets, trumpets and trombones and
3 a reed section initially consisting of two clarinets and later saxophones in the 1920s.

As the style spread and increased in popularity, the bands grew in size and sophistication, for example the King Oliver Band. One legendary musician, Louis Armstrong, went north with his unique style of solo trumpet playing and voice sculpted from asphalt, leaving behind the collective band playing associated with New Orleans.

SWING

This big band sound developed into swing in the 1930s. A truly cosmopolitan style with the compelling ingredients of strong riffs, authority of tone and elusive hesitating rhythms, the swing thing travelled the globe. The mixing of hot and sweet modes was central to the style. Hot jazz was represented by blistering solo playing while sweet jazz exploited the mel-

lower sound of the reed and brass sections. The saxophone added character to this carefully-arranged music and many famous names emerged from the swing era. Arrangers such as Glenn Miller created unique sounds and versions of popular songs and recorded soloists such as Benny Goodman and Lester Young remain popular today.

BEBOP, REBOP OR BOP

Reacting against the meticulously-arranged big-band sound of swing, bebop music was fast, complex, more free-form and usually performed in small groups. The name bebop is onomatopoeic, created from the short rhythmic phrasing of improvised saxophone or trumpet playing. New roles developed for some instruments – the double bass providing rhythmic counterpoint as well as melodic progression; drum patterns were more adventurous and complementary, with greater reliance on brushes and cymbals; while the piano playing was less intrusive, allowing space for the front-line horns to extemporise. In the smoky, all-night jazz clubs of the late 1940s and early 1950s, the small combo of piano, bass, drums, trumpet and saxophone became the typical band.

Depending on modern harmony with dissonant chords, classic rules were bent and almost

broken as more unusual notes became acceptable and denser musical textures developed. References to known tunes were injected into the complex weave of rhythms and other melodies for amusement. Caribbean rhythms were introduced and players accented the second and fourth beats in the bar rather than the traditional first and third. Later musicians accented off the beat altogether.

Great names such as Art Tatum, Charlie Parker, Lester Young and Dizzy Gillespie were central to the bebop movement and reading *To Bop or Not to Bop*, Dizzy Gillespie's notorious autobiography, brings this period to life.

With bop, jazz became recognised as a serious art form for the first time and the style evolved into the so-called modern jazz of the 1950s and 1960s.

Figure 1.2   *Harlem's Cotton Club*

COOL JAZZ, HARD BOP AND RECENT TRENDS

A lighter and more lyrical style of jazz known as cool jazz vied for popularity with hard bop in the 1950s. The relaxed rhythms of cool jazz provided the perfect backdrop and foil to hard bop, a dynamic New York jazz style with even more intensity and complexity than its forefather, bop.

In the 1960s Miles Davis began improvising on modes rather than traditional western diatonic scales and their harmonies, leading to greater freedom of musical structure and sound. Miles Davis also incorporated electronic rock music instruments, heralding a new jazz and a turning point for the future of style fusion. In the late 1960s Ornette Coleman developed a compositional theory in which harmony, tempo and melody were of equal importance. He became a central figure in the jazz avant garde, with its free playing and intensity of emotion.

Today all jazz styles are popular and jazz fusions such as acid jazz, soul-jazz and jazz funk celebrate the innovators of the past and other contemporary styles of popular music.

TASKS

- Create a chart of the history of jazz. Decade by decade list the key styles, musicians, stylistic features and examples of music.
- Select one jazz style and give a talk to your fellow musicians, playing musical examples where possible.

The 1950s

The world was recovering from the end of the Second World War and society was changing rapidly. Two new phrases hit America in the 1950s which were to change things for ever – teenagers and rock 'n' roll. Before the 1950s teenagers had no music (or money) to call their own. While Frank Sinatra set the bobby-soxers screaming and swooning in the 1940s, other crooners such as Bing Crosby appealed to an older generation which did not even recognise the existence of teenagers. Rock 'n' roll, and the freedom of youth it represented, became the strongest movement the establishment had ever witnessed.

 News headlines

Although the Second World War was over, peace was short-lived. The Korean War, France's war in Vietnam, the Suez invasion and the Hungarian Uprising all darkened the 1950s. In America Senator Joseph McCarthy of Wisconsin started a witchhunt against communists and communist sympathisers in all walks of life, and actors, writers and artists were summoned to appear before the Permanent Subcommittee on Investigations. Martin Luther King, a young black baptist minister and civil rights campaigner, began to promote racial equality and was involved in a black boycott of segregated buses in Alabama, forcing the White House to take notice.

The blatant racism in America hindered the development of popular music. Black R & B (rhythm and blues) for example, was denied airplay on white radio stations, but a breakthrough was initiated by the forward-thinking Cleveland D.J. Alan Freed. Realising that white teenagers would far rather listen to R&B than the light and classical music he was instructed to play by the management, Freed created an underground communication line. In 1951 he persuaded the racist management to give him a nightly show for white teenagers entitled Moondogs' Rock 'n' Roll Party. The show was an enormous success, attracting high ratings within weeks with its new style of presentation of jive patter, teenage humour and, of course, banned black music.

ROCK 'N' ROLL

The new music caused a sensation throughout the world. Young people, desperate for their own identity, immersed themselves in rock 'n' roll and the first pop music sub-culture. Fashion, dancing, shocking the establishment and the teen idol syndrome were as important to the rock 'n' roll movement as the music itself. The film industry began to acknowledge the teenager head on. When a leather-clad Marlon Brando roared onto screen as leader of a motorcycle gang in a film called *The Wild One* in 1953, and James Dean smouldered in *Rebel Without a Cause* in 1955, teenagers the world over identified with the stars and yearned for more.

A film called *The Blackboard Jungle* caused futher mayhem. Released in 1955 it featured good-guy teacher Glenn Ford battling for respect from Bronx hoodlums like Sidney Poitier. Over the opening credits, Bill Haley and the Comets played the song which was to become the great rock 'n' roll anthem – 'Rock Around the Clock'. The immediate media

Figure 1.3 *Bill Haley and the Comets*

exposure the film and song gained, communicated rock 'n' roll to the establishment as evil, delinquent and anarchic.

The music was raw, energetic, simply arranged and based on blues formats with light, fun lyrics. 'Shake, Rattle and Roll', 'Rip It Up' and 'See You Later, Alligator' were typical of the style and became further hits for Bill Haley and the Comets. With strong hooks and riffs these songs made you want to get up and dance and

Bill Haley, with his out-going personality and hair styled into a giant comma on his forehead, presented a distinctive image as lead singer.

Entertaining images for other perfomers became part of the rock 'n' roll sub-culture. Haley's cow-lick haircut seemed mild in comparson to singer and guitarist Chuck Berry, who slid and duck-walked his way across the world's stages playing a unique style of rhythm 'n' blues yoked with country runs and advertising slogans of the day. 'Sweet Little Sixteen', 'Roll Over Beethoven', 'No Particular Place to Go', 'Johnny B Goode' and 'Memphis, Tennessee' were Chuck Berry classics still played today.

Even more flamboyant was Little Richard who pouted, strutted and teased his audiences, often wearing make-up and flowing silks. Screaming the opening scat line 'a bop bop a loom op a bop bop boom!' of 'Tutti Frutti', he escalated the already-mounting hysteria of the older generation by introducing a new mystifying language exclusive to youth. Gene Vincent hit the television news headlines with his new song title 'Be Bop a Lula'. One newscaster asked the nation, 'What on earth does this mean?'

Meanwhile a Mississippi truck driver called Elvis Presely, ten years Haley's junior, was stunning audiences with his blues singing, wild dancing and dark good looks. After his first hit with the bluesy 'Heartbreak Hotel' in 1956, Elvis quickly became rock's first sex symbol. Presley was sensational on stage, causing riots and appealing to both sexes. He developed an outrageous and shocking act, including wrig-

gling his hips sexily to the music, letting his hair fall over his eyes and leering and grinning at the girls. All tame behaviour nowadays, but waist-down shots of Elvis the Pelvis were strictly forbidden on television.

Presley was nicknamed the 'King' of rock 'n' roll. His emotionally-charged distinctive voice and unique phrasing sold songs such as 'Jailhouse Rock', 'Hound Dog', 'All Shook Up' and 'Blue Suede Shoes' throughout the world, and sensitive ballads such as 'Love Me Tender' appealed to every generation.

Unlike many rock 'n' rollers whose fame was both found and lost within the 1950s, Elvis continued to be successful in the film and recording industries until he died. Even today millions listen to the sound and commemorate the life of Elvis Presley.

So the first pop sub-culture was born. Fashion, film culture, image and the role of the superstar all started with rock 'n' roll. This was to grow even greater in the 1960s.

TASKS

- Write a profile on three major rock 'n' rollers, including Elvis Presley, gathering pictures and information on their hit songs, lifestyles and images.
- Interview a relative or friend about life in the 1950s. Build up a backdrop on which to set the music. What were people wearing? What media were they into? What were the big news items of the decade? What are the differences between then and now?

The 1960s

The 'swinging sixties' represented a time of further change – morally, politically and socially. The youth movement, beginning with rock 'n' roll in the 1950s, was to find its expression in a freer, less class-conscious and more permissive society. Revolutions in fashion, music, literature and the arts were created and communicated to the media on a world-wide scale. Mini-skirts, thigh-length boots, the wet look, unisex long hairstyles, kaftans and beads all appeared on the world's high streets to shock and excite, and sexual and social taboos were eroded with the arrival of the contraceptive pill and the marijuana joint. The change of pace was so fast it left many of the older generation bewildered.

★ *News headlines*

Advances in technology were also transforming society. The world watched in astonishment throughout the 1960s as the American and Soviet space race unfolded. The Russians achieved a double coup with Yuri Gagarin, the first man in space, and two years later Valentina Tereshkova became the first woman in space.

The development of heart transplant surgery was another important technological advance which gave hope to many.

The youthful democrat John F. Kennedy was elected President of the United States in 1961 and was gunned down just two years later in the streets of Dallas. His brother, Senator Robert Kennedy, was also assassinated just after celebrating his success in the California primary election for the Democratic presidential nomination. The civil rights movement, led by Martin Luther King, fought on for equality but, tragically, Dr King was killed by a white gunman in 1968.

In the arts and media world Rudolf Nureyev, a leading dancer with Leningrad's Kirov ballet, defected to the west and Marilyn Monroe, American actress and sex symbol whose films included classics like *Some Like it Hot* and the *Seven Year Itch*, died in 1962. Her death was ruled as a possible suicide but is still shrouded in mystery, and Elton John was to write a hit song about her life called 'Candle in the Wind', later dedicated to Diana, Princess of Wales following her untimely death in a road accident in 1997. Another sex symbol of the 1960s was the French actress Brigitte Bardot, often compared to Marilyn Monroe.

Mickey Mouse celebrated his 40th birthday in the 1960s and films such as *Mary Poppins*, *The Sound of Music*, *Goldfinger* and *Butch Cassidy and the Sundance Kid* achieved box-office success. Pop art came to power with artists such as Andy Warhol and Roy Lichtenstein. Flourishing first in Britain and then in New York, a typical pop art show featured mass production images, comic strips and inflatable everyday objects and food.

Pop music began to reflect society and the art world. Using a universal language, it described and relayed to the world the most radical decade ever experienced.

TASK

- Prepare yourself for a study of 1960s music by creating a portfolio on the decade in small groups. Topics to research could include politics, the media, the arts and fashion.

MUSIC OF THE 1960s

The new trends created in the 1960s continue to influence rock musicians today and, in contrast to the1950s, Britain became a dominating force throughout the decade.

Skiffle was the first new style which had been developing from the late 1950s in Britain, through jazz traditionalists seeking to revive American country blues roots. Loose, rhythmic, high in energy, comprising acoustic guitar, washboard with thimbles and tea-chest bass, this music was playable by anyone anywhere and had immediate appeal for young people. In particular, jazz musician Lonnie Donegan made skiffle famous with his top-ten chart song 'Rock Island Line' in 1956. Donegan's music inspired skiffle groups to spring up across the country including one called The Quarrymen, initiated by the young John Lennon.

However, in the early 1960s skiffle ceased to challenge those groups who could play more than two or three chords. Some of these bands evolved into rock 'n' roll groups but with a more aggressive image, based on rebel heroes like James Dean and Marlon Brando.

Meanwhile an exciting new movement was gathering momentum in the North West of England. As a thriving port, Liverpool was at the cutting edge of the music scene with its direct access to new rock 'n' roll and R&B sounds via seamen in the Merchant navy. Local bands started playing a synthesis of American styles to young people desperate for dance music. This merging of musical styles soon developed into beat music which became known as the Merseybeat sound.

Intrinsic to the sound was the live club feel.

Figure 1.4   *British skiffle band featuring Lonnie Donegan*

The trendiest venue in Liverpool was the Cavern Club where many famous names of the 1960s performed including Cilla Black, The Beatles, Billy Fury, Gerry and the Pacemakers and The Swinging Blue Jeans.

TASKS

- Compile a list of beat groups around in the early 1960s and write a profile on three.
- Take one beat song and discuss the synthesis of styles as mentioned above.

THE BEATLES

With their original sound, excellent musicianship and song-writing talent, The Beatles stood out from their contemporaries at the Cavern Club. Discovered in Liverpool in 1961 by Brian Epstein, a local record shop manager, John Lennon, Paul McCartney, George Harrison and Pete Best impressed him with their unique musical combinations and commitment. Epstein immediately tried to sign The Beatles up with some major London record companies, but was turned down many times over. Eventually George Martin, head of Parlophone, recognised their talent with a signing in 1962, replacing Pete Best with Ringo Starr as drummer.

This major breakthrough represented two further important developments: The Beatles encouraged other artists to write their own songs and gain more control in production and they broke London's stranglehold on the music scene, making Liverpool the centre of attention. For a while A&R managers were frantic to sign up anyone with a guitar and a scouse accent. After learning the ropes of performing the hard way on the notorious Rieperbahn in Hamburg and meeting photographer Astrid Kirchherr who created their mop-style hair-cuts, Beatlemania swamped Britain and early chart-topping hits with new drummer Ringo Starr included 'Please, Please Me', 'She Loves You' and 'I Want to Hold Your Hand'.

The Beatles revitalised the British pop scene as never before and a study of their music tells the story of the 1960s generation. The group's earlier music had been based on rock 'n' roll. Simple tunes were coloured with the occasional interesting harmony giving force to straightforward lyrics about falling in and out of love. By the mid 1960s, however, The Beatles were setting new artistic trends. In 1964, 'A Hard Day's Night' was released as an album, a single and a documentary film – the first of its kind. In 1965 lyrics were becoming more complex and reflective. 'Yesterday' presented soul-searching lyrics and unusual harmonic changes. 'Paperback Writer' reflected the cut-throat world of publishing and tabloid journalism and 'Eleanor Rigby' commented on the universal theme of loneliness. 'Eleanor Rigby' also heralded an important progression in recording techniques and musical thought. A string quartet and collage effects were employed in the song and, for the first time, a merging of styles, cultures and even centuries was taking place in popular music.

In the late 1960s flower power and the peace movement affected the rock world. Fashions became soft and flowing and both sexes dressed in kaftans, Jesus sandals and wore their hair long. The Beatles became interested in Eastern mysticism and were particularly influenced by the Indian guru Maharishi Mahesh Yogi. They took part in transcendental meditation courses. In 1967 the album *Sgt. Pepper's*

Lonely Hearts Club Band was released. This album was a social commentary of the times through music and lyrics which broke new boundaries in five main ways:

1 it was a concept album, a new way of presenting an idea through a collection of songs;
2 the songs were linked with no pause between;
3 sleeve lyrics were included;
4 collage effects were used freely;
5 The Beatles had equal control in the studio.

The profound influence of this album, and others such as *Revolver* and the *White Album*, on both serious and popular music remains today. In a recent HMV Poll, albums of the Beatles scored highly.

By the end of the decade there was a great deal of friction in the band. Brian Epstein had died of a drugs and alcohol overdose and relations between band members were tense. The Beatles' last album and single, entitled *Let it Be*, was released in 1970.

Figure 1.5 *The Beatles in the* Sgt. Pepper's *era, June 1967*

TASKS

- Really get to know the music of The Beatles. In groups study three songs, one each from the early, middle and late 1960s. Jot down comments on the instrumentation, lyrics, style and unusual recording features of the times. Keep the information in a portfolio for the group.
- Although the names Lennon and McCartney are given equal billing on songs, in reality they rarely composed together. Lennon's songs were often intensely personal, whereas McCartney tended to use the third person and objective narrative. See if you can identify the real composer for the three songs you have selected above.
- Find out all you can about the producer George Martin. Start building up a new portfolio on music producers.

THE ROLLING STONES AND OTHER BRITISH ARTISTS

Back in the early 1960s, while The Beatles were promoting a positive and appealing profile both to fans and the media, a new London band called the Rolling Stones gatecrashed into the limelight. Refusing to conform in dress or behaviour, this band courted negative publicity. In August 1964 *The Mirror* lambasted The Stones by saying: 'If ever parents of Britain are almost united, it must surely be in their dislike of those shaggy-haired discoveries ... they are the anti-parent symbol'.

The music and image of the Rolling Stones and The Beatles were poles apart. While The Beatles looked to rock 'n' roll and smoother elements of black music for inspiration and were chiefly concerned with creating and performing music, the Stones sought out the rawest sides of blues and rhythm and blues to reinforce their equally important wild image. Mick Jagger, with his arrogant, electrifying and overtly sexual performances on stage, caused even more outrage than Elvis the Pelvis.

The Rolling Stones started out by singing R&B songs and other covers. Their first Top 20 hit, 'I Wanna Be Your Man', was written by The Beatles and soon further hits followed such as 'It's All Over Now' and 'Little Red Rooster'. Eventually Mick Jagger and Keith Richards began penning their own material and notorious songs such as 'The Last Time' and '(I Can't Get No) Satisfaction' burst onto the pop scene.

The Rolling Stones inspired a whole new R&B movement mostly based in London. Central to this movement was Alexis Korner, who idolised Muddy Waters and snubbed the blues purists by introducing electric guitars into his bands. More importantly, he formed a group called Blues Incorporated which many notable musicians including Charlie Watts, Jack Bruce, Ginger Baker, Long John Baldry and Paul Jones all passed through before establishing their own bands and identities. Great names like Eric Clapton, Georgie Fame, Jeff Beck, John Mayall and Steve Winwood emerged from the blues revival.

With The Beatles, the Rolling Stones, The Searchers, The Hollies, The Animals, The Hermits, Cliff Richard, The Dave Clark Five, Gerry and the Pacemakers and the phenomenal blues musicians referred to above, Britain seemed set to rule the world of pop music.

TASKS

- Research the Rolling Stones further by listing their hits and profiling the band, not forgetting their visionary manager Andrew Oldham.
- Write a profile of at least one other British group or solo artist chosen from those listed above.
- Listen to at least two Stones hits jotting down the instrumentation and blues elements within.

PSYCHEDELIC MUSIC

Emerging in the late 1960s psychedelic music or acid rock was deeply influenced by the acid drug culture. It was also inspired by The Beatles' album *Sergeant Pepper's Lonely Hearts Club Band* with its drug-oriented, surreal and dream-like qualities. A major feature of acid music was the light show which included visuals as well as music to recapture the whole LSD experience. In New York, a club called The Electric Circus enticed people into an enormous theatre in which songs would be lengthened to hours to recreate an entire acid trip. Performers like Jimi Hendrix would perform such ecstatic, sizzling and mind-blowing guitar that he would smash up his guitar just to keep the show on a high. This new direction was to encourage more theatre in rock music. British psychedelic bands included Pink Floyd and The Who with Pete Townsend, Roger Daltry and Keith Moon performing ferocious, exciting and often unpredictable music.

TASK

- Write a profile and listen to the music of one major psychedelic group or artist choosing from The Grateful Dead, Jefferson Airplane, The Who or Jimi Hendrix.

BACK IN THE USA

Meanwhile, in the USA, several big names and new music movements were emerging. The Beach Boys, for example, created surf music and sang in close harmony to a subtle rock beat. Songs written by Brian Wilson about Californian good living and sun-kissed sea and sand like 'Fun, Fun, Fun', 'Surfin' USA' and 'I Get Around' became international hits. Another close-harmony group, originally appearing in the late 1950s, were the Everly Brothers. Starting out as country singers with hits such as 'Bye, Bye Love' in 1957, the Brothers had further success into the mid 1960s with 'Wake Up Little Suzie' and 'All I Have To Do Is Dream'. With the advent of The Beatles, they bravely restyled their clothes, brushed their hair forward and hit the world with 'Love Is Strange'.

Another force on the American music scene during the decade was Roy Orbison. Dressed in black, scarcely moving a muscle and singing strong, tragic ballads Orbison flourished first in 1960 with 'Only The Lonely'. Other dramatic songs included 'Runnin' Scared', 'It's Over' and 'Oh, Pretty Woman', which became a huge hit, attracting even more acclaim in the 1990s as the title song of the film *Pretty Woman* starring Richard Gere and Julia Roberts.

Folk and protest music

The preserving of popular song or music through the oral tradition has lasted for generations. Internationally, the form exists in various styles, but there are essential similarities such as the use of modes, and a simple but effective narrative. In the 1930s and 1940s Woodie Guthrie revitalised the culture of American folk music using popular melodies as a vehicle for social comment or news, laying the foundations for later major protest singers of the 1960s such as Bob Dylan, Joan Baez and Pete Seeger.

Bob Dylan initially used traditional folk instruments in his music, such as acoustic guitar and harmonica. Singing about controversial topics of the day, he appealed to the intellectual student generation of the 1960s who staged marches and demonstrations to alert the world to the horrors of racism and the bomb. Songs such as 'Blowin' in the Wind', 'The Times They Are A-Changing' and 'Masters of War' reflected the impassioned feelings of the decade and influenced pop music history by merging country with rock and creating a sound so distinctive and original.

TASK

- Listen to some protest music of the 1960s, taking note of the instrumentation and the issues expressed in the songs.
- Do songs today reflect society? Talk about this, considering artists such as Billy Bragg and Prodigy.

Soul

From the start of the decade, new dynamic black music was gathering force in two American cities. In Detroit soul music was released under the Tamla and/or Motown labels, while in Memphis, Tennessee, soul was published by Stax records.

The Tamla Motown labels were created by Berry Gordy Junior, a songwriter and producer from Detroit. A major centre for the car industry, Gordy created the name Motown by contracting Detroit's nickname Motortown, and immediately signed up The Miracles and their talented lead singer/writer, Smokey Robinson. The company grew quickly and bought up other ailing Detroit labels. By the mid 1960s, Marvin Gaye, Sam Cooke, Stevie Wonder, The Four Tops, The Temptations, Martha and the Vandellas and The Supremes

had all signed with Motown and become international names. Apart from Robinson and Gordy, intrinsic to the legendary Motown sound were songwriters Holland, Dozier and Whitfield who generated much of the singers' success.

The Motown sound is difficult to define. At this point in its development, the music contained a free-sounding gospel element coupled to smoothed-out R&B styles with carefully-arranged, sophisticated backings featuring brass and use of the latest studio technology.

The Stax label in Memphis was initiated by Jim Stewart and his sister, Estelle Axton. In 1959 they teamed up with New Yorker Jerry Wexler of the Atlantic label and formed a tentative partnership which strengthened as soul music gained in popularity. A unique feature of the Stax label was the in-house band of phe-

Figure 1.6   *A classic Motown girl group – The Ronettes*

nomenally-talented musicians called Booker T and the MGs. This band laid the foundations of the Stax or Memphis sound. Central to the sound was the electrifying guitar playing of Steve Cropper upon which singers like Otis Redding, Wilson Pickett and Aretha Franklin added their distinctive voices.

Hailed as the King and Queen of soul were James Brown and Aretha Franklin. James Brown gave power to soul as dance music (see funk in the 1970s) and belted out hits such as 'Prisoner of Love', 'I Got You (I Feel Good)',

'Say It Loud, (I'm Black and I'm Proud)' and 'Get Up I Feel Like Being A Sex Machine'.

Aretha Franklin, raised on gospel music, stunned audiences in 1966 with her inimitable rendition of 'I Never Loved A Man (The Way I Love You)'. Signing to Atlantic, she soon scorched into the charts with 'Respect' and 'Natural Woman'.

Soul injected black music right into the heart of mainstream pop and with singers like Diana Ross, James Brown and Stevie Wonder, its high status was secured for the 1970s.

TASK

- Listen to as much soul music as possible and discuss with your fellow musicians the characteristics of the soul style in each song. List all the songs you hear.
- Carefully make listings of Stax, Atlantic and Tamla Motown artists and songs. Start a new portfolio for major recording labels.

The 1970s

'Too beautiful to live and too young to die' pronounced Marc Bolan, poet, singer, androgynous aesthete and creator of glam rock. Although Bolan was describing himself, these words reflected the pop music of the decade when precious, ephemeral styles like new romanticism, glam, glitter and disco held momentary fame. Even punk rock, loudly and aggressively reacting against all that represented the establishment, lasted only a few years. Black music, however, proved to be more far-reaching.

MUSIC OF THE 1970S

The flamboyant, quicksilver pop culture trends dominating the decade did not endure the quality test of time. While entertaining, colourful, often stylish and boldly attention seeking, many lacked substance and sincerity.

Glam rock

First to strut onto the 1970s stage were the glam or glitter rockers. Following Marc Bolan's lead and reacting against hard rock and

politically-motivated folk music of the late 1960s, this theatrical and fashion-conscious sub-culture injected a sexual glamour into British pop music. Immediately attracting the new generation of impressionable teenagers, Marc Bolan, a beautiful pixie with a glitter-dusted face, adorned himself in Lurex, satin, velvet and feather boas singing enticing hits such as 'Hot Love', 'Bang a Gong (Get it On)', 'Ride a White Swan' and 'Telegram Sam'.

★ *News headlines*

In the international political world three different presidents came to power in the USA – Nixon, Ford and Carter. In 1972 Nixon and Brezhnev signed the Moscow Pact which aimed to reduce the danger of nuclear war. In 1979, this aim was advanced when Brezhnev and Carter signed the SALT Treaty restricting each country's nuclear weaponry. At the Munich Olympics of 1972 when Mark Spitz won seven gold medals for swimming and Olga Korbut entertained the crowds with outstanding gymnastics, Arab guerrillas broke into the Israeli building in Olympic village with sub-machine guns blazing. Nine hostages were taken, and in the disastrous rescue attempt, all nine died. In 1973 top Nixon aids quit over the Watergate scandal. Nixon's famous quote rang out to the world, 'There will be no whitewash at The Whitehouse'.

Back in Britain, the Sterling currency (pounds, shillings and pence) was replaced by a decimal version. In 1973, the three-day week was introduced for many as trade union disputes paralysed the country with strikes at coalmines, railways and powerstations. In 1975 Margaret Thatcher became the first woman leader of a British political party and in 1979 she was elected first woman Prime Minister. Her first speech to the nation claimed, 'Where there is discord may we bring harmony ... where there is despair may we bring hope'.

The pop world mourned the death of Elvis Presley in 1977. The decade saw the passing of many other driving forces in the arts, including Agatha Christie, Maria Callas, Picasso, Bing Crosby, John Wayne, Charlie Chaplin, Marc Bolan, Janis Joplin and Jimi Hendrix.

In the film world *The Sting* became a huge box office hit, featuring music by Scott Joplin (brilliantly arranged by Marvin Hamlisch) and actors Paul Newman and Robert Redford. Martin Scorsese's controversial film *Taxi Driver*, however, shocked audiences by casting the young Jodie Foster as a child prostitute. Other key films of the decade were Coppola's *The Godfather* starring Brando and Pacino and *Apocalypse Now*, Forman's *One Flew Over the Cuckoo's Nest*, Spielberg's *Jaws* and Bertolucci's *Last Tango in Paris*. Meanwhile Opportunity Knocks, Upstairs, Downstairs and Dallas were the nation's favourite television programmes, and in 1974 streaking became *de rigeur,* particularly with undergraduates in the USA. In Britain streaking gained universal press when a young man appeared *au naturel* at Twickenham and on tabloid front pages across the world. These amusing incidents inspired a number one song entitled 'The Streak' with the intriguing opening line, 'There he goes – boogedie, boogedie'.

The glitter bandwagon travelled with several other stars, some only making a short journey into the current teenage pysche such as Sweet, Slade, Alvin Stardust and Gary Glitter, while Elton John, David Bowie and Rod Stewart demonstrated progressive talent, stayed longer and created new and individual roads in musical history. The androgynous fashions were common to all glitter rockers and intrinsic to the sub-culture. In addition to the romantic Bolan-inspired look, make-up, platform shoes, suits of sequins, flares and coiffured hair were adopted by both sexes.

Sweet launched their glam careers with superficial but highly-successful songs such as 'Wig Wam-Bam', 'Funny Funny' and 'Coco', but later changed to teen-terrace screamers such as 'Blockbuster', 'Teenage Rampage' and 'Ballroom Blitz'. Slade meanwhile, decided upon a more aggressive yob image from the start. Stomping, stamping and chanting, lead singer Noddy Holder screamed out, as if from a football terrace, 'Look Wot You Dun', 'Cum on Feel the Noize' and 'Mama Weer all Crazee Now'. Teenagers responded by waving scarves and banners, shouting out the choruses and swaying to the beat.

Two solo male glam protagonists were ageing rivals, Gary Glitter and Alvin Stardust. No spring chickens, Glitter and Stardust bravely jumped into unlikely youthful costumes to find fame. Gary Glitter squeezed himself into

Figure 1.7 *The Sweet – classic glam*

skin-tight Lurex and sequin suits, climbed into platform soles and teetered on to Top of the Pops singing 'Do You Wanna Touch Me?', 'I Didn't Know I Loved You Till I Saw You Rock 'n' Roll', 'I Love You Love Me Love' and 'Leader of the Gang'. In contrast, Alvin Stardust posed in long black leather gloves, chains and looked mean and menacing singing 'My Coo Coo Ca Choo', 'Jealous Mind', 'Red Dress' and 'You You You'.

By the mid-1970s glitter was disappearing. The unemployed, deprived and disaffected youth of the nation could find no solace in the glam movement. The street realism, which had fired and inspired rock 'n' roll and The Beatles, The Stones and soul music, was painfully absent in the obsessive narcissism of glitter which began to give way to the angriest music in pop history.

Punk

Hard, brutal, noisy, fast, primitive, furious and played around two chords with sustained dissonance, punk rock shocked and excited more

than any other style before. The true voice of youth had arrived in the 1970s, empowering a seething and sorely resentful movement.

Malcolm McLaren, art student and boutique owner, was the instigator. After travelling to the USA to manage a band called The Dolls, he returned to Britain crammed with ideas to change the course of pop music. First he changed the name of his 1950s style boutique, Let it Rock, to Sex. Next he threw out all the 1950s gear and instead sold ripped T-shirts held together with safety pins and bondage wear. Teenagers flocked and McLaren soon heard about a new band called The Swankers which encapsulated his dreams of the new music. With a quick change of line-up and name, The Sex Pistols were ready for London.

Arrogant and offensive, lead singer Johnny Rotten made Mick Jagger look like a cuddly teddy bear. Gate crashing their way into parties, clubs, the London Underground, anywhere, The Sex Pistols gradually acquired a cult following. Punk, like skiffle, could be

Figure 1.8   *Punk – The Ramones*

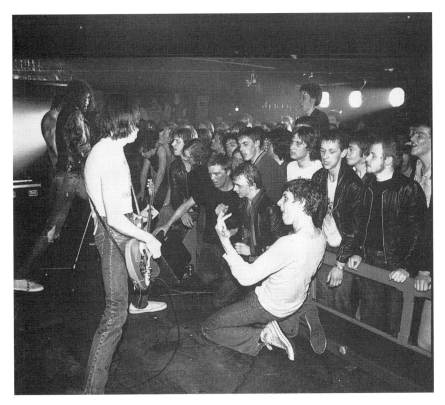

played by anyone, and bands did not require sophisticated gear and expert musicianship. The music began to spread across the western world and the young malcontents in Dusseldorf, Stockholm, New York, Rome and London crowded out the gigs and thrived on public disapproval. The media hysterically reported the anti-social elements of the punk culture: spitting, pogoing, swearing, violence, extreme body piercing, spikey haircuts and general unrest and mayhem. Bands such as The Buzzcocks, The Vibrators, The Slits, The Ruts and The Damned were inspired by The Sex Pistols but Johnny Rotten continued to lead punk's most repellent band. Their first single 'Anarchy in the UK', hurled into the charts on word of mouth, but EMI soon dropped the band after colourful swearing on television. 'God Save The Queen', released by Virgin was released next, offending royalists and traditionalists alike in the build-up to Queen Elizabeth's Jubilee celebrations. 'Pretty Vacant' followed but meanwhile other more mellow and politically-motivated bands such as The Clash '(London's Calling),The Jam and The Stranglers began to appeal to a wider, more mature and socially-conscious market.

TASKS

- Research the music of the punk era, profiling at least two of the bands mentioned above.
- Malcolm McLaren and Vivienne Westwood (fashion designer) were instrumental in creating the punk culture. Find out all you can about them.

Heavy metal

Thrash, heavy and death metal provided another escape vehicle for youth in the 1970s. First used by beat novelist William Burroughs in his novel *Naked Lunch*, and then again in Steppenwolf's hit 'Born to Be Wild', the term heavy metal symbolises hugely-amplified and ecstatic solo guitar music, accompanied by screaming singing and blues-based riffs.

The style began as heavy rock, with performers like Hendrix and Page who excited audiences with loud and fast electric guitar enhanced with feedback or wah-wah effects. 'Purple Haze' by Hendrix was a forerunner of the style. Speed and expert playing were tests of metal quality and innovative electric guitarists like Hendrix, Page, Ted Nugent and Eddie Van Halen developed legendary status.

Vocalists, although less important, also adhered to the heavy metal image code. Macho, aggressive, and often dressed in black leather ready for dare-devil motorbiking, lead male singers included Robert Plant and Steven Tyler, and important bands of the decade were Led Zeppelin, Black Sabbath and Iron Maiden.

Harder core metals, called thrash and death developed later. Thrash metal is faster, noisier and more frenetic than heavy metal, and death metal, as the name suggests, deals in the macabre, the sinister and the deadly.

TASKS

- Choose one metal band from the 1970s and another from the 1990s, and discuss any similarities and differences.
- Punk and heavy metal are the two most recent pop cultures you have studied. While they were both important to the 1970s music scene, could you argue that they matter today? Spark a debate!

Disco

The first movement to spring from the dance floor, disco culture embraced fashion, dancing and music. Originating in Paris after the Second World War, when dancers would swing and jitterbug at venues housing rich libraries of popular discs, the term discotheque was a coined neologism combining the French *disque* (disc) and *theque* (library). Disc libraries for dancing soon travelled to Britain and the USA, but true disco music and its culture emerged in the 1970s.

Disco fashions (returning in the late 1990s) were designed to attract the spotlights and to sparkle. Sequins, satin, glitter, lurex and PVC were standard fabrics for both sexes. Women wore short skirts and tight tops like boob tubes, while men sported bright three-piece suits with tight flared trousers, big-collared shirts and flashy jewellery such as chains or medallions.

The disco sound combined a variety of musical styles with electronic techniques. Strong rhythms in 4/4, carried by drums or bass, never dipped below 70 beats a minute (normal pulse rate) to keep the music constantly stimulating. Requiring the use of bigger sound systems, disco music incorporated the use of multi-tracking skills. Combined with a full symphony orchestra, and special effects like sirens and whistles, these layers of sophisticated musical strands created a rich and luscious sound.

Disco music spread across the globe reaching new markets. The Philadelphia disco sound linked black soul music to classical symphony textures. German disco featured strong violin, synthesisers and whistles. Disco versions of the tango, cha cha and samba promoted Latin-American music internationally, and disco arrangements of classical music gave the genre a cross-generational popularity.

Dancing was exciting, intricate and serious. Young people lived for Saturday nights on the disco floor and the whole movement was encapsulated in the hit film *Saturday Night Fever* starring John Travolta as Italian stallion Tony Manero. A working-class boy from Brooklyn, New York, Tony Manero's mundane existence was transformed every Saturday night by immersing himself in disco culture and dancing in particular. The film made John Travolta a superstar, and disco a fever.

The most exciting dance of all, however, was the hustle. An American invention, the hustle was created by young black youths in East Harlem without the money to gain entrance into rock concerts or smart discos. This dance style rejuvenated touch dancing, complex athletic moves involving spinning a partner in the air, and footwork aspects of the foxtrot and jitterbug. In 1975, Van McCoy and the Soul City Symphony produced the hit instrumental song 'The Hustle', which promoted disco music and the Latin feel to the world. Some pop historians argue that this song alone initiated the success of the disco craze.

Lyrics reflected the exciting, pleasurable and escapist feel of the music. Disco classics include Sister Sledge's 'Lost in Music', 'He's the Greatest Dancer' and 'We are Family', the Bee Gee's 'Stayin' Alive', 'Night Fever' and 'You Should be Dancing'.

Disco influenced the course of popular music in three main ways: 1) it gave new prominence to the artistic role of producer; 2) it promoted black music into mainstream music culture and 3) paved the way for later developments in the club music scene such as hip-hop, rap, house, acid jazz and techno.

TASKS

- Watch *Saturday Night Fever*. Listen to and list all music on the soundtrack, noting distinctive features about each song.
- Interview a disco dancer from the 1970s. Ask about fashions, dance steps, favourite discos, television, radio programmes and magazines. Try to build up a picture of 1970s disco culture.
- Research then define the role of music producer. Profile at least one producer associated with disco and add this information to your portfolio for music producers. Add any other names you have come across so far.
- From now on, when discussing music, always take a note of the producers involved.

Soul and funk

Black music established itself with strength and dignity in the 1970s and moved far beyond the sounds associated with the 1960s. Solo artists such as James Brown, Aretha Franklin, Diana Ross, Marvin Gaye, Lionel Richie and Smokey Robinson performed individual interpretations of soul music, which fast became a broad rather diluted term. These musicians continue to influence popular music today, and the essence of the original soul sound can be found in many categories of music from pop ballads to rap.

One style of music aimed specifically at the dance floor was funk. This sound originated in New Orleans where pianists created left-hand grooves known as 'funky' and bass players experimented with rhythmic patterns to complement the piano and drums. Essentially, therefore, funk is bass driven, highly syncopated and polyrhythmic – ideal for dancing. In the late 1960s and early 1970s, James Brown pursued funk/soul for dancers and characteristics began to emerge for the new style. Looser song structures, percussive use of all instruments to evoke the rediscovery of African roots among American blacks, punchy but fractured bass lines (incorporating the slap-bass technique), choked rhythm guitar and repetetive lyrical elements were the main ingredients.

James Brown performed major funk/soul dance hits spanning three decades. 'I Got You (I Feel Good)', 'Hot', 'Body Heat', 'Give it Up' or 'Turn it Loose, Say it Loud, I'm Black and I'm Proud' and 'Make it Funky' are only some of the golden dance tracks from *Soul Brother Number One*. Incredibly prolific, with 800 songs in his repertoire, Brown changed the course of dance music and made an indelible impression on artists from Prince to Michael Jackson.

Other classic funk tracks include Lee Dorsey's 'Everything I Do Gonh be Funky (From Now On)' and Funkadelic's 'One Nation Under a Groove'.

TASKS

- Listen to some classic soul tracks of the 1970s. Choose either one funk band or solo artist and write a short presentation on their contribution to popular music, playing relevant examples.
- In groups, choose three songs from the charts. Discuss and take notes on soul features present in the music.

Reggae

The quality of black music was sustained during the 1970s, in contrast to other superficial attention-seeking pop cultures such as glam or new romanticism. Reggae, influencing the work of several artists across the globe, stemmed from African and traditional Caribbean music. Known in Jamaica as mento in the 1940s, the music, originally performed by travelling musicians on guitars and percussion, was inspired by local worksongs, spirituals, the calypso, rhumba and merengue. Transformed by New Orleans and R&B styles in the 1950s, early characteristics were heavy syncopation and a strong brass section.

This new R & B influenced style, known as ska, (and in Britain as bluebeat) grew quickly, establishing Kingston, Jamaica as an important recording centre. Toasting, a strand of ska in which DJs would add vocal effects and aphorisms over the music, developed into dub which involved DJs in the practice of manipulating pre-recorded tracks. Later both toasting and dub moved into the studio for more commercial gain.

In the mid-1960s, ska shifted the brass emphasis to the bass and rhythm guitars, and lyrics became more socially aware. In 1966, the Jamaican heat wave slowed down the ska beat altogether to create rock steady, and the new electric sound began to attract white audiences. Reggae soon began to infiltrate the charts. Desmond Decker achieved a number one hit with 'Israelites' in 1969, and Dave and Ansell Collins hit the top slot in 1970 with 'Double Barrel'.

Bob Marley attracted interest in the USA initially through penning songs such as 'Stir it Up' for Johnny Nash, who also introduced

Figure 1.9 *Bob Marley and the I Threes backing singers*

him to Britain. Marley became the biggest exponent of reggae music worldwide and further songwriting successes included 'I Shot the Sheriff' covered by Eric Clapton, reaching number one in 1973, and his own album, *Natty Dread*, featuring the eternal 'No Woman, No Cry'.

Central to the reggae style was Rastafarianism. Burra drumming, quotes from Rasta scriptures and political philosophies of Marcus Garvey were incorporated into the music of Rastafarian groups such as the Wailers, Burning Spear and the Abyssinians. These elements, in addition to drug-induced tempos and language, pervaded reggae music in the 1970s.

One band drawing on reggae features was Police. Lead singer, bass player and chief songwriter, Sting, drummer Stewart Copeland and guitarist Andy Summer performed reggae-influenced songs in the late 1970s such as 'Roxanne', 'Walking on the Moon' and 'Message in a Bottle'. The band split up in 1984.

TASKS

- Research the Rastafarian cult, including Burra drumming, in order to understand the reggae culture in more depth.
- Write 300 words on the life and works of Bob Marley.
- Listen to the late 1970s songs of the band Police and discuss in groups the reggae features present in the music.

The 1980s

'LOADSAMONEY!' bawled Harry Enfield in a television ad in the mid-1980s, symbolising the greed and excess of a decade riddled with yuppies, Hooray Henries, DINKYS, nerds, couch potatoes, lager louts tabloid TV, and buzz words such as networking, thirtysomething, cellulite, photo opportunity and the telling phrase, call my people. The 1980s in reality had almost forgotten about people as

takeovers, mergers, leveraged buy outs and mega-mergers created billionaires overnight.

In the pop world, however, the rejuvenation of the quality song, the emergence of the singer/songwriter and the development of recording techniques and electronic instruments meant that music progressed positively into the 1980s and 1990s.

News headlines

The decade began abruptly when the SAS stormed the terrorist-occupied Iranian Embassy in Knightsbridge, London, after Iranian gunmen, demanding the release of political prisoners in Iran, started to shoot the hostages. The gunmen killed the Iranian press attaché, dumped his body on the steps outside then threatened to murder a hostage every 30 minutes. The Middle East War continued to wage throughout the decade.

In December 1980, rock fans across the world mourned John Lennon, murdered late at night outside his home in New York. Mark Chapman, requesting Lennon's autograph earlier that day, shot the musician five times at point-blank range. The decade witnessed further killings and attempted assassinations: President Anwar Sadat of Egypt was shot down by automatic fire during a military parade; Swedish premiere Olaf Palme was gunned down in the street, and the Prime Minister of India, Indira Ghandi, was shot dead by her Sikh bodyguards as she walked in the gardens of her New Delhi home. The night before her death, Mrs Ghandi told a political rally, 'I don't mind if my life goes in the service of a nation. If I die today, every drop of my blood will invigorate the nation'.

Closer to home Peter Sutcliffe, known as the Yorkshire Ripper, was charged with the murder of 13 women, and in Dublin 49 people, mostly teenagers, died after a fire gutted The Stardust Club on St Valentine's Day. The financial negotiations of Britain's entry into the European

Community continued in teeth-bearing fashion as the country tried to clarify its involvement.

Attempted assassinations were made on President Reagan and Pope John Paul II. In 1984, an IRA bomb, intended to massacre most of the British Cabinet in Brighton at the Tory Party Conference, devastated the Grand Hotel and killed three people, narrowly missing the Prime Minister Margaret Thatcher. The 1980s also witnessed the Falklands War when British task forces were sent to the south Atlantic.

In the mid-1980s, the music business came to the aid of Africa's famine victims. Initiated and driven by Bob Geldof, Band Aid, a large group of top rock musicians, produced the single 'Do They Know It's Christmas?' for the starving refugees of Ethiopia, innocently caught up in a bitter civil war. In 1985, 160 countries watched internationally-renowned musicians Phil Collins, Paul McCartney, Dire Staits, David Bowie, Mick Jagger, Tina Turner, Queen and many others perform at Wembley Stadium, London or JFK Stadium, Philadelphia raising 40 million pounds for Africa. This time the operation was called LIve Aid.

In Britain the decade saw the wedding of Prince Charles and Lady Diana Spencer in 1981 and the births of Prince William (1982) and Prince Harry (1984). One 1980s morning, Her Majesty the Queen was surprised to find on waking up one Michael Fagin sitting dishevelled on her bed, slurping a bottle of wine stolen from the Palace, and asking for a cigarette and a chat. Security for the Royal Family was immediately questioned.

News headlines

While unemployment tipped the three million mark, sales of *The Sun* newspaper rose by 540 000 thanks to the tabloid Bingo War. Big money was also being made by the paper's owner, Rupert Murdoch who bought *The Times* and *Sunday Times* from the Canadian-based Thomson organisation. The Brixton and Toxteth riots, however, claimed by black leaders to have stemmed from years of heavy-handed racist policing, provided a stark contrast to 1980s sordid excesses such as lager louts provoking football violence at home and abroad.

In the arts and media world, Channel Four was launched along with breakfast TV and blockbuster glamorous television series such as *Brideshead Revisited*, *Smiley's People* and *Dynasty*. *Chariots of Fire*, *The French Lieutenant's Woman*, *Tess* and *Ghandi* were major films of the decade drawing from modern history or literary works, and *Ghandi*, directed by Sir Richard Attenborough and starring Ben Kingsley, collected eight Oscars for Britain. *Crocodile Dundee* and *ET*, meanwhile, were huge box-office hits. For young people, Teenage Mutant Ninja Turtles, Cabbage Patch Kids, Barbie dolls, Nintendo and The Smurfs were the latest crazes.

The 1980s bade farewell to many prestigious talents: Steve McQueen, Peter Sellers, Bob Marley, William Walton, David Niven, Sir Ralph Richardson, Count Basie, Sir John Betjeman, Eric Morecambe, James Mason, J.B. Priestly, Richard Burton, Laura Ashley, Rock Hudson, Orson Welles, James Cagney, Simone de Beauvoir, Henry Moore, Cary Grant, Andy Warhol, Fred Astaire and John Huston.

The Silicon micro-chip inspired creative computer experts to develop electronic games and computerised watches, sound systems and video recorders. Information Technology developments spread worldwide as links became possible between televisions, telephones and computers and similar innovations in the rock world were to add depth and interest to popular music in the 1980s.

MUSIC OF THE 1980S

Three major developments took place in the 1980s which were to change the course of popular music history: the emergence of the personality singer/songwriter, the progressive use of synthesisers, samplers and computers in music, and the pop video as an essential promotional tool. Several new dance-generated trends were also created in addition to stadium rock, which involved top-name musicians performing in huge audience-capacity venues.

New romantics and electro pop

The decade began with a few ephemeral hangovers from the late 1970s. One of these was the new romantic movement. Mainly disco influenced, this culture promoted an outrageous but sophisticated and elegant image, with the pop video being central to its success. The most notorious new romantic, tutored by punk instigator Malcolm Maclaren, was Adam Ant. Modelling himself on Prince Charming, the red indian and the pirate, Ant stormed into the charts with hits such as 'Stand and Deliver' and 'Goody Two Shoes'. Incorporating a tribal drum sound, initially used by Gary Glitter to appeal to adolescents, Adam and the Ants impressed audiences briefly along with other new romantic bands such as Spandau Ballet, Duran Duran and Visage.

One band, while adopting the cultural trappings of the new romantic movement, concentrated on the innovative development of electropop. Human League quickly established themselves as leaders in the field of electronically produced music incorporating synthesisers and samplers. With lead singer Phil Oakey's dark and menacingly-performed lyrics and Kraftwerk-influenced synthesiser textures,

Human League were highly acclaimed for their music across the pop world. A major hit for Human League which has been covered several times is 'Don't You Want Me?'

TASKS

- Profile at least one of the new romantic bands mentioned above.
- Find out all you can about the German band Kraftwerk, listen to their music and discuss their contribution to present-day pop.

Break dancing

Involving dare-devil dance routines, particularly during instrumental breaks, this more meaningful dance craze began in the New York ghettos of the Bronx and Brooklyn. The verb 'to break', used by inner-city black kids, meant to express anger openly and loudly, and like many strands of pop culture, break dancing became a forceful communication vehicle for young people.

In 1983, an edition of *In Performance*, published by the Brooklyn Academy of Music, described break dancers as 'twirling around the axes of their upper bodies like human coffee-grinders, using fast pedalling footwork, twisting belly-up, belly-down, finishing with elaborate leg pretzels'. Dangerous and exciting, an exclusive in-crowd feel to break-dancing groups soon developed. Part of the thrill was knowing that any outsiders would incur serious injury if they attempted the expert moves.

The Wigan Casino became the centre of break dancing in Britain, attracting teenagers across Britain every weekend in the late 1970s and early 1980s.

Electric boogie

Providing the perfect foil to break dancing was electric boogie. With moves like robotic popping, moonwalking, and mime-like hand-waves, there was no fear of this dance breaking bones. Michael Jackson brought fame to moonwalking in particular, but the roots of electric boogie are to be found in the comic mime routines of Shields and Yarnell in the late 1970s. Having studied with Marcel Marceau, they were professional mime artists who managed to broadcast a show on CBS TV one early 1980s summer. Shields and Yarnell introduced audiences to a robotic couple called the Clinkers who moved by popping and told stories. Within weeks young blacks were imitating the style and telling their own stories, but to dance music.

Rap (and hip-hop)

Not all dance-based trends were ephemeral. One form, originating 20 years earlier and still continuing today, is rap, also known as hip-hop. Essentially this significant black music dance genre involves the vocalist (the rapper) speaking in rhythm and rhyme over the manipulated backing music (the hip-hop). Although reggae toasters and dubbers, club DJs and concert presenters have talked over and manipulated music for years, true rapping emerged in the mid 1970s along with other ghetto open-communication channels like break dancing, underground freedom writing and graffiti. The genre, as we know it today, is a profound socially-conscious art form, drawing from wide-ranging contemporary creative media.

The rap story began in the late 1970s when artists like Grandmaster Flash, a major Bronx

Figure 1.10   *Public Enemy and the SIW's, 1995*

spinner, developed a unique style which quickly attracted large audiences. Flash's novel music-editing techniques involved cutting (segueing tracks on the beat), phasing (altering speeds) and back-spinning. He began working with rappers such as Kurtis Blow and the Furious Five, launching himself as a rap/hip-hop artist with Sugarhill Records in 1980. By 1982, Grandmaster Flash's 'The Message' had brought rap music to the charts.

While rap's main themes are dancing and partying, there is often a political thrust or sociological comment behind the lyrics. Brother D's 'How We Gonna Make The Black Nation Rise?' and Public Enemy's 'It Takes a Nation of Millions To Hold Us Back', are typical of political rap of the 1980s and 1990s. Rap began to conquer racial barriers, however, when white artists Ian Dury , Blondie and The Clash incorporated rap techniques into their music. In 1987 white rappers The Beastie Boys hit the Top Ten with their single '(You Gotta) Fight For Your Right (To Party)'.

One of the biggest names in 1980s rap was M.C. Hammer, who became the first rap artist to win a Grammy award in 1990.

A hard-core rap called gangsta rap emerged in the late 1980s, taking over as the dominating style in the 1990s. With violent lyrics delivered aggressively, gratuitiously touching on rape and killings, and urban musical collages of sirens and gunshots, this rap sub-culture has been heavily criticised by many sectors of society. Several rap and hip-hop artists have rejected all gangsta elements, but the genre has inspired some of the biggest pop names, for example Ice Cube and Snoop Doggy Dogg. A gangsta dress code of baggy clothes and head bandanas emerged for serious fans, which became banned in some schools.

TASKS

- Create a dictionary for rap. Firstly define the following terms: spinning, back-spinning, segueing, phasing, scratching, sampling.
- Create a list of all the rap/hip-hop artists mentioned above, adding any others you know.
- Discuss the copyright problems of sampling in a group, referring to Chapter 7 on this area for extra information.

House, acid house and into rave

Taking its name from Chicago's Warehouse, a club for black gay culture, house music has the essential ingredients of fast but deep drums and bass with heavy reverb, a combination of urban and jungle sounds and tribal rhythms. The music developed from revved-up disco beats mixed with Latin, African, or the Philadelphia sounds spun by Chicago DJ Frankie Knuckles.

A more psychedelic form was created when it came to London in the mid 1980s. Hypnotic and enticing, this variation on the Chicago style included bites of TV chat and other media, and DJs adding spaced-out grooves. Along with techno, acid inspired the 1990s rave scene.

The Stone Roses and The Happy Mondays, an indie band hailing from Manchester, embodied the acid house sound. Led by Shaun Ryder, and featuring Bez who danced and shook maracas, The Happy Mondays hooked the club scene with their heavy bass and drums, spaced-out grooves and hints of 1960s psychedelia. The band hit in Britain with singles like '24 Hour Party People', 'Tart Tart' and, in 1990, 'Pills 'n' Thrills and Bellyaches' attracted American attention. Shaun Ryder formed Black Grape in 1993.

Although drugs are associated with acid house and the rave scene, the term acid is, in fact, Chicago slang for sampling or stealing someone else's music. British underground music entrepeneur, Genesis P. Orridge, spotted the word acid on some Chicago house music, and believing it referred to LSD, released the British version of house as acid house.

The era of the solo singer/songwriter

During the rock 'n' roll era and the 1960s, it became normal for bands to perform and record their own music. Apart from a few exceptions, however, it had been rare for solo singers to pen their own songs. In the 1970s artists such as Michael Jackson, Phil Collins, Kate Bush, Peter Gabriel, Prince, George Michael and Elton John created music intrinsically linked with their personalities, and while growing in status in the 1970s, the 1980s saw them flourish and expand to reach stadium rock stardom. They continue to influence and lead the way today not only in music, but in ownership and control of their work.

A major player in this field is Michael Jackson. An immensely-talented songwriter, singer, arranger, producer and dancer, he is also a superbly astute businessman who has created the biggest persona in pop history. The projected

Figure 1.11   *The techno and rave scene*

image of child-like vulnerability belies his worldliness and obsession with control.

Originally a performer in his family group, The Jackson 5, Michael's outstanding talent ensured he quickly progressed from band member to lead singer. With Michael's high staccato voice, the Jackson 5 soared to success rivalling another family dynasty of the 1970s, The Osmonds. Michael soon became more popular than the group, and a few solo 1970s hits were released such as 'Rockin' Robin' and 'Ben', a slow original ballad penned by Michael. A meeting with veteran producer Quincy Jones in 1978 was to prove a major turning point in Michael's career and a catalyst to the Michael Jackson phenomenon we know today.

In 1979, *Off The Wall*, produced by Jones, enabled Jackson to become the first solo artist to release four top-ten hits from one album. 'Off the Wall', 'Don't Stop Till You Get Enough', 'Rock With You' and 'She's Out of My Life'

displayed Jackson as a dance artist as well as a sweet soul man, attracting huge mass appeal.

International fame and success arrived with *Thriller*, another work produced by Jones, which became the biggest-selling album of all time. With 45 million sales worldwide and major hit singles from the album such as 'Billie Jean', 'The Girl is Mine' and 'Beat It', Jackson was the first artist to achieve the number one slot in every western country. The added acclaims which *Thriller* brought of topping both the singles and album charts in R&B and pop simultaneously, winning 8 Grammy awards and breaking through the racist boundaries with videos for MTV, secured Michael Jackson's role as a major force in pop music history.

The album *Bad*, released in 1987, with a video directed by Martin Scorcese, yielded five number one hits and in the 1990s major works such as *Dangerous* and *HIStory* maintain his unique status.

TASK

- Write a profile on at least one of the following singer/songwriters: Phil Collins, Kate Bush, Elvis Costello, Randy Newman, Prince, Elton John or George Michael.

The 1990s

The present and most immediate decade is always difficult to describe and place in context. Only with more time shall we be able to analyse fully the fundamental changes it has made on society, in arts and in politics.

★ News headlines

The decade began euphorically when Nelson Mandela was released after 27 years of imprisonment. The last bastion of imperialist white majority rule, South Africa witnessed Mandela fight for the end of racial prejudice and become an international leader as President of the African National Congress.

In Europe history was being made. Communist rule ended in East Germany and the Berlin Wall was demolished. The USSR announced the end of the Cold War, while the aftermath of the Romanian Revolution and the overthrowing and shooting of President Ceausescu still reverberate. In 1991 hard line communists attempted a coup in the USSR, but the resistance was led by Boris Yeltsin, who after Gorbachev resigned was elected President of the new Russia.

Civil war, however, continued to darken the early 1990s in Yugoslavia, as Slovenia and Croatia fought for independence. Between 1992 and 1993, Serbia tried to maintain federation, while Czech and Slovak became separate states.

At home successes for equal opportunities arrived in the early 1990s when the Church of England agreed to the ordination of women, and Amnesty International pressed to free men and women imprisoned because of their sexual preferences. Equality in the workplace also become of major concern in the 1990s, spurring sensational tabloid news stories.

Press intrusion, an issue argued over for decades, hit hearts internationally in 1997 when Diana, Princess of Wales was tragically killed in a car accident in Paris, after allegedly being chased by paparazzi. While it is still not clear if the paparazzi were to blame, the invasion of privacy into peoples' lives and the unfair stress it creates, continues to spark fierce debate.

In the arts and media worlds a return to feel-good films and easy-listening music, looking unashamedly back to the 1960s and 1970s for inspiration, became fashionable. Films such as *Four Weddings and a Funeral*, *The Full Monty*, *Brassed Off* and *My Best Friend's Wedding* have not only promoted British culture, and its film industry, but created an interest in all that is traditional. Other major films of the 1990s were Scorsese's *Cape Fear*, Jonathan Demme's *The Silence of the Lambs*, Spike Lee's *Malcolm X*, Spielberg's *Schindler's List* and *Jurassic Park*, Disney Studios' *The Lion King*, Zemecki's *Forrest Gump*, Mel Gibson's three-hour epic *Braveheart* and Anthony Minghella's *The English Patient*.

In music we mourned Freddie Mercury, lead singer and songwriter for Queen. Immensely talented and much missed in the rock world, Freddie's voice soared over the unique Queen sound of glam rock mixed with heavy metal and intricate, almost classical harmonies achieved by multi-tracking Mercury's voice. Major hits included 'Another One Bites the Dust', 'We Are The Champions', 'Radio Ga-Ga' and 'Bohemian Rhapsody', which remained in the charts for nine weeks in 1976, with its ground-breaking conceptual rock video. An Aids benefit concert was held in tribute to Mercury in 1992.

MUSIC OF THE 1990s

While the development of dance music has sparked increasingly sophisticated use of technology, incorporating electronic sounds generated by samplers, controlled by computers and manipulated by musicians, the rest of the rock world has gone retro. In line with other pop cultures such as fashion and film, pop continues to draw from music of the past.

Raves and techno

While discos were the mainstream dance venues in the 1970s and early 1980s, undergound places for dancers called raves took over in the early 1990s. Raves were all-night psychedelic parties for dancers who heightened the effects of partying and dancing by taking the hallucinogenic stimulant Ecstasy, also known as E. Dancers would move and get high to techno music at raves, and the whole movement was instigated by Detroit DJ Derrick May. By the early 1990s a large cult audience had developed and major labels were signing and promoting techno exponents such as 808 State, Moby and Messiah.

The music is entirely computer generated, fast and furious. The harder the techno, the faster the beat. DJs utilise samplers, turntables, TV and radio bites, drum sequences, fragments of songs, and so on to create an endless frenetic array of sounds for dancers.

Other major dance styles, emerging in the 1980s and developing in the 1990s are trip-hop, jungle, bhangra, ambient, house, drum 'n' bass and speed garage.

TASKS

- Create a chart for dance music. For each decade (start at the beginning of the century), list the major dance forms of the day.
- Choose one of the many 1990s dance forms above and discuss in groups the differences and similarities between this and disco music.

Easy listening

Retro culture has established itself in an unprecedented way in the 1990s. The sub-culture draws from the fashion, art, film, soul and disco movements of the 1960s and 1970s along with a general interest in The Beatles.

Melody, sweet pop harmony, lush orchestration and easy rhythms are back in vogue. Frank Sinatra, Burt Bacharach, Dionne Warwick, and the superbly-arranged music of easy-listening singers from the past such as Ella Fitzgerald are inspiring both original songs and cover versions from artists as diverse as Bjork, Brand New Heavies and Oasis. A sophistication coupled with simplicity is present in the easy-listening music of today, and it appears in a wide range of styles.

Britpop

In Britain, bands with a retro feel are generally linked to the phenomenal Britpop movement. British artists from the past such as The Kinks, Squeeze, The Beatles, The Sex Pistols and The Who have influenced and inspired current artists to create new, accessible and appealing music with a distinctive British sound. Oasis, Blur, The Verve, Texas, Ocean Colour Scene, Pulp, Primal Scream, The Charlatans and Supergrass have reinstated Britain as a world centre for quality pop music.

Two of these bands vied for media success in particular: Oasis and Blur. In August 1995, Blur's 'Country House' beat Oasis' 'Roll With It', a Lennon-influenced song, to number one. Shortly afterwards, Oasis won all wars with their rivals when their LP *(What's The Story) Morning Glory?* hit number one in the album charts, becoming the top-selling CD in Britain in 1995. The music of The Beatles, punk rock and The Smiths influenced the songs of this pop rock CD, and attracted mass market appeal, particularly with 'Wonderwall' and 'Champagne Supernova'. Amusingly, Mike Flowers Pops created an easy-listening version of 'Wonderwall', enabling the song to chart twice.

TASKS

- Listen to the original version of 'Wonderwall' performed by Oasis and then compare it to Mike Flowers' arrangement. Jot down the differences.
- Choose any three bands from the Britpop movement and discuss influences from the past with your fellow musicians.
- Predict the popular music trends for the next ten years.

Country and country 'n' western music

Throughout the history of popular music, country has steadily developed. Like folk music, country has existed for generations, but is now associated solely with America, even though the form began when British white settlers came to the USA with ballad songs, taking root in places such as Kentucky and Tennessee. Words and styles were adapted as time progressed to describe local characters, happenings and culture giving the music a live and relevant feel.

Instruments initially were simple and usually portable, for example the banjo, harmonica, fiddle and single-stringed bow. By 1900 country music had divided into two categories: string-band music (the origins of blue grass and hillbilly) and vocal harmony music. By the 1930s, however, the development of recording techniques and radio widened the influences on the style, and the term country began to dissipate in meaning. The Grand Ole Opry radio show, broadcast weekly from Nashville, Tennessee, secured a new centre for country music.

The style continued to develop. In the late 1930s, singers such as Roy Acuff performed solo with a pop-like band while others, particularly from Texas, incorporated blues and jazz into the country sound. By the 1940s and 1950s, improvisational elements derived from blues and jazz appeared in most country music, ensuring mass appeal and commercial success. At this point the genre became known as country 'n' western music. But the traditions of the Grand Ole Opry Show continued unabated. While blues and rock 'n' roll had hit the world with driving beats, drums were barred from the Opry stage.

In the 1960s, artists such as Hank Williams, Loretta Lynn and Webb Pierce popularised the honky-tonk style while rockabilly singers like Jerry Lee Lewis and Johnny Cash promoted a revival of country roots. The folk protest movement, involving Bob Dylan, brought country to a new young student generation concerned with political issues of the day. The simplicity of the music provided the perfect vehicle for strong messages.

In recent decades country 'n' western has become a major force on the music scene, with its

Figure 1.12   *Country and western music flourished in America*

own charts, record labels and television stations. Dolly Parton, Tammy Wynette and George Hamilton IV shot to stardom in the 1970s and remain popular today, while Garth Brooks and Trish Yearwood are representative of the 1990s.

TASK

- List as many country and country 'n' western artists as you can, decade by decade, taking note of hits as you go.

The musical

Another major development of twentieth-century popular music is the musical. Today, London's West End and New York's Broadway offer both recent and established works of this ever-popular genre. It is the most eclectic form of stagecraft, drawing from diverse sources: popular literature or poetry, for example *Guys and Dolls* or *Cats*, the classics such as *Kiss Me Kate*, rock music as in *Hair* or sociological observations such as the anti-hero in *Pal Joey* or New York street gangs in *West Side Story*.

The term is, in fact, an abbreviation of musical play, and the form originally appeared as light stage entertainment, often transforming into films from Broadway productions. Early stage musicals, later to become films, were Jerome Kern's *Showboat* and Ira and George Gershwin's *Porgy and Bess*. The first Hollywood film musical was *The Jazz Singer of 1927*, starring Al Jolson. Other early film musicals included *Top Hat* with Fred Astaire and Ginger Rogers, *Meet Me in St Louis* with Judy Garland and the famous, *Oklahoma!* starring Gordon MacRae. Premiered first on Broadway, and created by Richard Rodgers and Oscar Hammerstein II, *Oklahoma!* became one of the most successful musical comedies of all time. This was the first musical they collaborated on and many more followed: *South Pacific*, *The King and I*, *The Sound of Music* and *Carousel*, all appearing first on Broadway.

In the 1950s Hollywood film studios were reeling from the impact of television. The film musical, however, continued to attract even more fortune. Songs could be pre-sold to audiences through radio, the jukebox and television, ensuring box office success for the film musicals. Lavish stage productions turned into even more opulent screen spectacles, and moviegoers across the world flocked to see *Annie Get Your Gun, Showboat, Gentlemen Prefer Blondes, Kiss Me Kate, Guys and Dolls, Singin' in the Rain* and *Seven Brides for Seven Brothers*.

During the 1960s, realism entered the musical as it did elsewhere in the pop world. *Sweet Charity*, first appearing in 1964 on Broadway about a dance-hall hostess with a heart of gold, dealt with the harsher sides of life. With sensational songs like *Big Spender, Rhythm of Life* and *If They could See Me Now* and splendid direction and choreography by Bob Fosse, this stage and screen musical became a major success of the decade. Other key musicals of the 1960s included *The Sound of Music, Paint Your Wagon,* and *Hello, Dolly!*

Musicals in the 1970s took a nostalgic turn. *Grease, Cabaret, Fiddler on the Roof, A Little Night Music* and *1776* all evoked the past. *Cabaret* changed traditional perceptions of the musical, both on stage and screen. The origins of the work, (directed by Hal Prince with lyrics by Fred Ebb and music by John Kander), stemmed from Christopher Isherwood's semi-autobiographical book *Goodbye to Berlin.*

Tough, acid and satirical, it was the first musical to confront and celebrate the ambiguity of life. Homosexuality, using people, Nazism, decadence and transvestism are all dealt with honestly and expressively. *Cabaret* also used music in an exciting new way: characters did not burst into song, to explain feelings. Instead striking, at times savage songs, were perfomed in the sleazy Kit Kat Club, providing a logical place for music.

Jesus Christ Superstar, the first of the Lloyd-Webber/Rice creations, opened on Broadway in 1971 and was translated onto screen in 1973. *Evita* became a further hit for this partnership, becoming a film in the 1990s, starring Madonna.

In the 1980s, *Starlight Express*, written by Andrew Lloyd Webber and Richard Stilgoe introduced highly-technical stage effects into the musical. Peformers act and sing on roller blades, skating around the audience to produce an exciting atmosphere. The West End of London still shows many of the musicals mentioned above, with some running since the moment they were created.

No section on the musical would be complete without listing the chief composers of the genre. Richard Rodgers, Oscar Hammerstein, Jerome Kern, Cole Porter, Kurt Weill, Meredith Wilson, Irving Berlin, George Gershwin, Noel Coward and many others have made an invaluable contribution to the history of popular music.

TASKS

- Watch at least three film musicals from the early, middle and later periods of the genre. Discuss the common traits.
- Some of the early musicals seem old-fashioned nowadays. Why is this? Consider, for example, the role of women in such works as *Kiss Me Kate* or *Seven Brides for Seven Brothers*.
- Try to arrange an outing to view a stage musical. List all the elements which are involved in the creation of the production.

Figure 1.13   *Nöel Coward*

Figure 1.14   *Elvis Presley*

END OF SESSION ASSIGNMENT

- Create a radio programme, suitable for young people (aged 16 to 25), on the history of pop music, starting with rock 'n' roll in the 1950s. The programme should be exactly 30 minutes long.

- Create five groups, each comprising a DJ, researchers and script writers. Each group should be given a certain decade to present, including relevant musical examples. The scripts should be lively, entertaining and informative without a second of 'dead time'. The time allotted for each group will be exactly five minutes.

- One DJ should be appointed to top and tail the show and insert patter between the decades. You may wish to select appropriate introductory music for the programme.

chapter 2
HISTORICAL DEVELOPMENT OF FORMS AND STYLES

Labelled classical music, serious music, oldies' music, and worst of all, posh music, this genre is recognised by all. Like popular music, it is celebrated by those who understand and denigrated by those who don't, but both genres exist in our lives in advertising, as background music to film or as muzak, whether we actively seek to listen or not.

While pop stars and cultures attract lively tabloid headlines and huge financial rewards, the music of the concert hall has until recently maintained a low profile. Nowadays promotional techniques are changing, and with innovative new radio stations like Classic FM and specialist arts television channels, this genre and its history is surprising and informing many of the uninitiated.

So hold on to your seats, and prepare for an exciting journey. If you thought sex appeal, glamour and outrageous behaviour were the copyright of the rock world, a major shock is in store. Likewise, you will discover powerful, evocative music which expresses deep emotions of universal experience.

Forms and styles

Considering the development of key forms and styles through the eras, enables a deeper understanding of the genre, and a comparison with popular music.

Every creative product is built upon forms and styles to ensure easy communication, coherence and meaning. In music even the most abstract combination of sounds has order and distinctive expression. So what is a form exactly, and how does it compare to a style?

Form is the structure around which style is created. In classical music, for example, sonata form is divided into three main sections each with a particular role to play, but a Beethoven sonata from the late classical period would sound quite different to a sonata composed by Hindemith in the twentieth century. The difference is a matter of style. Similarly two songwriters working to the same pop song format would create entirely different sounds because of individual style and interpretation. Like popular music, we shall be looking at the current cultures surrounding the music, starting with the renaissance period.

Renaissance music

Generally speaking, the renaissance or 'rebirth' refers to the great revival of art, literature, music and learning beginning in Italy in the fourteenth century and flourishing in Europe by the sixteenth century. The aim of this intellectual movement was to push the boundaries of education as far as possible and produce the 'renaissance man', conversant in the humanities, mathematics, science, arts, crafts, geography and sports. Vital to this movement was the emphasis on questioning, scepticism and free thought.

The new spirit spread quickly with the development of printing, geographical discovery, and the revival of interest in classical Greek and Roman culture which inspired great works from writers Petrach and Boccaccio and artists such as Leonardo da Vinci, Michelangelo and Dürer. Other figures in the renaissance period included the famous politicians, Machiavelli and Bacon, poets Ariosto and Tasso, physicist Galileo, astronomer Copernicus and writers Shakespeare, Sidney and Marlowe.

RENAISSANCE MUSICAL STYLE

Musicians embraced the new era's vitality and adopted a more free and expressive style. The renaissance sound was rich and fluent with musical strands blending together smoothly within a homophonic or polyphonic texture.

The distinctive style of renaissance music is partly achieved through instrumentation. The sackbut, lute, cornett, crumhorn, virginal, clavichord, viol, recorder and shawm are typical of the period, and many of these instruments developed into the modern versions we play and hear today. The viols, for example, evolved into the string family, and the sackbut eventually transformed into the trombone.

Secular instrumental music flourished boldly after a long period of sacred vocal compositions. In particular, jolly dances and suites of dances became popular: often a fast dance with three beats to the bar would follow a slow dance with two beats in the bar, such as the combination of pavane and galliard. Other dances of the renaissance and baroque periods were the allemande, sarabande, courante and the bransle, nicknamed by Shakespeare as the 'French brawl'.

Another stylistic characteristic of renaissance music was the use of modes. Inherited from ancient Greece via the middle ages, modes consisted of twelve sets of eight-note scales. All have Greek names and may be represented on the white notes of the piano, for example the Lydian mode, starting on F. This mode, favoured by Chopin in the romantic period, consists of F G A B C D E F. The modern version of this scale is F major which has a B flat instead of B natural.

By the end of the seventeenth century, modes were reduced to two: major and minor, but they reappeared later during the romantic, nationalist and impressionist periods, and are in use today in much folk and popular music.

TASKS

- Start a portfolio for musical instruments. Era by era, list the most important instruments and their developments.
- Try to attend a concert of renaissance music in which the performers use authentic instruments.
- Play the following three modes on the white notes of the piano or keyboard:

Lydian, starting on F
Dorian, starting on D
Ionian, starting on C
Aeolian, starting on A

- Write a very short tune based around one of the modes.
- Listen to some folk music to hear the use of modes in a more popular context.

RENAISSANCE FORMS

Freer forms in both sacred (religious) and secular (worldly) music were encouraged. Important and distinctive forms were polyphony and homophony, the madrigal, the mass and the motet.

Polyphony and homophony

Music in two or more parts which are independent and of equal status can be described as polyphonic. These separate and equal parts move in different directions at different times with an emphasis on melody and rhythm, which in the renaissance period dominated the harmony. Polyphonic music implies the use of counterpoint or contrapuntal forms such as fugue in baroque times. The adjectives polyphonic and contrapuntal, and nouns polyphony and counterpoint, are interchangeable and apply to the music of composers such as Palestrina, Lassus and Byrd.

The opposite of polyphony (literally many sounds) is homophony, in which one part dominates and the others accompany.

The madrigal

Still popular today, the madrigal is an unaccompanied secular vocal composition set to poems for several parts. Early madrigals are in strict form but by the sixteenth century the introduction of word painting, chromaticism, imitative polyphony and a sense of drama give way to less restrained writing. Freer rhythms, the use of modes, independent part writing and intense emotion are the distinctive stylistic traits.

One of the most famous madrigals was written by Thomas Morley:

> Now is the month of maying
>
> When merry lads are playing
>
> Fa la la la la la la la la
>
> Fa la la la la la la
>
> Each with his bonny lass
>
> Upon the greeny grass . . .

The reference to pastoral scenes and the fa la chorus capture the essence of renaissance freedom and vitality. Another secular vocal form using the fa la refrain is the ballett, which originated in Italy around 1600. The main distinction between the two forms is that the madrigal is polyphonic while the ballett is mostly homophonic with strong dancing rhythms.

The fa la chorus is rather like the affirmative yeah, yeah we get in pop music. Another typical phrase of the times was 'with a hey and a ho and a hey nonny no', again reinforcing the sentiments of a song with scat-like meaningless words.

Prominent composers of the madrigal in Italy during the renaissance were Monteverdi and Marenzio and English composers (who tended to create around stricter forms) were Morley, Weelkes and Wilbye.

TASKS

- Listen to three madrigals. In groups discuss the characteristics of style as described above.
- Next discuss the sentiments of each song. Are there any common traits? Are there similarities to the pop songs of today?
- Try writing the lyric for a madrigal using the language of the times.

The mass

The celebration of the Eucharist or Holy Communion, the chief Christian sacrament when bread and wine are consumed in memory of Jesus Christ, is commonly known in the Roman Catholic Church and certain Protestant churches as the mass.

The service is taken in any one of three forms:

1 **high mass** (missa solemnis) consisting of five variable plainsong passages performed by a choir, deacon, sub-deacon and other ministers, and five extended invariable pass-ages performed by the congregation, called the ordinary of the mass;

2 **sung mass** (missa cantata) which is similar to **1** but without the deacon or sub-deacon and

3 **low mass** (missa privata or missa lecta) normally performed by a priest and clerk.

In music, however, the term refers to the setting of the invariable ordinary of the mass. The five sections are always the Kyrie, Gloria, Credo, Sanctus with Benedictus and Agnus Dei.

Figure 2.1A *A fourteenth century illustration showing drum, pipe, shawm, fiddle, psalter and sackbut*

Figure 2.1B *An early treble or tenor viol*

The mass developed as a musical composition around 1430, incorporating existing plainsong melodies and common openings for each movement. In the renaissance period, Palestrina and Monteverdi were notable composers of the mass, but the form inspired many later musicians such as J.S. Bach, Haydn, Mozart, Schumann and, in the twentieth century, Bernstein and Lloyd Webber, who were normally associated with popular music.

TASKS

- Try to arrange an outing to hear a mass by any composer, not necessarily from the renaissance period.
- Under headings of the five sections of the mass, jot down brief descriptions of the music, mentioning the different emotions expressed and subject matters.

The motet

Flourishing in the thirteenth century, the motet is commonly a short piece of unaccompanied sacred music for three or four voices based on an existing plainsong melody sung by a tenor. Between 1300 and 1450, composers such as Machaut and Dunstable perfected the isorhythmic motet which was usually in three parts woven around the tenor line. Each part had the same rhythmic pattern applied to successive divisions or repetitions of the melody. Motets at this time were either secular or sacred. In the renaissance, motets were sacred, unaccompanied and based on a plainsong tenor line. The text was in Latin and each part had the same words. In keeping with the philosophy of the period, composers added freer elements such as imitation and new themes.

TASK FOR END OF THE RENAISSANCE PERIOD

- Arrange a renaissance day out with your fellow musicians. Use your imagination for an enjoyable and informative day. You could, for example, go to an art gallery to admire some renaissance works, read some Shakespeare over coffee and sing a madrigal before lunch!

Baroque music

The term baroque has an intriguing history. Nowadays it refers to the dynamic artistic and architectural movement originating in Rome around 1600, and flourishing throughout Europe until the early eighteenth century. Originally, however, baroque was a term of abuse, coined at a time when certain aspects of seventeenth-century art were out of critical favour. At this point baroque meant grotesque and over elaborate.

Taking root particularly in Catholic countries, the style became deeply associated with the new Catholic church, expressing a grandeur and strength inherited from high renaissance. This style was perfect for conveying intense religious feeling and artists such as Bellini and Rubens were devout Catholics.

The lavish eloquence so typical of the baroque was also attractive to secular arts. In France, for example, the style reached its greatest heights at the court of Louis XIV. His palace at Versailles housed exquisite baroque sculpture, landscape, architecture, painting and decoration. The concept of several arts joining together to form a 'total work of art' was another characteristic of the period.

In music, the term describes the works and style of the period which spanned 150 years. From the birth of opera and oratorio to the death of J.S. Bach, baroque music fired future generations of composers with ideas and gave them solid foundations on which to build.

Early baroque composers were Monteverdi, Lully and Purcell, who were all involved in the development of opera in Italy, France and England respectively. Later baroque composers include J.S. Bach, Handel and Vivaldi. Still popular today, this music is performed at sell-out concerts around the world.

TASK

- Research J.S. Bach and one other composer from the following list to prepare for a study of the baroque musical style: Handel, Vivaldi, Monteverdi, Purcell, Lully.

BAROQUE MUSICAL STYLE

The baroque sound is identifiable by its instrumention, harmony and rhythmical and melodic phrasing. The most typical instrumental feature was the figured bass (also known as thorough bass or basso continuo) played by a keyboard or other chordal instrument, with actual bass notes often performed by the cello. Baroque ensembles were held together by the basso continuo, appearing on musical scores as figures indicating the harmonies. A certain degree of improvisation was involved for continuo players.

Figure 2.2A   *Theorbo player*

The viols, associated with the renaissance period, developed into the violin family and the orchestra as we know it today, was beginning to emerge. Clavichords, harpsichords and organs were the keyboard instruments which characterise the era, and much music was composed for them alone, for example J.S. Bach's *48 Preludes and Fugues* which demonstrate the use of all the major and minor keys on the chromatic scale.

Sequences of chords dominated the harmony, and modes began to wane by the seventeenth century. Energetic rhythms and a walking bass drove the music forward while long flowing melodies were contained in balanced groups. The rich baroque sound, whether communicated through solo works or larger forces still stands the test of time.

Figure 2.2B   *A clavichord*

Figure 2.2C   *The lute*

BAROQUE FORMS

Certain forms dominated the era. These were binary and ternary forms (music in two or three sections), variations, ritornello form (literally meaning returning theme), rondo and the fugue. One important structure, especially popular for variations, was the ground bass. This was a constantly-repeated bass line over which changes of harmony or melody could occur. This concept developed into the ostinato in classical music and the riff in pop music. Nearest to the unchanging ground bass in popular music is a blues riff over which musicians improvise.

These structural elements were used for much larger baroque forms such as opera, overture, oratorio, concerto grosso, polyphony and the fugue.

Opera

This dramatic form, in which most characters sing with an instrumental accompaniment, evolved from a combination of precursors such as liturgical dramas of the middle ages and sixteenth-century Italian court entertainments. Present day opera stems from the Florentine Camerata, a group of musicians, artists and scholars led by Count Bardi. The Camerata's thoughts on music determined the origins of opera and the two main beliefs were that

1 vocal polyphony destroyed poetic meaning and
2 words when set to music should be recited without too much interpretation.

These beliefs combined into a new vocal communication vehicle called recitative – the style of operatic singing for dialogue and narrative which is more closely related to dramatic speech than song.

Monteverdi's *Orfeo* is an example of the Florentine philosophy, but goes far beyond earlier forms by hinting at developments for the future. A lavish orchestra, the use of expressive recitative, the creation of contrasting strophic songs (songs with verse and chorus), choral writing, early forms of arias and duets were all combining to express intense human emotion on a grand scale. Opera sparked mass appeal and the form quickly spread and developed.

Lully incorporated ballet into the genre which was to remain in French opera until the nineteenth century. Purcell presented England with its first true opera, *Dido and Aeneas*, which was greatly influenced by the masque. Later a standard form of aria emerged called the da capo aria. Literally meaning 'from the top, the da capo aria comprises three sections: the first' a contrasting second, and a repetition of the first.

Opera began to take flight, attracting new interpretations in the classical period.

TASKS

- Listen to extracts from both of the early operas mentioned above. In particular try to identify recitatives and arias. At this stage there are quite subtle differences, which become more obvious later.
- Start a new portfolio for opera. List operas and composers by era.

Figure 2.3   *A baroque interpretation of a scene from* Dido and Aeneas

Overture

Initially there were no introductions to operas, except perhaps a flourishing fanfare to bring the audience to attention. Composers quickly sensed that listeners required more preparation for an opera, and that introductory scene setting could increase excitement and anticipation for the musical drama ahead. This concept was later developed by Mozart in the classical period and Wagner in the nineteenth century.

Two types of introduction became standard: The French overture and the Italian overture. Both types had three movements. The French overture was always slow, quick, slow while the Italian is the opposite – quick, slow, quick.

Oratorio

A large form closely related to opera is the oratorio. The single most important difference is that oratorio is sacred, whereas opera is secular. The term originated in the late sixteenth century when St Philip Neri decided to hold a more popular style of service in an oratory – hence the term, oratorio. Composers like Carissimi adopted opera forms, in particular the chorus, which began to reflect and, in some cases, comment upon the dramatic action. This added tension, force and excitement to the work. Schutz, J.S. Bach and Handel were major exponents of the genre in the baroque period.

TASKS

- Research oratorio by listing composers and their main works in this genre.
- Listen to extracts of the most famous oratorio of all time, Handel's *Messiah*.
- In the twentieth century, Quincy Jones, the prolific songwriter, producer and arranger created an oratorio entitled *Black Messiah*. Celebrating the history of black music, *Black Messiah* reflected the forms of Handel's *Messiah*. After listening to this radical work, jot down a comparison of both oratorios in terms of style and form.

Concerto grosso

The characteristic orchestral form of baroque times was the concerto grosso. Paving the way for the solo concerto the term is Italian for great concerto. In the baroque period the concerto grosso involved contrasts between the full orchestra, called the ripieno, and a small solo group of instruments, called the concertino. Ritornello form was often used in the concerto grosso to highlight the opposing sections by including a recurring theme (the ritornello) for the full orchestra. Linked together by continuos, the concerto grosso comprised several movements, for example Allegro, Adagio, Minuet and Trio and other dance movements.

To provide even greater contrast, the solo concerto was developed. Initially the violin was chosen as the solo instrument because so many composers played it and knew the capabilities. Torelli's solo concertos normally had three movements (the central one being slow) with solo themes discreetly accompanied by the orchestra. These themes were separated by orchestral ritornelli. J.S. Bach and Vivaldi also wrote solo concertos, but the form was to develop more significantly during the classical period.

TASK

- Listen to J.S. Bach's *Brandenburg Concerto No 1* or *2*. Jot down the orchestration, number and type of movements and any typically baroque features you notice. Try to obtain a musical score for this exercise.

One of the most famous works of the period is Vivaldi's *Four Seasons*. Depicting each season through a concerto, radical and progressive thinking is demonstrated as Vivaldi pioneers the embryonic forms of solo concerto and programme music, and uses lighter textures more prevalent in classical music. This hooky and vibrant music is much used by advertising and continues to sell well today.

TASKS

- Listen to Vivaldi's *Four Seasons*, preferably with a score so that you may read the written descriptions of the music.
- Discuss in groups how Vivaldi communicates the narrative through music.

Polyphony and the fugue

While the Florentine Camerata were opposed to vocal polyphony for opera, instrumental works embraced and developed the forms. The most prevalent polyphonic form was the fugue, and the master of it was J.S. Bach. Starting simply, but developing into a complex labyrinth of sounds, the fugue is a contrapuntal composition for two or more voices, of equal importance. The voices are built around a subject which is introduced and imitated by each voice in turn, reappearing frequently throughout the composition in various guises.

The first entry, called the subject, is introduced in the home or tonic key. The second entry, called the answer, starts a fifth above or a fourth below. Other voices then enter in the same manner, but they may be delayed by a codetta. After all the voices have entered, the exposition (or first section) is complete.

Thereafter, the subject continues to appear, but in different keys, or by augmentation, diminution, inversion or other means.

TASKS

- Augmentation, diminution and inversion are important musical terms which you should know. Look them up in a musical dictionary, and be aware of them from now on.
- Listen to J.S. Bach's *Toccata* and *Fugue in D* minor which has been used countless times in advertising and film. Toccata is from the Italian verb toccare, to touch, and indicates a rapid solo instrumental piece showing off the performer's technique.
- Create a new portfolio for forms. Era by era, list the major forms. By the end of your study of classical music, you will have a comprehensive overview of the development of forms.

Classical music

The true meaning of the term classical music refers to the works of Mozart, Haydn, Beethoven and others composing between 1750 to around 1810. These two dates are important to remember: late baroque composer J.S. Bach died in 1750, and romantic exponent Chopin was born in 1810. Shifting away from the characteristically solid and sombre music of the baroque era, classical music and its forerunner, galant, introduced lighter elements without losing richness.

In the art world, rococo developed from baroque and partly reacted against it. Equivalent to the galant style in music, rococo art was lighter, often intentionally playful, and was initially communicated through interior decoration. The first rococo painter was Watteau, and artists Boucher and Fragonard brought the style to its peak in Paris, which replaced Rome as the international capital of the arts world.

By the 1760s, interest grew towards neo-classicism in France but in central Europe, the rococo movement flourished until the end of the eighteenth century. While baroque art was largely sacred, rococo tended to be more secular.

Reacting against the frivolity of rococo, neo-classical art looked to ancient creations of Greece and Rome for inspiration and depth.

The new movement responded to the increasing scholarly knowledge of antiquity, and the excavations of the Roman towns Pompeii and Herculaneum, which had been buried by an eruption of Mount Vesuvius, stimulated interest further. Rome returned as the arts centre, and artists from Europe and America travelled there to work for long periods and absorb the atmosphere. Neo-classicism aimed at order and clarity, but there were many shades of interpretation drawing from ancient artistic trends. Chief exponents of the style were Jacques-Louis David, Claude-Nicholas Ledoux and John Flaxman.

The galant

Like rococo art, galant music represents the transition period between baroque and classical, and is roughly dated between 1730 and 1770. In music this can be simply understood as marking the differences between the works of J.S. Bach and his sons C.P.E. and J.C. Bach and the early works of Haydn and Mozart. Many of the stylistic traits emerging in galant music were adopted by classical composers. Light homophonic textures (as opposed to polyphonic), elegantly ornamented melodies, simple tonic and dominant harmonies and clear, balanced phrasing are characteristics common to both genres.

In keyboard music, one of the most important aspects of galant was the Alberti bass. A left-hand broken chord figuration, the Alberti bass became a common feature in the classical period. Listen out for this in all keyboard music of the time.

TASK

- Try to listen to some keyboard music of C.P.E. Bach or early Haydn, noting all of the galant traits mentioned above.
- Prepare yourself for a study of classical music by researching the composers Mozart, Haydn and Beethoven. Include their main works, their dates and brief notes about their lives.

CLASSICAL MUSIC STYLE

Developing from the galant style, classical music is embodied in the works of Mozart, Haydn and Beethoven. The style radically changed the course of musical history, influencing future generations of composers and giving much enjoyment to millions.

Textures are homophonic and lighter, further enchanced by balanced phrasing, formal order, clarity of expression and restraint. The music was not without passion, however. Haydn, for example, influenced by the Mannheim School, incorporated sudden contrasts of quiet, almost inaudible passages with bombastic loud music in his symphonies.

Dynamics were part of the increasingly contrasting elements in classical music. Themes, rhythms, timbres, moods and even keys shifted, changed and developed within a single piece, while grace and beauty still predominated.

The instrumentation of classical music was also a distinctive part of the style. The orchestra increased in size and became more balanced with woodwind developing its own section identity. The four orchestral sections which continue today were established: strings, woodwind, brass and percussion, and the harpsichord continuo fell out of use.

The string quartet and the introduction of the piano are instrinsic to the style. Early piano works of Haydn and Mozart demonstrate thin textures which became richer, denser and more powerful with Beethoven.

Figure 2.4   *G.F. Handel, 1685–1759*

CLASSICAL MUSIC FORMS

The ideals of order, balance and clarity were communicated directly through form, the most important being sonata form. Like the fugue in baroque times, this was a structure upon which larger forms were created.

Sonata form

Essentially this musical form comprises three main sections: exposition, development and re-capitulation.

In the expositon, or first section the composer introduces two ideas which form the basis of the music. These two ideas are known as subjects, and are different in character and key. They may also consist of a group of ideas rather than single themes. The first subject is stated in the home or tonic key, and after a bridge passage, the second subject appears in a new but related key, such as the dominant, or relative major, if the home key is minor. Occasionally the exposition is repeated.

Figure 2.5   *W.A. Mozart, 1756–1791*

The development section literally develops the material introduced in the exposition. The subjects may modulate into new keys (always avoiding the home key), or combine together to create an exciting dialogue, or appear in inversion. The tension increases as developments mount, reaching a climax when the instruments herald the return of the home key as the music moves into the recapitulation.

In the recapitulation the subjects of the exposition are restated but in a slightly different way. The first subject reappears in the home key as before, but after a different bridge passage, the second subject also appears in the home key. The form is often concluded with a coda, or tailpiece.

An easy way to remember sonata form is to consider the sections as if they were part of a three-act play.

In Act 1 the two main characters are introduced and the scene is set.

In Act 2 the plot thickens and develops. The characters experience new situations: they might fall in love, argue and separate, or even commit murder!

In Act 3 the characters reappear in a semblance of normality, and the denouement occurs. While the characters are essentially the same, experience has left its indelible mark.

Sonata form is intrinsically linked with classical music, and often structures the first movements of larger orchestral classical forms such as the symphony or solo concerto. Sonata form is also known as first-movement form and occasionally, compound-binary form.

TASK

- Read over the information on sonata form again. Enter the form in your portfolio, and draw a diagram to help you understand.

The symphony

This orchestral form in four movements developed from the baroque concerto grosso, the Italian overture (favoured by Scarlatti in fast-slow-fast form) and the suite. The four movements comprise: first movement (usually in sonata form); a slower second movement; a minuet and trio, and a finale. C.P.E. Bach, Stamitz and Gluck of the Mannheim School were early composers of the form, and it flourished and developed in the hands of Haydn, Mozart and Beethoven.

Haydn's twelve *London Symphonies* represent a culmination of output with a large classical orchestra consisting of pairs of flutes, oboes, clarinets, bassoons, horns (sometimes more because they were much favoured by the composer), trumpets, timpani and strings. Beethoven not only increased the orchestra further in his symphonies, but also created more technically difficult parts for the players. Beethoven also presented a unity of mood, joined movements together, tended towards a narrative programme and even introduced vocal elements. The symphonies of Beethoven directly influenced Liszt's symphonic poems, Berlioz' *Romeo and Juliet*, and indirectly many works of the future.

Figure 2.6   *Handel (extreme right) conducting an oratorio*

TASK

- Immerse yourself in classical symphonies by listening to as many as you can. Beethoven's *Fifth Symphony* is a good place to start.

The solo concerto

In contrast to the baroque concerto grosso consisting of the ripieno and the contrasting concertino, the classical concerto presented a platform for a solo performer and full orchestra. In the first movement (again often in sonata form) an opportunity arose for the soloist to display their virtuosic talent in the cadenza. Improvised at first, cadenzas were later written out fully by Mozart and Beethoven.

By Mozart's time, the figured bass had become obsolete, although a harpsichord or piano was still included in the orchestra, even in keyboard solo concertos.

TASK

- Choose an instrument you like and then find a classical solo concerto for that instrument. Listen to it.

Opera

This form continued to develop in the classical period and different styles began to emerge. Opera buffa was Italian-style comic opera dealing with lighter subjects and everyday characters. A fine example of this genre is Mozart's *The Marriage of Figaro*. Based on a play by French writer, Beaumarchais, the opera tells of Figaro, a popular barber of Seville, who becomes a valet to Count Almaviva. Figaro intends to marry Susanna, the Countess's maid, but the Count so enjoys flirting with Susanna, he refuses Figaro permission to marry the woman he loves. Figaro, however, considers himself equal to his social superiors and the opera cleverly explores all aspects of love while ridiculing the class system. The same character appears in another important Beaumarchais play, *The Barber of Seville*, providing the inspiration for one of Rossini's operas. These plays caused offence and outrage amongst the aristocracy of Paris in the 1780s and represented part of the intellectual atmosphere leading to the French Revolution of 1789.

Opera seria, in contrast, was more serious and formal, involving an heroic or mythological plot with leading roles often given to castrato singers. Characters were noble and arias elaborate with the libretto in Italian. An example of this style is Mozart's *La Clemenza di Tito*.

Another significant composer of opera was the German composer Gluck who influenced Mozart, Beethoven and, later, Berlioz. Gluck believed that the philosophies of the Camerata should be reinstated: virtuosic elements should be abandoned to enable dramatic truth and simple expression. In addition, Gluck created overtures which prepared the audience for the drama ahead, utilised the orchestra to heighten or lessen the drama according to the words, and avoided marked differences between recitatives and arias. Two of Gluck's operas which

Figure 2.7 *Act II from Mozart's* Magic Flute

demonstrate this philosophy are *Orpheus and Eurydice* of 1762, and *Alcestis* of 1767.

Sonata

Not to be confused with sonata form, the single word sonata is simply a three or four-movement work for a solo instrument with or without piano accompaniment. A similar composition for three instruments is called a trio sonata.

A feature of the sonata, in common with many other large classical forms, is that the first movement is in sonata form.

Mozart developed the idea of having three contrasting movements, while Beethoven added the scherzo, a fast and jolly movement in 3/4 time.

TASKS

- Listen to any of Beethoven's piano sonatas, examining the sonata form used in the first movements.
- Other light forms associated with the classical period are divertimento and serenade. Listen to Mozart's *Eine Kleine Nachtmusik.*
- Investigate the popularity of classical music today. Interview your peers, parents, grandparents and other age groups to examine the extent of interest in this genre.

Romantic music

Passion, excitement, fear, love, anger – these are natural emotions we all experience as part of human life. In the romantic period, artists sought to express those feelings as sincerely and as originally as possible, resulting in some of the most explosive music ever composed.

The romantic movement dominated all western arts from the late eighteenth century until the first half of the nineteenth century. Writers such as Victor Hugo and George Sand, painters like Turner and Goya and musicians such as Chopin and Schumann found a new freedom of expression, and for the first time the arts were linked more closely together, each taking inspiration from the other.

In some ways, the romantic era reacted against classical principles. In the quest to convey a new outlook on life and art, novel forms, styles and techniques were required to give the movement full rein. This was in direct contrast with the classical period which respected the past. However, some aspects of the romantic movement did celebrate bygone times, albeit in a nostalgic, sentimental way. This small movement was known as romantic classicism.

Typical romantic themes across the arts were: the extreme pain and pleasure of love; nature, in particular wild, exotic or mysterious landscapes; dreams and nightmares; fairytales and legends; the macabre; literature of the past such as Shakespeare, and nationalism. At every turn, these themes provided vehicles for intense emotional expression.

TASK

- Guess some changes about to take place in musical history. Now read on to see if you were right!

Figure 2.8   *Landscape by Caspar David Friedrich*

ROMANTIC MUSICAL STYLE

The romantic movement, promoting self-expression and freedom of thought, pushed the boundaries of all musical elements to communicate in a striking new language.

The orchestra grew even larger. The brass section, now comprising four horns, three trumpets, three trombones and a tuba, increased its stature in the orchestra by the weighty addition of the tuba and the invention of the valve system, which gave the instruments greater flexibility and range. The woodwind section also increased in size to three flutes, oboes, clarinets and bassoons, and new additions the piccolo, cor anglais, bass clarinet and double bassoon offered more volume, timbre and expressive

possibilities. The string section grew to balance the other sections, with one harp or more adding richness and exoticism to the string textures. This modern orchestra, full of character, richness and depth provided the perfect channel for romantic fervour.

An emphasis was placed on the virtuoso performer/composer and society regarded the artist as rather a remote genius, even though more realism was present in music than ever before.

Melodies were lyrical, powerful, evocative and song-like, incorporating expressive chromaticism. With the upsurge of nationalism, folk idioms were introduced into melodies, such as the modal Lydian fourth in the music of Chopin, along with folk rhythms. Harmonies were richer, modulations were plentiful and chromaticism, a truly romantic characteristic, added tension, uncertainty and drama as the sense of key began to dissipate. Thrilling dynamic and pitch contrasts, bold discords, the introduction of rubato (literally meaning robbed time), and the uninhibited promotion of the virtuoso performer, all aided the expression of fierce emotions.

TASK

- Research the life and works of Chopin and one other romantic composer, choosing from Schubert, Schumann, Liszt, Wagner or Weber.

ROMANTIC FORMS

The new movement demanded freer forms to communicate the expressive style. The solo concerto developed in the romantic period with the virtuoso performer requiring more brilliant and technically difficult parts to show off to increasingly appreciative audiences. Paganini, who composed at least five violin concertos, played with such demonic ferocity that some believed he was inspired by the devil! Liszt, on the other hand, wooed his audiences with passionate renderings of his piano works and sexy looks, causing some women to faint with passion.

Programme music

It would be wrong to assume, however, that romantic music was unstructured. Under-pinning all romantic music is a new concept of form, influencing future generations of composers. The combination of arts in particular, inspired the radical thinking behind programme music. Describing a poem, story, painting, landscape or emotional experience, the form and style of programme music is dictated by extra-musical subjects. Hinted at with Vivaldi's *Four Seasons*, composers such as Berlioz, who wrote *Symphonie Fantastique* and Richard Strauss, who composed *Don Quixote* and *Till Eulenspiegel's Merry Pranks*, developed the form and introduced radical pictorial possiblities in music. Liszt called composers of programme music 'tone poets'.

TASKS

- This new form spurred many composers to turn to literature and the arts for inspiration. Listen first to some romantic programme music such as *Don Quixote*, studying details of the story in advance.

Recurring motifs or themes

One way of increasing tension and drama in programme music was to create strongly identifiable motifs which would return throughout the music in various guises.

A motif, or motive is a short independent melody or rhythmic unit which may be as brief as two notes or longer, and is repeated. A musical theme is normally a melodic group of notes which forms the basis or chief idea in a composition by repetition and development.

Figure 2.9   *Delacroix's 'Liberty Leading the People', 1830*

For example, in sonata or rondo form, a theme may also be known as a subject. Therefore, theme and motif are similar in definition, but generally a theme is longer and of greater importance to the form of the whole composition, while a motif (which may form part of a theme) is shorter and less structurally important.

In romantic programme music the concept of both the motif and theme developed significantly. Berlioz, in his *Symphonie Fantastique*, created an idée fixe (fixed idea) which was a recurring theme common to all movements. This fixed idea reflected the story and was changed and varied for dramatic effect. You can imagine, therefore, how this theme is transformed in Berlioz' work sub-titled *Episodes in the Life of an Artist*, with the five movements called Reveries – Passion, A Ball, Scene in the Country, March to the Scaffold and Dreams of a Witches' Sabbath.

Liszt's term for a theme's changing character, which he used in his symphonic poems, was the metamorphosis of themes.

Wagner became associated with the term leitmotif, which was introduced into musical language by H. Von Wolzogen when discussing Wagner's *The Ring*. The leitmotif (or leading motif) is again a recurring idea, this time symbolising an object or character, feeling or situation. The device strengthened the dramatic significance of Wagner's work by recalling at will the audience's memory of thoughts and actions. The result was a heightening of emotions in the vocal line as well as in the orchestral commentary, and an intense audience experience.

Wagner radically changed the course of opera with this new method of composition and his music dramas, more of which we will study later.

Lieder

Intrinsic to the romantic period was the development of the song and the role of the piano. In lieder, the German plural for lied or song, mood and expression were paramount with the piano acquiring equal status to the singer. Schubert wrote some of the most famous, for example the typically romantically themed 'Erlkonig' (Erl King), telling of a forest spirit stealing the soul of a child. A frenetic night horse ride, demons, an anxious father and a terrified son are all captured in the dark and menacing music. Schumann also wrote lieder and, like Schubert, song cycles – sets of songs. In 'Women's Love' and 'Life of 1840', he created songs from a woman's point of view describing courtship and marriage, having children and bereavement.

TASK

- Listen to Schubert's 'Erlkonig' and discuss in groups how the meaning is conveyed both through the singer and the piano part.

Opera

The magic potion of artistic ingredients in romantic opera sparked several turning points in the genre. In France three kinds of opera dominated: grand opera, lyric opera and opera comique. The term grand opera was originally used to distinguish between serious opera and opera comique which involved dialogue. Later the term implied any type of opera on a lavish scale. Several grand operas were written by composers of other countries, for example Rossini's *William Tell*, Wagner's *Rienzi* and Meyerbeer's *Les Hugenots* which vividly portrayed a key chapter in French history.

Lyric opera offered a midway platform between grand opera and operetta. This genre aimed at depth without pomp and complexity, and two major exponents were Gounod and his pupil Bizet, composer of *Carmen*. This lyric opera tells of the doomed and fatal love affair between Don Jose, a Spanish sergeant, and Carmen, a gypsy working in a Seville cigarette factory. The combination of romantic realism, humour and powerful melodies attracted a mass international audience, and much later in 1943, a new version of *Carmen* hit Broadway. Created by Oscar Hammerstein II, *Carmen Jones* appeared with new lyrics and an all-black talented cast, but this time the story was set in the USA. The music of famous arias such as 'Habanera' and the 'Toreador Song' remained but with different words. Bizet's opera holds the record for the number of films it has inspired – a spectacular fourteen.

Meanwhile opera comique siezed the public's imagination when Offenbach's satirical *Orpheus in the Underworld* was premiered in Paris in 1858. The craze soon spread to Vienna, and in London the light operas of Gilbert and Sullivan became highly fashionable in the 1870s and 1880s.

Certain composers, however, preferred to remain loyal to the Italian style and composers Verdi, Bellini, Donizetti and Rossini significantly developed several aspects of the genre. Verdi, particularly in works such as *Il Trovatore, La Traviata, Otello* and *Falstaff*, increased the expressive potential of the orchestra and gave realistic drama more importance. Rossini, with his gift for accessible melody evident in *William Tell* and *The Barber of Seville*, broke conventions of recitative and solo vocal improvisation. Bellini, who died at only 34, contributed expressive melodies to opera which enabled the performer to display both the voice's natural appeal and acquired technique. These exquisite melodies were much admired by Chopin, whose piano melodies paid tribute to Bellini's lyricism.

In Germany Wagner, a composer, librettist and set designer, was influenced by the romantic movement and all of the current developments in the genre, particulary grand opera.

He believed that opera should combine all the arts equally calling his works music dramas. In 1848 Wagner was forced into exile for having liberal sympathies during the revolutionary uprisings. He headed firstly for his friend and composer Liszt in Weimar, but was soon forced to leave Germany completely. Later, after settling in Zurich, Wagner began to realise the vast operatic cycle of four music dramas, *The Ring of the Nibelung*.

The Ring, Tristan and Isolde, The Mastersingers and *Parsifal* illustrate Wagner's theory and philosophy of opera. The fusion of the arts (in which the music did not dominate the drama), the legendary subject matters written in emotional and powerful verse, the heightening of tension by association using the leitmotif, intense expression from the orchestra to aid and at times replace words, and the overall symphonic unity of the works were the key elements which altered the meaning of the genre and rendered the term opera inadequate.

In addition, Wagner's inventive harmony was considered revolutionary. It undermined tonality and paved the way for a new generation of composers in the twentieth century.

TASKS

- In your portfolio on opera, jot down the various types present in the romantic period, with examples of composers and works as stated above.
- Now, in the order they are mentioned above, try to listen to extracts from each type, ensuring you research the storylines beforehand.

THE ROMANTIC TWILIGHT

The pace of change quickened considerably towards the end of the nineteenth century. The traditions of western tonality, questioned by Wagner, added to the altering perceptions of opera, symphony, the orchestra and the artist in relation to society.

The upsurge of nationalism offered composers the chance to react against the German musical domination of Wagner, Brahms and Beethoven. While French and Italian composers maintained their independence during this time, other European writers asserted individuality by finding a nationalist voice. By drawing on folk melodies, rhythms, history, culture or landscape, composers could express patriotism through operas, programme music and symphonies.

In music, nationalism can be traced back to Glinka's opera, *A Life of the Czar* in 1836. By 1860 the movement had hit Norway, Russia and Bohemia. In Russia a group of composers known as The Five strongly supported the cause. Balakiref, Cui, Borodin, Mussorgsky and Rimsky-Korsakov were the members, and *Boris Gudunov*, an opera composed by Mussorgsky, became established as the greatest Russian opera ever composed. The libretto, also written by Mussorgsky, was based on Pushkin's *Boris Gudunov* and Karamzin's *History of the Russian Empire*.

Towards the end of the nineteenth century the movement spread to Spain with Albeniz, Granados and De Falla, Finland with Sibelius, and England with composers Elgar and Vaughan Williams. Moving into the twentieth century, Bartok and Kodaly initiated the nationalist musical movement in Hungary, Villa-Lobos in Brazil and Chavez in Mexico.

These nationalist composers enhanced the styles of the romantic era by incorporating folk scales, rhythms and melodies into the music to create unusual textures, and by utilising the orchestra in a new and expressive way they told stories and communicated a love of their country through music.

TASKS

- Explore nationalism by listening to music from at least two countries involved in the movement. With your fellow musicians, try to establish exactly what makes the music nationalistic, by discussing and taking note of aspects such as rhythm, melody, harmony, instrumentation and subject matter.
- Are there any nationalist composers today working either in the rock or classical field? Jot down names and works, for example the Super Furry Animals from Wales or The Proclaimers or James MacMillan from Scotland.

Figure 2.10 *A 1916 production of Wagner*

Into the twentieth century

Veering towards the twentieth century, the developments in travel, medicine, science, technology and the arts provoked whirlwind changes across the world, and composers increasingly sought to reflect these sociological and artistic transformations in new and accessible ways.

In the late nineteenth century, significant advancements in all spheres of life took place. Darwin wrote *Origin of the Species*, Mendel founded genetics, Pasteur discovered bacteriology and Lister introduced antiseptic surgery. In the world of technology, excitement was rife when Bell invented the telephone, Edison the lightbulb, Benz the automobile and Lumiere the cinema.

Major works of literature were changing viewpoints and widening horizons. Tolstoy's *War and Peace* and Dostoyevsky's *Crime and Punishment* educated the world on Russian thinking, while other writers such as Oscar Wilde were shocking society with their honesty, sexuality and wit.

In the art world, Monet's painting, 'Impression, Sunrise', gave its name to the radical and influential movement called impressionism. Later, expressionism was to react against it, challenging even more strongly all that had gone before.

The communications industry was also advancing. By the turn of the century film was developing, print media was expanding and Marconi had transmitted his first radio signals across the Atlantic.

An Austrian neurologist called Sigmund Freud, however, was to create a profound impact across all the arts and the history of twentieth-century ideas. Known for his development of psychoanalysis, Freud believed that studies of the unconscious mind, such as dream analysis and free association, were highly significant in the understanding and treatment of neurosis. In particular, the repressions which dominate the subconscious, were held by Freud to be closely connected with infantile sexuality. In 1900, Freud published his notorious book, *Interpretation of Dreams*. Freud's radical thinking influenced the work of several artists, writers and composers in the twentieth century.

TWENTIETH CENTURY MUSICAL STYLES

The key styles at the turn of the century were impressionism, expressionism, nationalism, jazz, blues and ragtime. A significant fusion of arts and cultures began to emerge as travel became popular and class-ridden attitudes less entrenched. Rather like the popular music of today, styles co-existed more happily, drew from each other and reflected the ever-changing times.

Impressionism

Artists such as Monet, Renoir, Degas, Pissaro and Manet aimed to capture this new modern life on canvas and concerned themselves with painting in the present. They sought to seize the truth in a moment. Degas tried to arrest that impossible 'now' moment by painting quick movements of ballerinas, but he also portrayed the victims of modern city life such as drunks and prostitutes.

To capture these transitory scenes artists had to paint at speed, some using broad brushstrokes (like Manet) to hint rather than state. To the traditionalists these paintings appeared unfinished but to certain musicians and writers they were an inspiration.

Figure 2.11   *Impressionist art inspired early twentieth-century composers*

Debussy and Ravel are the two composers we associate with the movement. Debussy was profoundly aware of all the arts, in particular impressionist painting and symbolist poetry. An early success for Debussy was the orchestral *Prelude à L'Aprés-Midi d'un Faune*, based on a poem by Mallarmé which explores the mystical world between dreaming and waking, imagination and reality. The music depicts a summer afternoon spent by a faun, a mythical creature, who through a haze sees nymphs in a forest. Is it all a dream, or does the faun really witness this pastoral scene? No one really knows, and in line with impressionist painting, the music hints but does not state.

The characteristics of the style which create this dream-like sound, this seizing of a momentary scene, are typical of Debussy's music generally and can be classified as impressionist music features. The whole tone scale, use of modes, fragmentary melodies coloured with parallel fifths, ninths, thirds and fourths dissipate the sense of key and produce a vague unconscious feel. Free rhythms, duplets against triplets, influence of the orient and unresolved chords add exoticism, and a sense of liberating the mind into uncharted realms.

The music was spacious, all-encompassing and evocative, ignoring the dogmatic rules of harmony. The orchestra grew larger, but was used more subtly. Shimmering textures, harps, unusual combinations of timbres and detailed tiny shades of dynamics for the vast array of instruments ensured interest and tension throughout the music.

TASKS

- Listen to *Prelude à L'Aprés Midi d'un Faune*, taking note of the impressionist features in the music. Then discuss with your fellow musicians how the dream-like quality of the music is achieved.
- Listen to Ravel's famous work, *Bolero*. Discuss how interest is maintained throughout the music.
- Ensure you view some impressionist paintings either by going to an art exhibition or by borrowing some art books.

Expressionism

While impressionist works depicted what the artist saw, expressionist works sought to show what the artist felt. The term was first applied to artists such as Kandinsky and Nolde, but Dutch painter Van Gogh, who expressed sorrow as well as joy, is often viewed as the innovator of the movement.

Immersed in the darker sides of their personalities, painters such as Edward Munch were deeply influenced by Freud and his exploration of the unconscious. The famous painting by Munch, entitled 'Angst', epitomises the movement and the Freudian belief of neurosis stemming from childhood trauma.

Expressionist art soon influenced Schoenberg and his students, mostly because he was closely associated with Kandinsky and other Blaue Reiter painters (a group of more spiritual expressionists). Since expressionism was so personal, the art form rejected extra-personal aspects, and in music this meant traditional forms and techniques. A direct link was formed, therefore, with atonal music through which neurosis, alienation, hysteria and depression could be conveyed in a new language.

Two key expressionist works by Schoenberg were *Erwartung*, an atonal opera for one singer, and *Pierrot Lunaire*. A revolutionary expressionist work, *Pierrot Lunaire* is based on a set of intense and rather graphic poems by Giraud. The music requires reciting voice and a quintet.

The reciting voice, known more generally as sprechgesang or sprechstimme, continues to shock today. In *Pierrot Lunaire* the singer is directed to 'give a pitch exactly, but then immediately leave it in a fall or rise.' An 'x' on the note stem is the standard indication that sprechstimme is to be used, and the result is a tortured sound, ideally suited to expressionism.

Pierrot Lunaire influenced chamber music considerably by introducing unconventional instrumental forces, and small-scale theatrical works by increasing dramatic possibilities.

TASKS

- Listen to 'Der Kranke Mond' ('The Sick Moon') from *Pierrot Lunaire* preferably with a score to enable you to see the indications for sprechstimme.
- Try to arrange to view some expressionist art by visiting a gallery or locating some art books.
- Make sure you really understand the major differences between impressionism and expressionism by jotting down a paragraph of information on both.

Serialism

While expressionism conveyed for the first time the essential vulnerability of the human condition through a disquieting new language, it had certain limitations. A reliance was placed upon drama to provide unity and coherency in a work, since the traditional elements of form had been abandoned. Tonality, harmonic movement, melodies and their development held no importance in expressionism, and therefore extended forms of interest and meaning presented problems. Also, other types of emotions required communication through music. A structural and tonal chaos began to grow. Order and a new direction were vital.

During the years of the Second World War and beyond, Schoenberg immersed himself in literary work, lecturing, conducting and experimenting with atonal music. Eventually, in 1923, he composed *Five Piano pieces, Opus 23* and *Serenade* for chamber ensemble using a new technique – serialism.

Also known as twelve-note, twelve-tone or dodecaphonic music, serialism presented a radical and lasting new modern language.

All the chromatic notes of the scale are specially selected to form a twelve-note theme, known as the note row or series. In traditional music, this operates like a key with its own scale and harmony.

After the row is fixed upon, each of the twelve notes must be played in their complete specified order. There are four main ways in which the row may appear:

1 forwards;
2 backwards (retrograde);
3 upside down (inversion);
4 upside down and backwards (retrograde inversion).

The series can occur on any one of the twelve pitches, so therefore has 48 forms (12 × 4). In addition, any note of the row can appear on any octave, and chords can be formed, providing the notes are used consecutively and simultaneously. For example notes 1, 2 and 3 could be heard together if they were followed by 4, and so on.

Serialism provided the basis of several works, but few were totally in this style. Schoenberg's two students, Berg and Webern, developed his principles further, especially Webern who wrote sparse but expressive strict serial music.

In the 1950s an even stricter type of serialism, called total serialism, emerged with avant garde composers Stockhausen and Boulez. All elements of music, including pitch, duration (note values), dynamics, tempos, articulation and timbre were subjected to the control of Schoenberg's serialist principle. An example of a work in this more extreme form is Stockhausen's *Gruppen*.

TASK

- Borrow the score of Berg's *Violin Concerto* so that you may see the original tone row. Play the tone row over several times, then play it backwards. Read the introduction for other background information and write down a brief paragraph on the inspiration behind this work.
- Listen to the music and then discuss both the serial and traditional tonal elements within.

Neo-classicism

While Schoenberg and his students advanced the concept of serialism, other composers sought to re-establish past styles and forms and present them in a modern language. Neo-classicism flourished as an influential movement throughout the twentieth century, with the Russian composer Stravinsky as a leading figure. Drawing on the principles of balance, diatonic and chromatic harmonies, structured forms and smaller instrumental groupings, Stravinsky proved that 'Music of the past animates and informs the present'.

While the term neo-classicism implies drawing only on the classical period, Stravinsky and Hindemith happily used baroque, renaissance and early music forms and styles, such as fugues and sacred vocal polyphony. To inject a modern feel, unusual and frequent mixtures of time, keys, rhythm and instruments were created. Sometimes Stravinsky would use more than one key simultaneously. This technique is called polytonality.

Two works by Stravinsky in the neo-classical style are *Oedipus Rex* and *Symphony of Psalms*.

Figure 2.12   *A performance of Stravinsky's* Rite of Spring, *1920*

TASK

● Listen to either of the above works and make two headings: old and modern. Jot down all the forms and styles which fall into the respective categories.

One of Stravinsky's most exciting works is *The Rite of Spring*, which caused uproar when it was first performed in Paris in 1913. Written for a vast orchestra, the work tells of a series of pagan rituals culminating in a young girl's voluntary self-sacrifice. The story is communicated fiercely through throbbing and jerky rhythms, pounding discords and striking new combinations of instruments. Listen to the 'Dance of the Youths' and Maidens then discuss why this music caused so much outrage. Also write a brief paragraph on Stravinsky's associate Diaghilev, who founded the Russian Ballet Company.

Chance

After 1945 and the upheavals of the Second World War, rapid sociological changes occurred, particulary the impact on society of new technology and Eastern philosophies. A new generation of composers emerged who began to reject the traditional classical vehicles of expression. Orchestral instruments and forms were less frequently used as composers sought to communicate real life through everyday sounds and electronic media.

Central to the avant garde school was the polymath John Cage, who studied counterpoint with Schoenberg in the 1930s and non-western, folk and contemporary music in New York with American composer Cowell. In addition to music John Cage studied art, architecture and most importantly, Eastern philosophies and Zen Buddhism.

The *I Ching*, the Chinese book of changes, inspired the chance music John Cage was to compose from the early 1950s.

In aleatoric or chance music, the composer chooses to leave the music in an indeterminate state. This random element may be partly controlled, for example by pre-writing sections which could be performed in any order at the throw of a dice. In contrast, where chance is central to the composition, almost anything could happen. John Cage's famous silent piece, 4′ 33″ is an extreme example in which life's sounds are heard as they naturally occur at that moment by chance.

Several composers interpreted chance in different ways. Cowell devised 'elastic notations' which were musical fragments to be assembled by the performers, Berlioz used 'mobile form' which involved whole freely moveable sections, while others such as Stockhausen would simply give the performers advice or offer a collection of symbols, a poem or a drawing for open interpretation. Pitch, speed, dynamics and tempo could also be left to choice and chance.

TASK

- Create your own chance music. Firstly ask your fellow musicians to be silent for a specified amount of time, for example three minutes. Record that 'silence' then discuss the sounds heard.
- Now gather as many musical instruments as you can to allow for a vast choice. Ask your group members to select one instrument each. Now choose some complex emotions, for example neurosis or anger, set the tape recorder running and ask them to play in that vein for two minutes. Don't worry if there are people in your group who cannot play an instrument: this deepens the chance element!

Prepared piano

Cage invented a whole new orchestra of sounds suitable for the twentieth century by inserting everyday objects such as spoons, forks, pieces of cardboard or screws onto or between the strings of the piano. This became known as the prepared piano.

A striking piece in this style is *Amores I, Solo for Prepared Piano,* which requires nine screws, eight bolts, two nuts, and three strips of rubber. Precise indications, lasting several paragraphs, are given as to the size and position of each object so that the desired sound is accurately achieved. Scored traditionally, with ele-gant, balanced phrasing and almost classical melodic lines, the music shocks when heard as it presents the opposite of what is expected. The score, therefore, becomes only a means of instruction to the performer, and as Cage said in the introduction to *Amores, I:*

> The total desired result has been achieved, if on the completion of the preparation, one may play the pertinent keys without sensing that he is playing a piano, or even a prepared piano. An instrument having its own special characteristics, not even suggesting those of a piano, must be the result.

TASK

- Obtaining permission from the owner of a grand piano, experiment with a little prepared piano music by collecting a few household objects and inserting them into any strings. Record the effects.
- Listen to *Amores, I* if you can and jot down your immediate reactions to the piece. Compare them with your fellow musicians.

Electronic music

In 1942 Cage composed *Imaginary Landscape No 3* which employs audio frequency oscillators, a variable-speed turntable for the playing of frequency recordings, a generator whine, electric buzzer, and amplified coil of wire and an amplified marimba. Electronic music was beginning to emerge combined with real-life industrial sounds.

In Paris, also in the 1940s, Peter Schaeffer coined the phrase musique concréte (or concrete music). He believed that music of the past was abstract because written symbols were employed as the starting point. Music of the future, he maintained, is therefore concrete as new technology with pre-recorded real or instrumental sounds are used to activate the creative work. Initially this term was used in contrast to electronic music which is composed entirely with synthetic sounds, but Varese and Stockhausen quickly combined both styles, and the term fell out of favour.

In purely electronic music, the sounds may be all pre-recorded on tape or manipulated live in a concert hall. A synthesis of cultures, centuries, styles and philosophical depth became possible through new technology and electronic music.

TASKS

- Raid your local music libraries for any music by Stockhausen, Varese or Boulez. Establish first whether the music is purely electronic, musique concrete or a combination of both. Then discuss with your musician friends the variety of sounds within and their effect on the listener.

Figure 2.13 *John Cage, 1950s*

GALAXY OF THE TWENTIETH CENTURY

Several other composers have also made an indelible impact on the development of forms and styles in the twentieth century. British composer Benjamin Britten injected more realism into opera and dealt with human suffering and isolation on a grand scale in *Peter Grimes.* Also from Britain, Michael Tippett fused popular music styles, particulary jazz and blues, into his work, to represent music as a universal and accessible means of expression in his celebrated oratorio, *A Child of Our Time.*

Hungarian composer, Bartok altered our perceptions of concerto when he created the vibrant *Concerto for Orchestra,* acknowledging the unique qualities of all instruments while injecting folk rhythms and melodies into the music.

Carl Nielson employed progressive tonality in the symphony by beginning and ending on different keys and the symphonies of Vaughan Williams, Prokofiev, Walton and Shostakovich developed further this essentially classical form by adding different movements and expressing their individuality.

In the USA Henry Cowell coined the term 'tone clusters' from their look on the page. Playable on the piano, the tone cluster was achieved by placing the fist, forearm or fingers across several adjacent notes. Cowell also invented the 'string piano' heard in *Aeolian Harp* where the piano strings are plucked or strummed while certain keys are depressed silently. He was also the innovator of the prepared piano, later advanced by John Cage.

Hindemith and Kurt Weill, who were influenced by Brecht, created gebrauchsmusik or utility music which could be played by amateurs and included idioms from everyday life.

Meanwhile Satie and Milhaud invented furniture music intended for performance outside the concert hall which could be listened to or ignored. This was a precursor of the ambient music later developed by Brian Eno.

Composers experimented more adventurously with sound as the century progressed. Messiaen, the French composer and organist, drew on a colourful array of sound sources from bird song (for which he is most famous), Indian music and oriental percussion to plainsong. Stockhausen began to evoke mystical philosophies in his work, seeking spatial effects and sounds which were alien to the west. Composers, as in the generations before, continue to seek new ways to attract us, their listeners.

Figure 2.14   *The premiere of Brecht's* Baal, *1926*

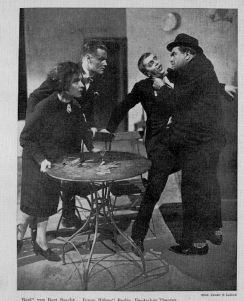

END OF CHAPTER ASSIGNMENTS

- Having read this whistle-stop tour of classical music, which way is music going to go now? Discuss and jot down your opinions on one page.
- Classical music appears to be a man's world. Argue and discuss with reference to this chapter and classical concerts you have attended.
- Try to address the problem of gender imbalance in the history of music by researching some contemporary female composers such as Sally Beamish and Imogen Holst. Write a page on each.
- From all the pieces you have listened to, which inspired and excited you most of all? Create a short radio-style debate, in which each group member states their views and then debates with the others. Choose a presenter and record the show with appropriate extracts. Ensure everyone is well prepared beforehand, and dream up a name for the show which would appeal to a mass-market audience.

chapter 3
PERFORMING MUSIC

Whatever instrument you play or musical style you favour, performance is the goal we all strive towards. Specific instrumental, technical and vocal skills require hours of practice, dedication and excellent instruction – by teachers, peers and other musicians. This chapter does not attempt to cover this area but offers general guidance which may be useful to all performers starting out on a life in the limelight.

Vision

It is important to plan ahead and have an artistic vision of what you or your group wish to communicate to an audience.

Once you have this vision you must ensure you remain focused. If you are forming a group it is important that all band members have similar aspirations and levels of commitment.

Aim for your own individual or band sound that is instantly recognisable whatever material you are playing. Do not feel you have to avoid influences or be deliberately different from everything else. Establishing an identity can be a subtle thing. Even if your set is made up entirely of covers of other peoples' songs, you can do them in your own way and still be unique.

Early on you will need to recognise your strengths and accentuate them:

- What makes you different to other acts?
- What do you do better than anybody else?
- What will an audience remember about your set?
- What will encourage them to see you again?

If your vision is of recording deals and world tours bear in mind that the single most attractive attribute of an unsigned act is a strong local following and fan base. If there is a 'buzz' about the act companies may become interested.

To be successful your vision may change – but the fact that you have a vision will not.

TASKS

- Draw up a ten point list of your strengths and unique features.
- Find three words to describe your act or sound.

Selecting material and interpretation

Selecting material should be the first and foremost decision you make.

The main choices to consider are whether you will perform:

- original material
- covers
- a mix of original and covers
- material in a particular genre

TASKS

- Write down four set lists corresponding to the above.
- Describe each song in terms of form, style, rhythm and mood.

Medium for performance

The medium you choose to perform through may depend on practical considerations or the availability of others. Formats to contemplate are:

Solo performance	Can you accompany yourself and communicate with the audience?
Solo act with Backing/session Musicians	Can you direct others clearly and timeously – have you got the authority and organisational skills necessary?
Solo act with Recorded backing	Can you record the backing yourself and would you enjoy performing without camaraderie?
Duo	Will the extra musician merit half the profit?
Trio	Will you be three equal partners or a front person and two backing musicians?
Quartet/group	Do you all share the same vision and have equal commitment and energy?
Collective	Fashionable, but would you enjoy the looseness and lack of personal control?
A mixture of all	Do you have the technical, musical and interpersonal skills to achieve this?

TASK

- Analyse the ensemble of the Top 20 chart acts at the moment. Are they solo artists, duos or trios, and so on. Which appeals to you the most? Try to describe their style, for example dance, soul, boy band, girl band, pop aimed at younger audiences, pop aimed at older audiences? Describe the instrumentation used: for example 2 guitars, bass, drums & keyboards, brass section, string quartet, synthesizer based, sample based, vinyl mix, computer sequenced.

Working in groups

1 Always consider your reason for performance – is it; profit, personal communication, popularity, artistic endeavour, rebelliousness or assessment for qualification?

2 What are your restricting factors – working to a commission, the intended venue, budget, equipment available, time scale or legal factors?

3 What is the required impact on intended audience? Consider if your act is fit for your purpose, does it have a climax, variety, relevance, and suit current taste and trends?

4 When formulating a performance always consider the alternatives, try them and then choose the best after evaluation.

5 Work with different forms of stimulus – everyday events, personal experiences, trends, literature, politics, philosophy, humour, advice, fun, and so on.

6 After you have established personal and group aims, and decided how decisions will be made, draft and plan the whole endeavour. This can be revised, but it is important to have a guide and direction rather than just waiting for something to happen.

If you wish to lead and direct a group the following may provide a tick list of issues to consider:

- develop a personal or group vision
- select appropriate material for performance
- identify the potential of available performers
- allocate roles within a group or team
- prepare a rehearsal schedule and timetable
- arrange or provide resources and spaces
- liaise with technical support
- manage time effectively and work to deadlines
- set standards
- communicate effectively
- encourage and develop the work of others
- solve problems
- create coherency
- deal with unforeseen circumstances
- be ambitious but realistic

Practice regime

We all know that practice make perfect – but
what constitutes perfect practice?

Here are some guidelines:

Be punctual	Be ready to start – many bands waste time by playing around at the beginning of a rehearsal, a sure sign of amateurism in the worst sense of the word. You are there to do a job of work.
Be prepared	Learn songs and parts before rehearsals rather than during them, as this saves time and minimises strain on other band members. Write down and copy chord sheets and/or lyrics before the rehearsal rather than scribbling them down while everyone waits around. Tape ideas and hand out cassettes before the rehearsal.
Be equipped	Always pack spare strings, sticks, cables, power supplies, fuses etc. – the last thing you want is a long wait while someone 'nips home' or to the local shop for simple spares.
Be quiet	You need to hear each other and not strain the voice or more importantly your ears. Acoustic rehearsals can be of great use – it is easier to communicate ideas, there is less strain on the ears and they can be held in the comfort of your own home without annoying neighbours. This is especially useful for vocal rehearsals because the whole band doesn't have to grind slowly to a halt to go over a short vocal phrase until it is correct.
Be economical	Only practice the bits that need practice – don't always start at the beginning of a piece of music but focus on the bits requiring work. Make it a rule to use practice time solely for rehearsal and arrange other times for discussion of a non-musical nature. So many valuable hours can be wasted over petty arguments (often financial) that can easily take place elsewhere.
Record your ideas	A simple cassette recording, or the jotting down of ideas, chords, notes or rhythms can provide excellent material to be worked on before the next rehearsal
Evaluate	What works and what doesn't, and why. Start with an idea, research and develop it, rehearse and develop it further, discuss the work and develop it further, review and refine the work. Always establish and maintain standards. Try not to be over sensitive – constructive criticism is important – so learn how to give advice and opinions rather than insulting or hurting other musicians. Learn how to take advice or ideas without 'throwing a moody'. Effective communication is very important and does not happen by itself. Work at being honest but supportive of each other and yourself. In a group situation try not to gang up on one individual – how would *you* like it?
Relax !	Practice is hard work. Rather than overdo it just do it regularly. Three or four hours three times a week is good – eight hours once a week is bad.

TASKS

- Draw up a wallchart of ten golden rules for the rehearsal room.
- Plan a rehearsal timetable for the month ahead.
- Analyse past rehearsals that were less than fruitful – what went wrong?
- After any particularly successful rehearsal make a note of why you were so productive – was it the time of day, preparation done beforehand, material worked on, atmosphere, and so on.

CVs

CV stands for Curriculum Vitae – a record of your experience and qualifications.

CVs should be prepared as soon as possible and updated at regular intervals.

Companies and individuals provide this service at a cost but anyone with access to a word processor should be able to do their own.

Here are the main ingredients of a standard CV:

- Name
- Address and phone number (including STD code)
- Date of birth
- Educational establishments attended and qualifications gained
- Work experience
- Interests

Organise the information in chronological order and try not to leave periods out – this can lead to suspicions about your whereabouts.

Keep the tone direct, clear and factual and don't lie – whatever anyone says. The truth should be enough.

Make it easy to read, not too informal or 'chatty' and try not to sound too arrogant!

Always use white A4 paper in case photocopies are needed, and ask the permission of referees if they are to be included.

Once this is done you must remember to update it whenever you achieve anything. This is why a word processor is better than a typed version. Make sure you save it carefully, label the disk and keep it safe but findable.

BAND CV AND PORTFOLIO

The first page should be factual and give the contact addresses and basic information.

The rest can be as imaginative and impressive as you can make it.

Make the presentation clear and spacious and easy to follow. Include newspaper reviews, pic-

tures, posters, tickets, videos, badges, T shirt designs and so on.

If you are just starting off why not invent your own tongue in cheek versions – but make it clear you are aiming at humour rather than deceit.

TASK

- Make up your own CV and one for any group or act you wish to perform with. Update your CVs at monthly intervals. (If you have nothing to add after three to six months start questioning the strength of your artistic aspirations.)

PRESS RELEASES

These should be simple, straightforward and informative. The basic ingredients are details of forthcoming engagements, recording sessions or record releases and general news and gossip about the act. It may be appropriate to add a brief biography for a new act. Try to make them economic, clear and entertaining. Any photographs of the band or artist help if they are of a good quality. If you are on a tight budget resist the temptation to include a fuzzy, confusing photocopied portrait and stick to well written text (see page 186).

TASK

- Compile a press release for your act. It should only take up one side of A4 paper but include a gig list and short biography that creates interest.

Making a demo

While not wishing to belittle the importance of well produced CVs and publicity handouts, most pubs and clubs will expect a demo tape before considering any acts. Demo CDs or videos will certainly impress but are probably not cost productive if you are handing dozens out and receiving one or two gigs.

A demo cassette should contain your three best songs and display contrast and professionalism. The first song is the most important because employers rarely listen to more than one track if they do not like the first one. Indeed the first 20 seconds has to impress them, so make sure the opening makes an impact and encapsulates your style and character.

Professional studios are well versed in demo tape preparation and after asking around you should be advised on the best one locally. Meet the engineer before starting recording and play him or her the rehearsal tapes of your chosen three songs to give them an idea of the set-up required. If you can afford it plan to spend a day recording each song and a day to mix them down. It is advisable to leave a gap between recording and mixing down when you can take the rough mixes away and listen to them carefully before committing the final mix to master.

An impressive and eye-catching cassette cover is a good idea, but make sure your name and contact number is clearly displayed. The same information should be written on every cassette as they are often separated from their cover carelessly.

Bulk copying of cassettes should be included in your budget. Make sure they are all of the same quality or you risk throwing gigs away needlessly.

Set list – pace of repertoire

It is worth putting some thought and research into constructing your set list. Eventually you should have several set lists for varying lengths of gigs. The more common are: 30 minutes, 60 minutes and the most common is 2 × 45 minutes.

Have these prepared and rehearsed before accepting work and always ask about the expected playing time before accepting a gig.

A set list needs contrast and shape and here are some combinations:

- loud/quiet
- fast/slow
- rhythmic/melodic
- dense/sparse
- relaxed/tense
- serious/humorous

The first song needs to have impact, but more importantly needs to be a number that you are confident about playing.

It is often wise to take advice from friends about set decisions. The song the band may enjoy playing isn't necessarily the one the audience enjoys listening to.

With experience this job becomes easier – if you are observant and analytical you can remember which songs work well in which order. Sometimes the exact same songs in a different order can result in a totally different reaction from an audience.

Try to build each set up to a climax point about three quarters of the way through. The final numbers can then be more intimate *or* 'anthemic' sing-along numbers, presuming the audience is on your side after being won over by the pace and shape of your set.

Quiet numbers may not stand a chance early on when the attention of the audience has not been grabbed. Be careful not to play your big 'show stopping' number too early on because you will have difficulty following it!

Always have an encore in mind in the lucky event that one is demanded. If you are short of material repeating your first number is acceptable, especially if it has impact and you are happy to be remembered by it. It may become your 'theme song' and there is no shame in repeating material the audience enjoys.

Finding work

Now you have a well rehearsed set and a demo tape you are ready to find gainful employment. Route one is to approach friends and contacts and beg for the opportunity to play. Route two is to mailshot your marketing pack to all the local venues. At the risk of sounding cynical, most venues are only interested in attracting large numbers of paying guests into their establishment. If you have a fan base, lots of friends and/or exceptionally large supportive families, by all means mention this!

Always follow up posting information with a phone call or personal visit. Try to be friendly, businesslike and cheerful as you pester people, and don't take rejection or lack of enthusiasm personally. Try to make a note of names you need to target and build up a rapport with them. If they are not interested in you ask them why and accept any criticisms constructively rather than antagonising future contacts through arrogance. You often have to invest a great deal of effort and time for little result.

No-one said that this was an easy business to get into. Patience and perseverance will reap rewards eventually.

Be prepared to undertake early work for little or no reward – this is part of your training and is more for your benefit than for the audiences.

Sometimes unscrupulous venues operate a 'pay to play' system whereby performers pay £50 to £100 in exchange for tickets that they can sell to friends. Think very carefully before accepting any such 'deal'. Thankfully this practice is dying out.

TASK

- Assemble a publicity pack containing: demo tape, band or personal CV, reviews, posters/flyers and an introductory letter.
- Create a database of possible venues within a reasonable travelling distance. Include addresses, telephone numbers and contact names if possible. Update both as necessary.

The venue – equipment and sound check

On arriving at a venue the first consideration should always be health and safety.

If the electrical fittings seem dangerous or the stage is unsafe do **not** perform.

Two almost essential support staff for your act are a sound engineer and a roadie.

The sound engineer should attend rehearsals to become familiar with your material and then control on-stage sound levels.

The roadie should organise transport, setting up and packing away equipment and any on-stage problems such as broken strings, faulty leads and equipment failure.

Both should become valued members of your team – never consider technical support as second class citizens. Experience will teach you that you rely on backstage personnel as much as on-stage colleagues.

Considerations are:

Venue

Location	Will you be able to get there on time? Will it be financially viable?
Access	Visit the venue at a quiet time and establish where to park and the shortest/easiest route to the stage. What time will you need to arrive to be able to set up without having to climb over punters or fight your way to the stage?
Atmosphere	What type of venue is it? What style of music are the locals used to? Is it friendly and or safe? Imagine turning up at a Country and Western Club with a rap act or vice versa! Always check the type of music required before turning up.
Merchandising	Will you be able to supplement your meagre gig fee by trying to off-load your exclusive T-shirts, badges or cassettes?

Space

Performance space	Try to plan your stage set-up before the gig. Where is the power supply, and can you reach it?
Audience capacity	Be realistic about the size of venue you should be playing. A meagre crowd in a hanger of a venue or a 'backroom' with friends and fans being turned away are equally disappointing.
Acoustics	The quality of your performance is greatly affected by the natural acoustics of the venue. Hard floors and walls will reflect sound and reverberate the music, soft carpeting and clothed bodies will absorb sound and require greater amplification. Volume levels need to be calculated anew for each performance space. A sound engineer or friend out in the audience can advise you on levels. Do not expect the mix to be the same as when you were practising or at the previous gig.
Sightlines	Obvious, but important. At each venue check what can be seen from around the audience space. Take care not to stand where you are obscured by a pillar, or PA cabinets. You want a place with maximum visibility for maximum effect.

Technical Facilities

PA	Always check whether there is a house PA or if you need your own. If the latter is the case make sure the size of your system is appropriate for the venue. Small venues may require a 100 to 200 Watt rig, medium size halls – 200 to 500 Watts and large venues 500 Watts to 2K Watts. Check the usual magnitude of PA when booked for the gig.
Microphones	It is usual for vocalists to use their own microphones, even if house mic's are available. Buy the best you can afford and look after them. They are easily damaged and simple to steal!
Lighting rig	A simple lighting system can make a big difference to your act. Systems are becoming more compact and affordable all the time.
Changing space	Do not expect the 'star' dressing room during your early career. Try to respect the fact that others will want to use the same space and be wary of leaving valuables that may 'walk' while you are on stage.
Wardrobe	What you wear depends on the image you are trying to project. Simple but striking additions to normal clothes can be as effective as grandiose costumes.
Catering	On your world tour catering will be provided. Until then check the normal procedure at each venue.

TASK

- Select a few venues that promote live music and comment on the considerations mentioned above. Rate each section out of ten for suitability for your act to give an overall ranking.

SOUNDCHECK

All bands need to soundcheck. The further you are down the bill the less time you will be allocated. Accept this and use your limited time economically. Be businesslike and organised.

It is important to establish a good working rapport with the sound engineer. Set your backline (guitar and keyboard) amplifiers at an appropriate level and try not to alter them mid set. Work out a set of simple hand signals to communicate changes from stage quickly. This usually comprises pointing at the instrument requiring change and raising or lowering a flat hand in proportion to the volume increase or decrease required. Never antagonise or annoy your sound engineer and be prepared to adhere to 'house rules' regarding times, changing spaces and 'housekeeping'.

Communication and the audition

If it is your job to talk to the audience you have a very important role to play. Use the space well and perform to the whole audience rather than to a small section of it. Work out what you are going to say beforehand rather than making it up as you go along, then practise making it sound spontaneous – remember this is show business! If comments or phrases work well, use them at other gigs but pretend they have just entered your head.

Always maintain eye contact with the audience and treat them as friends. Take your time, ensure movement and speech are slightly exaggerated and clear and avoid mumbling. Keep it simple but remember that simplicity is a difficult thing to achieve.

Try to sound natural and relaxed and always project your personality and respond to the situation rather than reading from a script. Acknowledge audience support with humble thanks – always react to their encouragement and remember that they are the customers and deserve respect.

Never be shy or intimidated by an audience. Don't be overawed by hecklers – you should be in charge as you have the microphone and the stage. With experience you will pick up some witty retorts but try not to be offensive or arrogant. Charm will win people over quicker than spite. Take care never to attempt humour and fail. If in doubt ask a friend for an honest opinion of your comic talents and remember that timing is all important.

Never look embarrassed or phased. Don't signal displeasure in your own or group members' performance to the audience. Often mistakes would go unnoticed to the audience had not three quarters of the band turned to the keyboard player and pulled faces and laughed.

Look as if you are enjoying yourselves and are committed to what you are doing. Audiences need to be led – if the singer looks impressed with the guitarist's solo the audience will tend to follow suit (within reason). Even if you have heard it hundreds of times before and often better you should play the part. Leave petty squabbles until the band are alone.

Performance anxiety

Stage fright can be a disabling experience. Sometimes it is the rational fear of embarrassment due to the knowledge that your performance has not been prepared fully. This problem is straightforward to cure – practise and rehearse more diligently!

More often the agitation is more difficult to pinpoint, explain and remedy.

If you are affected by nerves calculate whether it has a positive or negative effect on your performance. The performer who is almost (or sometimes literally) sick with worry before a performance but then goes on-stage and does well has probably benefited from their discomfort. This type of anxiety is positive. If a performer suffers physical tension that inhibits and spoils their performance it is obviously a negative force that can lead to personal and artistic frustration.

Everyone suffers anxiety – it is a healthy part of human psychology that creates the will to improve, work hard and impress. Stage fright can manifest itself in various ways – nausea, perspiration, loss of memory, trembling fingers and frequent visits to the toilet to describe but a few. The first step to controlling the symptoms is to banish any feelings of shame about being nervous. Everyone who has been called upon to stand up in front of an audience understands these fears.

Just as the anxiety is very personal and unique to each individual, the remedy must be just as idiosyncratic. Some performers have their own rituals before each performance – which order they dress in, relaxation or vocal exercises, what they eat or drink, a list of checks (usually ending with checking that your flies are done up!)

If this does not help matters, try to analyse the root of your anxieties. Are they:

FEAR OF MEMORY LOSS

Try to memorise music through the inner ear, in your mind rather than by finger-memory or by repetitive practice. Sing through the opening 8 bars or so of each piece to be performed, but concentrate on the rhythmic pulse and mood of the piece rather than worry about specific notes. If you prefer you can prepare an 'aide-memoir' of the details of the beginning of each piece. Presume that once the beginning has been accomplished you can relax into the piece and concentrate on communicating musical emotions and entertainment rather than technical details.

FEAR OF TECHNIQUE FAILURE

Logically anyone should be able to play as accurately, as quickly and to reach high notes as easily during performance as they do when rehearsing. If this is not the case it is usually because the performer is not as relaxed as they should be. At the end of the day you have nothing to fear but fear itself. Try not to worry about that top F sharp or that semi-quaver passage. Concentrate instead on the overall musical effect you intend to communicate. Often slight technical mistakes pass unnoticed to the great majority of the audience, but if you or group members grimace and look flustered, everyone realises a mistake has been made and shares in your discomfort. It is unfair to put the audience in this situation, so remain calm and remember that the foremost message is the music and emotion, and not your personal feelings.

FEAR OF BAD INTONATION

We can all hear when someone else is out of tune, the trick is to actually listen to our own tone and correct intonation quickly. To do this we must be relaxed and confident. The more you worry about being out of tune the more difficult it will be to correct it.

FEAR OF EQUIPMENT FAILURE

Check all connections and set-ups carefully before starting a performance and have spares readily available. It is useful to have a systematic check list, either mental or written, that you go through each time. Once this is done be reassured that you have done all you can. Strings are going to break eventually and technology will always let you down when you desperately need it not to. When this happens try not to panic – be good natured and quickly right the wrong. Most audiences will sympathise with your plight and may be more responsive and emphatic to the rest of the performance.

FEAR OF NOT IMPRESSING THE AUDIENCE

The competitive nature of our society and education systems leads to the need to succeed and the confusion of personal worth with musical accomplishment. Again it is important to remember that you are the same person before and after a performance and will not lose friends and respect if it is less than perfect. Other performers realise the stress you will be under and non-performers can appreciate readily that they would not wish to be put in a similar situation.

Great performers always seem to be relaxed and full of confidence. This leads to a 'chicken and egg' situation. Are they great performers due to the fact that they can control their nerves, or is the absence of stage fright due to the fact that they are 'great' performers? The truth probably lies somewhere between the two. Without the fear of failing it is doubtful whether an individual would achieve great things. On the other hand, if their fears prevented them from realising their potential there is every chance they would fall by the wayside.

Concentrate on the positive aspects of your performance rather than the defects, appear to be enjoying the situation you are in and remember the enjoyment of the music in rehearsal and endeavour to share this with your audience. Always imagine you are 'giving' rather than being tested.

THE PRESSURE OF BEING A 'PERFECTIONIST'

Unfortunately perfection in musical performance is extremely difficult to achieve, although the pursuit of perfection is almost essential for success. Try not to have a fixed idea of your ideal performance, but enjoy the challenge to constantly improve. Concentrate on the journey rather than the idealised destination.

One of my teachers advised me always to make at least one mistake when performing ('it gets the audience on your side and convinces them that the music is challenging – just as a tightrope walker will always feign a near fall to "work the audience"'). Ridiculous advice really, but more often than not the reverse psychology ensures a faultless rendition or the odd tiny slip can be played without losing momentum or confidence.

Surely your most critical audience is your teacher, friends or group members. They know exactly how the music should sound and what you are capable of. Why then is an audience often more frightening? They are there to enjoy your performance and you should allow them to do this.

Try to imagine the situation the listener is in – the poor examiner who has to listen to a seemingly endless stream of worried candidates, the audition panel who have a very difficult task of discerning between similar performances, the adjudicator who has to assess a snapshot of someone's musical endeavours and sum them up and justify their choice almost instantaneously, the audience who have their own lives to lead, their own concerns and wish to put them all aside and be uplifted by a performance, the critics who aim to be informative, accurate and entertaining, and so on. If you can sympathise with the listener and try to communicate with them through music, if you are prepared and honest, how can they be disappointed with you?

Another important concept to bear in mind is that the music itself is the important factor during a performance. Your only pressure is to be true to the composer. If people do not enjoy what they hear they are not criticising you as a person. Most of them do not know you at all. Tastes differ and if your endeavours are not to their liking, do not take it personally. Be analytical and professional about it rather than personally traumatised. Was it your playing that was bad or the fact that however well you performed your programme that particular audience would not have enjoyed it. Another important idea is to put everything down to experience and learn from it. However uncomfortable bad gigs are, they teach us and help us to ensure it will not happen again. Always try to understand what went wrong – was it choice of material, inappropriate venue for your material, technical problems, your lack of enthusiasm or any other factor?

TASKS

- Keep a diary of rehearsals and practice sessions. When you are pleased with your musicianship try to remember what elements came together to create this.
- Make a list of your worst fears concerning live performance. How rational are these fears?
- Make a pre-gig checklist to alleviate worry about equipment failure.
- Investigate relaxation techniques – which do you feel more comfortable with and works the best for you?

EVALUATION – REVIEWS

We never stop learning and can all learn from others. It is a good idea to see as many concerts as possible. After each one write a review from your viewpoint and then compare this to the reviews of friends or in newspapers and magazines. Opinions always differ. Before attending a gig listen to recordings of the artists and compare how their recorded and live work differs.

You should welcome reviews by others and accept constructive criticism as part of the job.

If an audience doesn't appreciate you try to analyse why this is. Do you need to present yourself(ves) differently, aim for a different audience, or keep persevering to educate your audience to your way of thinking.

Always learn from you audience – they may be right sometimes.

Remember even the worst of gigs can be of use if you can learn from it. Too many people believe fatalistically that it is all down to chance and luck, but the wisest words on the subject were from the famous sportsman who when asked if all his success was down to luck replied 'yes – and the funny thing is the harder I work at it the luckier I get!'

SCHUMANN'S ADVICE

Figure 3.1   *Robert Schumann, 1810–1856*

Robert Schumann (1810–1856) gave the following advice to the young musician: Translations (*in italics*) are ours!):

- Never tinkle! Play pieces thoroughly and never by halves. *Never mess about – if you are going to play music, do it!*

- Take pains to play easy pieces well; this is better than the indifferent performance of more difficult music. *It is better to play a simple piece well than a difficult piece badly.*
- You must seek to advance so far as to understand any music on paper, without

playing or singing it. *Hear music in your head rather than a mechanical test of finger agility – this is the difference between a musician playing a piano and a typist typing.*

- When you play, never bother yourself about who is listening. *Play musically and with feeling whoever is listening. More importantly, listen to yourself carefully at all times.*

- Should anyone place a composition before you to play at sight, read it over first. *Think before playing any music. Don't be like a headless chicken running around without a sense of direction. This applies especially to improvisation and soloing.*

- You should by degrees learn to know all the important works of the great masters. *Respect the music of previous generations. Learn from it and do not be blinded by the fashions of 'here and now'.*

- Do not judge a composition in a single hearing. First impressions are not always correct. *Listen carefully and repeatedly to new music and don't judge it on first impressions.*

- Do not imagine that you are the only person in the world. Be modest. *As true today as it always has been.*

- There is no end to learning. *Never think you know it all – you don't!*

TASK

- Make your own 10 points of advice for musicians.

chapter 4
MUSICAL EQUIPMENT AND TECHNOLOGY

Introduction

It could be argued that a harpsichord, piano or keyed trumpet are examples of music technology, but this chapter will try to describe the main elements of technological change that have flourished since the 1960s.

Some of the information will be outdated before the ink is dry, but new machines tend to owe design features to their predecessors and general concepts will be abiding.

Using the maxim that 'you don't need to know how a clock works to tell the time' technical information is scant, but all musicians should understand how sound is modelled and manipulated in order to take advantage of the greatest advances in music that have occurred during our lifetime.

Classical composers would have relished the opportunities afforded to musicians today, apart from maybe J.S. Bach who once proclaimed that the new-fangled pianoforte would never catch on!

Safety

Most music technology is powered by relatively low currents but it is imperative that all musicians treat equipment with the utmost respect, just as we treat our acoustic instruments with care (on the whole!).

By far the most precious pieces of equipment are your ears, and there is a real danger of damaging them irreversibly through shameful lack of care. I am often told '... if it's too loud, you're too old' but, whimsical as this may be, it is worrying that so many young and/or stupid musicians risk losing everything by 'pumping up the volume'. It's not big and it's not clever, so don't do it.

Before the lecture gets too vitriolic and pages are flicked on to avoid it, here are ten points as a quick check guide to safety:

1 **Avoid damage to your ears**
   Turn the volumes down before connecting and switching on equipment as a matter of course, especially in confined spaces and when wearing headphones, and be aware of the dangers of aural fatigue when using them for extended periods of time.
2 **Ensure liquids and food are kept away from equipment at all times**
3 **Check that plugs are wired correctly**
4 **Avoid strain on leads and connections**
5 **Do not overload power sockets**
   Devices that cut out currents *before* you receive a shock are a good investment.
6 **Use extra plug boards and extension leads**
   Problems usually occur when amps are placed too far away from power points causing strain and the risk of being tripped over.

7 Make sure equipment is earthed correctly

The earth connection provides a path for currents to escape down if the live wire works loose and threatens the user. It is a vital safety feature and must not be removed – even if it is suspected of causing 'hum'.

A buzzing amp or speakers usually points towards a poor earth. If buzzing stops when you touch the strings of an electric guitar, microphone, stand or metal case of a keyboard the equipment is not properly earthed. Switch everything off straight away, check the mains plug first and then work your way through the system.

8 Adopt a strict regime for switching equipment on/off in a logical order

Switch on:	Switch off:
keyboard	**power amp with volumes down***
computer	mixer with volumes down
effects	recorder with volumes down
recorder with volumes down	effects
mixer with volumes down	computer
power amp with volumes down*	keyboard

* NB: power amp should always be last on and first off with the volume to zero to avoid power surges and blown speaker cones.

9 Avoid strains from bad posture

10 Avoid damage to your ears
   (Safety for musicians begins and ends with this one!)

TASKS

- Compile a step-by-step switching on and switching off checklist for the equipment *you use regularly.*
- Draw the inside of a power plug demonstrating the correct wire connections.

The physics of sound

Sound is what we experience when vibrations or tiny changes in pressure travelling through the air move our eardrums (See Figure 4.1a).

If you have difficulty visualising this, imagine a stone being dropped into water. The ripples spread outwards and form recurring waves. A stick landing on a drum skin will send a sound wave of air particles that cannot be seen but can be heard when they vibrate or move the delicate membrane in the inner ear.

Figure 4.1A   *Vibrations or changes in air pressure travelling through air and moving eardrum*

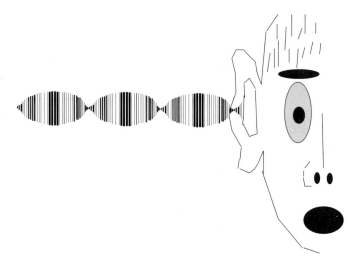

TASK

- What vibrates to give the following sounds (Answers on page 94.)

Sound
1 snare drum   4 tuba
2 guitar   5 voice
3 electric guitar

If sound waves are random or irregular we hear noise. If they are ordered or regular we hear a sound of definable pitch, or a 'note'.

When a note is played on an instrument we ac- tually hear the fundamental pitch plus other notes called partials or overtones sounding with it at lower volumes. The pattern of these partials or overtones determine the character of the note.

Figure 4.1B   *Fundamental (A below middle C) = 220 Hz   First harmonic (A above middle C) = 440 Hz   Second harmonic (E second above middle C) = 660 Hz   Third harmonic (A second above middle C) = 880 Hz*

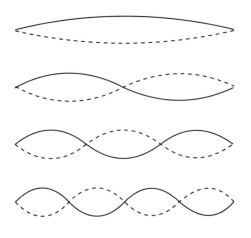

TASK

TASK

- To investigate this hold down the note 'C' above middle 'C' on a piano (not an electric piano!), without playing it. Now play middle 'C' with a single short loud note and release it. You should be able to hear the higher 'C' sounding quietly. This is because middle 'C' contains the note 'C' an octave above as one of its partials and this sets the string vibrating. Now investigate which other notes within this octave can be triggered by middle 'C' and order them into a table based on their strength of volume. This requires careful listening and a quiet room. These are the partials of the note 'C' on that piano. For answers, see page 94.

Fundamental
1   strongest partial
2   second strongest partial
3   third strongest partial
4   fourth strongest partial

Acoustics are a complicated business. To summarise:

- Sound is made up of several components.
- These components are called partials.
- Another word for partials is overtones.
- Harmonic or ordered overtones produce notes, enharmonic or random overtones produce noise.
- Partials, overtones and harmonics are three words that describe the same thing.

Waveforms

A sine wave is the simplest and purest sound wave. Sound waves or waveforms are the building blocks of all electronic sound.

Acoustic instruments produce very complex sound waves. They start from the same basic shapes but contain differing overtones and have individual envelopes.

The main waveforms are on page 88.

The sine wave is a pure tone (like the test tone or beep on the television when all the programmes have finished). The others are richer tones containing overtones or harmonic partials.

Below is a table listing waveforms, their harmonic characteristics, a description of their sound and instruments that feature the waveform fundamentally.

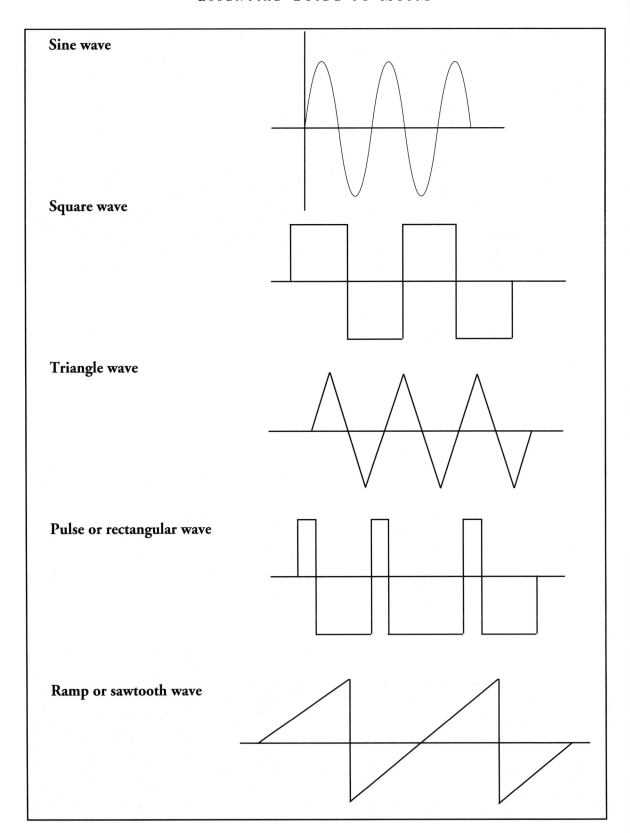

Sine wave

Square wave

Triangle wave

Pulse or rectangular wave

Ramp or sawtooth wave

Wave	Harmonic partials	Description	Instrument
Sine wave	No harmonic partials	Pure tone	Flute
Square wave	Odd numbered harmonic partials	Hollow	Clarinet
Triangle wave	Odd-numbered harmonic partials	Mellow	Sax
Pulse/rectangular wave	Harmonic partials depend on shape	Nasal	Oboe
Ramp/sawtooth wave	All possible harmonic partials	Powerful	Brass

TASK

- If you have the use of an analogue synthesizer and an oscilloscope, play all the waveforms into the oscilloscope and verify that they do produce the wave shapes shown in the figures. Listen to the sounds change as you add harmonics (using the filter) and the corresponding change in waveform shape.

The parameters of sound

The four most important elements of musical sound are:

- pitch
- volume
- timbre
- articulation.

PITCH

Pitch is the musical equivalent of frequency. Each repetition of a sound wave is called a cycle. The speed at which these cycles occur per second is called the frequency and is measured in Hertz – from Heinrich Rudolf Hertz (1857–1894).

The human ear has a range of about 20 to 20 000 Hz. 50 Hz is a very low pitch, 264 Hz is 'middle C' and 15 000 Hz a very high pitch. (1 000 Hz = 1 kHz.)

If you spin a plastic tube around your head the air rushing through it produces a sound. Investigate spinning the tube faster and the note produced should rise in pitch correspondingly.

TASK

- As we get older we lose the ability to hear high pitched sounds. Try this experiment to prove whether or not this is true. Using an analogue synthesizer to play a very high pitched note, vary the note using the pitch bend so it passes in and out of the audible range. Ask a group of people to raise their hand when they hear the note and lower their hand when it passes out of their range. Usually the younger members of the group will hear much higher frequencies than older members. Record your findings in a log.

The length of a string determines the frequency it vibrates at. If the length of the string is halved it will vibrate twice as fast, therefore the frequency will double and the note sounded will be an octave higher (see Figure 4.7).

Figure 4.7   *Pitch – frequency doubles = pitch rises by one octave*

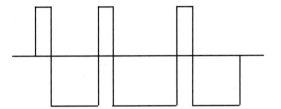
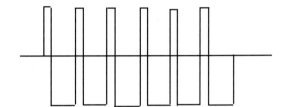

VOLUME

Volume is the musical equivalent of 'amplitude' – the height of the sound wave. The dynamic range of the human ear is divided into 12 steps called Bels. Each Bel can be divided into 10 decibels (or dB). Therefore 1dB is the faintest sound the ear can hear, 60dB is the volume of speech, 80 dB the volume of shouting and 120dB is the loudest the ear should have to tolerate. Amplitude is represented by the height of a sound wave (see Figure 4.8).

Figure 4.8   *Volume – increase the amplitude = increase decibels and volume*

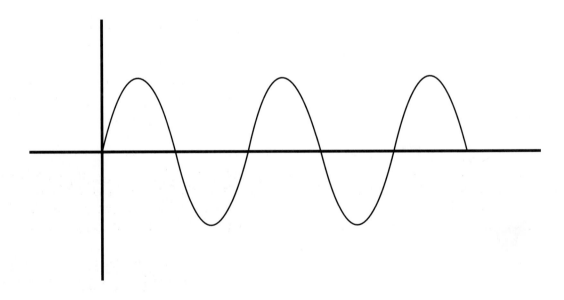

Social and night clubs around Britain often had decibel meters fitted backstage that would cut the power supplied to the band or disco if the volume went above 120 decibels. This seemed a great idea in terms of controlling musicians who revelled in the power of large PA's in the 1970s, it protected the musicians' ears and allowed the punters to talk above the music and order drinks and food without discomfort. Unfortunately although bands in the 1960s often played gigs with 30 watt amplifiers, the new solid state technology and transistor amps ensured groups would rarely get past the first chorus without suddenly being cut off. This used to ruin equipment and seriously annoy band members. Happily this practice has mostly died out, but it is wise to wear ear plugs if you are continually playing above 120 decibels. So many older musicians have already ruined their eardrums. Your ears are without doubt your most valuable asset – protect them!

TIMBRE

Timbre (pronounced tarmber) is the 'tone' of a sound or the shape of a sound wave, and is determined by components or partials made up of 'harmonics' or 'overtones'. These are a combination of waves on top of the main one at different pitches and volumes. Every musical instrument produces its own characteristic wave-shape and therefore its own individual timbre.

Articulation and sound envelope

Articulation is the shaping of sound over time: the beginning, middle and end of a note.

A sound rarely stays at the same volume throughout and has four main time parameters:

Attack	The start of the sound – the time taken to reach its maximum volume.
Decay	The time taken to move from its maximum level to the next level.
Sustain	The time taken at a constant level before release.
Release	The time taken to fade away after sounding.

(see Figure 4.9)

The attack is an extremely important part of the sound because the brain makes decisions about the sound from its attack rate more than any other feature of the envelope. A drum has a fast attack, decay, sustain and release, a trumpet has a relatively slow attack, fast decay, sustain as long as the player blows and a fast release. A cymbal has a fast attack, fast decay and a long sustain and very long release if allowed to fade away naturally (see figure 4.10).

Figure 4.9   *Envelope or ASDR (attack/decay/sustain/release)*

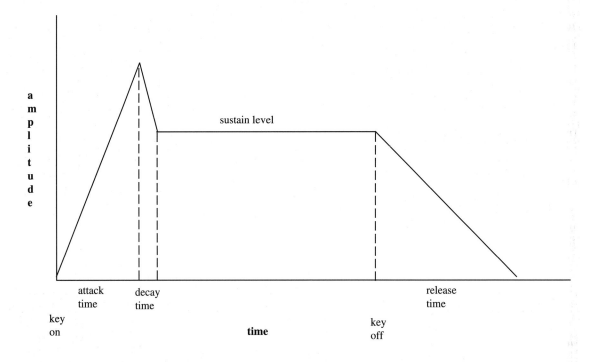

Figure 4.10   *Drum   Trumpet   Cymbal*

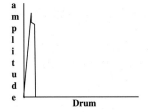

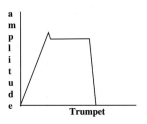

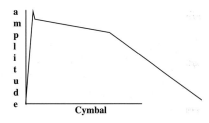

TASK

- Think about the following sounds and draw a sound envelope shape for each:
- violin playing a minim
- piano with the sustain pedal depressed
- organ playing a semibreve
- glockenspiel
- timpani
- wood block
- ride cymbal
- crash cymbal
- reverse cymbal
- a thunder clap

TASK

Describe whether the main difference between the following sounds is in pitch, volume, timbre or articulation (answers on page 94):

1 guitar/bass guitar
2 violin/double bass
3 guitar/electric guitar
4 male voice/female voice
5 flute/piccolo
6 plucked violin string/bowed violin string
7 scream/whisper
8 voice/trumpet
9 acoustic piano/electric piano
10 piano/harpsichord
11 nylon strung guitar/steel strung guitar
12 fretless bass guitar/fretted bass guitar
13 french horn/trombone
14 alto sax/tenor sax
15 clarinet/oboe
16 woodblock/xylophone
17 open hi hat/closed hi hat
18 ride cymbal/crash cymbal
19 bass drum/tom tom
20 oboe/cor anglais

Environmental colouration and fx

Sounds are always 'coloured' by the environment they are heard in. Investigate singing in a small carpeted room that dampens the sound or a tiled bathroom that reverberates the sound or a large empty hall that almost echoes the sound.

A sound without any coloration or 'effects' is called a dry sound. Here is a list of the most common effects applied to sound:

Reverberation	Simulates sound reflecting off a wall, that is many delays of the sound added to give ambience and the feel of music in a hall.
Delay	Sound stored temporarily then played after the original.
Echo	Separate copies of the entire sound in ever-decreasing volumes.
Equalisation	Filtering out or boosting low, middle or high frequencies like a fancy tone control.
Compression, limiting, expanding and noise gate	A process that boosts or lowers the gain to ensure the sound stays within a given dynamic range.
Chorus	Short delays with slightly altered pitch to give the effect of more than one instrument/voice playing at the same time.
Flanging and phasing	Very short delay that gives a sweeping sound as notes go in and out of phase with themselves.
Vibrato	Small and repeated variations in pitch.
Tremolo	Small and repeated variations in volume.

TASK

- Listen to a selection of songs recorded over the past 20 years and list as many effects used as possible.

Answers from page 86

What vibrates

1 (skin of drum and metal 'snares' underneath skin if touching)

2 (string and air in instrument)

3 (string and speaker cone)

4 (lips and air in instrument)

5 (vocal chords and air in mouth and body)

Answers from page 87

Middle C

1 (C octave)

2 (G fifth)

3 (F fourth)

4 (E third)

Answers from page 93

1 (pitch)
2 (pitch)
3 (timbre)
4 (pitch)
5 (pitch)
6 (articulation)
7 (volume)
8 (timbre)
9 (timbre)
10 (articulation)
11 (timbre)
12 (articulation)
13 (pitch)
14 (pitch)
15 (timbre)
16 (timbre)
17 (articulation)
18 (articulation)
19 (pitch)
20 (pitch)

chapter 5
COMMON MUSICAL EQUIPMENT

Microphones

MICROPHONE BASICS

A microphone is a transducer, a device that converts mechanical energy into electrical energy. Sound waves move a sensitive part of the microphone called the diaphragm and it is this mechanical movement that causes the electrical signal (see Figure 5.1).

Figure 5.1   *The parts of a microphone*

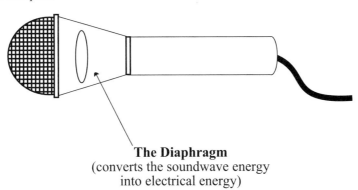

The Diaphragm
(converts the soundwave energy
into electrical energy)

Microphones are either directional or omni-directional. This means they respond to sound waves from only one direction or from any direction respectively. The most common form of directional microphone is the 'cardioid' – this has a heart shaped pick-up pattern (see Figure 5.2).

Figure 5.2   *Cardioid microphones pick up sounds within the heart-shaped area around diaphragm*

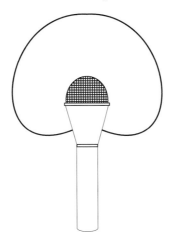

THE DYNAMIC MICROPHONE

A permanent magnet surrounds a coil of wire which is attached to the diaphragm. When the diaphragm moves, the coil cuts across the magnetic flux lines and a current is induced in the wire. The amplitude (volume) of the signal is proportional to the distance moved by the coil from its resting position, so the louder the sound the higher the current produced. The frequency is determined by the speed of the diaphragm reversing its direction.

THE CONDENSER MICROPHONE

Condenser microphones work on electrostatic rather than electromagnetic principles. The 'capsule' consists of two delicate plates that form a capacitor (once known as a condenser). When sound waves cause the diaphragm to move the capacitance of the capsule varies and discharges and charges proportionally with the waves' amplitude and frequency. The capacitor in the capsule has to be charged up initially so most condensers have to be phantom powered. This is an external voltage, often sent down the microphone lead from the mixer. Because the signal requires boosting batteries are necessary within the microphone.

MICROPHONE COMPARISONS

	Good points	Bad points
Dynamic	Tough	Low output
	Relatively inexpensive	Poor dynamic range
	Self-powered	High frequency loss
Condenser	High-output	Fragile
	High dynamic range	Expensive
	Accurate response	Phantom powered

MICROPHONE TECHNIQUES

The two most important decisions when recording are choosing the correct microphone for the job and deciding the best position to place it.

DISTANT MICROPHONE PLACEMENT

The placement of one or more microphone at a distance of five or more feet will pick up the complete sound of the instrument and the natural reverberation of the acoustic environment. This technique is usually employed for the recording of a symphony orchestra, where the conductor acts as the mixing console balancing the various sections of the orchestra. A drum kit can be made to sound bigger if the microphones are placed at a distance. A saxophone can sound more haunting, and even a drum machine can be made to sound acoustic, if it is fed through speakers in a large studio and the resulting sound picked up by a pair of distant microphones.

There are however problems with distant microphone placement. The microphone will be more liable to pick up unwanted sounds and there may be problems caused by reflected sound bouncing back and interfering with the direct sound.

CLOSE MICROPHONE PLACEMENT

This is the technique often used in the studio where over-dubbing and controlled mixing require each sound to be isolated. In a multi-instrument recording session isolation is achieved by close microphone placement and screens to provide separate acoustic booths for individual players.

Much care has to be taken when using close microphone placement because all instruments generate sound from different areas. A singer can be made to sound completely different by moving the microphone from 1″ to 24″ away. The closer the microphone is, the more intimate, breathy and imposing the singer will sound. The further away they are from the microphone the more distant, natural and controlled the voice will be.

PHASE CANCELLATION

When a stereo signal is produced the sound waves should reach the ears in unison. If speakers are out of phase the air compression generated from one speaker will cancel out some of the signal from the other speaker.

STEREO TECHNIQUES

Using two microphones for stereo recording may cause out-of-phase problems resulting in a good stereo sound but no sound in mono due to the 180 degree phase difference. This can be rectified by either rewiring one cable at the XLR plug or using the phase switch on the mixing console.

Too many microphones picking up one source can also lead to problems. A good rule is to make the distance between any two microphones at least three times the distance between each microphone and the source. This is known as the 3:1 technique.

Another technique is the 'XY' or '90 degree' technique, where the heads of the microphones are almost touching and facing each other at 90 degrees. The 45 degree line through the middle of this angle points directly at the source. This technique works well because it recreates the way we hear stereo naturally through our ears. There are no phase problems because the microphones are close together.

MICROPHONE PLACEMENT FOR DRUMS

Use either specialist drum or 'general purpose' microphones such as the Shure SM57. At smaller venues do not mic the drums – it will only overpower other instruments. At medium size venues it may be advantageous to reinforce the bass drum or use one mic on the bass drum and another positioned above the hi-hat to give extra tightness to the overall stage sound. For large venues, and therefore large PA systems, mic the drums up as follows:

Bass drum	Place a specialist, high-pressure mic inside the drum between ½ inch to an inch away from where the beater strikes the skin.
Snare drum	Place general-purpose microphone 2 or 3 inches above the rim of the drum pointing at the centre of the skin.
Tom toms	Place microphones as with the snare.
Hi-hat	Place microphone above hi-hat aimed towards the edge of the top cymbal – never between the gap!
Cymbals	Cymbals will be picked up by the other microphones and do not need separate consideration.

MICROPHONE PLACEMENT FOR AMPLIFIER CABINETS

For larger venues you may need to place microphones in front of smaller guitar, keyboard or bass cabinets or combos. Place the microphone an inch or two away from the speaker grille aimed at the centre of a speaker cone.

DI

Direct Injection (or DI) is where a guitar, bass or keyboard signal is fed into the microphone input of a mixing desk using a DI box which matches the impedances of the instrument signal and desk input.

TASK

- Describe, using diagrams if appropriate, the situations you may use the following in:

- a cardiod microphone
- a condenser microphone
- distant microphone placement
- close microphone placement
- the 3:1 technique
- the XY technique
- distant microphone placement with a cardiod microphone
- close microphone placement with sound booths
- the phase switch on a mixing console
- phase cancellation effects

PA systems

A 'PA' can be one of two things: a Public Appearance by a celebrity or a Public Address system for amplifying voices and instruments for gigs. We will dwell on the latter!

The PA system does three things:

- Step 1 **convert** sound into an electrical signal
- Step 2 **increase** the amplitude of the signal

- Step 3 **convert** the larger and/or modified signal back into sound

The most common examples of this are:

Step 1	Step 2	Step 3
Microphone	PA amplifier	PA speakers
Guitar pick up	Guitar amp	Guitar speaker
Record needle/deck	Amplifier	Speakers

Interestingly, the microphone and speakers are more similar than we imagine. In fact, a pair of headphones can be used as a microphone (albeit a very poor quality one) but do not try this the other way around!

Figure 5.3   *How a microphone works*

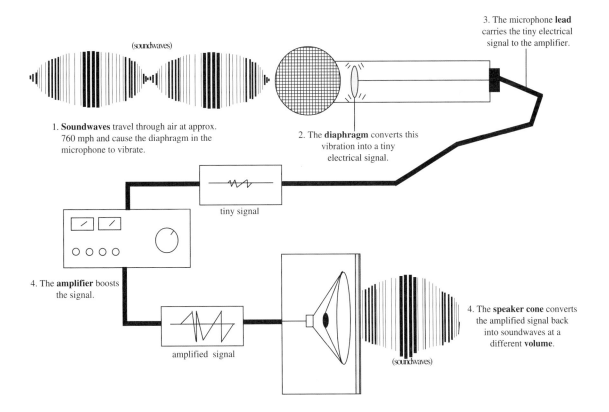

(soundwaves)

3. The microphone **lead** carries the tiny electrical signal to the amplifier.

1. **Soundwaves** travel through air at approx. 760 mph and cause the diaphragm in the microphone to vibrate.

2. The **diaphragm** converts this vibration into a tiny electrical signal.

tiny signal

4. The **amplifier** boosts the signal.

amplified signal

4. The **speaker cone** converts the amplified signal back into soundwaves at a different **volume**.

(soundwaves)

Combo amps

Electric guitarists often use combination amplifiers or combos, which combine amp and speakers in one, portable box.

Electric organ players sometimes use dedicated speakers with a rotating speaker cone or horn at the top to give that distinctive swirling or chorus effect. Hammond organs and Leslie cabinets give a classic combination and are worth mentioning by name.

Foldback or monitors

Foldback or monitors are speakers, usually floor cones, that send some of the amplified signal directly back to the musicians so they can hear the full stage mix clearly. They are obviously at a much lower volume than the output from the main stage speakers.

Headphones

Headphones are simple and inexpensive, but a good quality pair are a precious boon and well worth spending that little extra on. Treat yourself to a decent pair and you will be rewarded.

Electric pianos

Electric pianos vary greatly. Early examples such as the Fender Rhodes had a distinctive sound but required tuning and were not very stable. Nowadays the term digital piano is a more accurate description. The sounds are very realistic and common features include:

Feature	What it means
88 keys	7 octaves and a minor 3rd.
Velocity sensitive keys	The harder you hit them the louder the note sounds.
Weighted keys	Similar to a piano action.
Semi-weighted keys	Partly similar to a piano action.
MIDI	Can be linked to computers and other MIDI equipment.
Voices	Extra sounds such as harpsichord, organ, strings, and so on.
Sequencer	Allows you to record the piano internally.

Digital pianos will never replace traditional acoustic instruments, but they do have advantages and also disadvantages when compared to their ancestors:

Acoustic piano

Advantages	Disadvantages
Distinctive sound	Needs regular tuning
Fully weighted action	Not portable
Attractive build	Not MIDI compatible
Ageless and enduring design	Only one sound

Digital piano

Advantages	Disadvantages
MIDI compatible	Action not natural
Portable	Sound not unique
Variety of sounds and fx	Can become obsolete
Does not require tuning	Not as hard wearing
Relatively inexpensive and consistent quality	

TASK

- Compare the advantages and disadvantages of electric and acoustic guitars and electric and acoustic basses in the same way as above.

RECORD DECKS

Record decks have evolved into an instrument in their own right when operated by skilful hands and musical DJs. They have two turntables as opposed to the one found in home hi-fis, and a varispeed feature that allows DJs to alter the tempo of a track slightly to match the BPM (beats per minute) of two separate records. A mixer allows the user to switch and mix between the two tracks and a simple array of effects such as delay and sample may also be included.

CD PLAYERS

CD (compact disk) players play back digital recordings. Terminology and specifications will be better understood after reading digital and sampling sections to be found later in this chapter.

CASSETTE DECKS

Cassette decks were originally designed for use in cars but have become widespread. Professional decks will allow better noise reduction than the standard home systems, but their basic operation is the same.

DAT

DAT is digital audio tape. Its operation is similar to that of a cassette and they are available in similar lengths (60, 90, 120 minutes). The sound quality is much higher but care must be taken when recording not to exceed the gain level. Unlike tape, sounds recorded when the gain or vu meters are in the red will not be stored.

MINI DISC

Mini disc recorders look all set to replace four-track cassette multi-track recorders. They have several advantages – quick access to any location markers (that is the tape does not need to be rewound or forwarded to the beginning of the next song), non-destructive editing and bouncing of tracks and all the features of a nor-mal porta studio cassette system (varispeed, punch in/out and limited eq and mixing fa-cility).

The synthesizer

Theoretically all electronic devices that pro-duce sound could be considered as synthesizers (electronic organs, electric pianos, drum ma-chines, toys and so on) but it is easier to con-sider four basic synthesizer types:

- Subtractive
- Additive
- Sampling
- Composite

Additive synthesis	Two or more signals added together to produce a new sound.
Subtractive synthesis	Found in analogue synths – a rich sound source (noise, pulse wave) is filtered to produce a new sound.
Sampling	Digital storage of any sound – but usually an acoustic one.
Composite synthesis	Uses both sampled and synthesized sounds.

ANALOGUE/DIGITAL

One of the most confusing aspects of music technology is the difference between analogue and digital. Digital means encoded in numeric form or computer-based, while analogue refers to electrical equipment controlled by voltage changes.

An analogue signal varies smoothly whereas a digital signal varies in jumps – from one num-ber to the next (see Figure 5.4). Analogue sounds are therefore often perceived as being 'more natural' but unstable and inaccurate, whereas digital sounds are more synthetic, easier to store and more stable.

Figure 5.4   *An analogue signal and its digital representation*

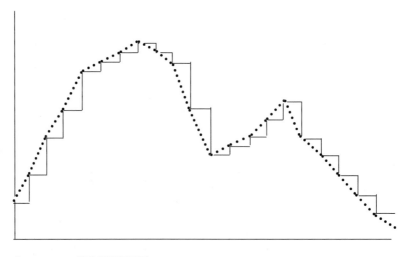

Key: • • • • • = ANALOGUE SIGNAL
         = DIGITAL SIGNAL

The accuracy of the digital sound depends on how often it takes reference points or 'samples'. A course digitisation will not be accurate, but a very 'fine' digitisation will be very accurate. The same applies to sample rates and CD players.

Some examples to compare are:

Analogue	Digital
Vinyl record	CD
Cassette tape	DAT
Fender Rhodes piano	Digital piano
Multi-track cassette recorder	Mini disk recorder
Moog synthesizer	Yamaha DX7
Analogue synthesizer	Virtual reality synthesizer

THE ANALOGUE SYNTHESIZER

Early commercial analogue synthesizers were mostly **monophonic** – that means they could only play one note at a time, not chords. Later analogue synthesizers had 4, 6 or 8 note **polyphonic** capability.

The main components of an analogue synthesizer are:

Voltage Controlled Oscillator	or	VCO		
Voltage Controlled Filter	or	VCF		
Voltage Controlled Amplifier	or	VCA		
Envelope Generator	or	ENV	or	ADSR
Low Frequency Oscillator	or	LFO		
Performance Controllers				

(See Figure 5.5)

Figure 5.5   *The analogue synthesizer*

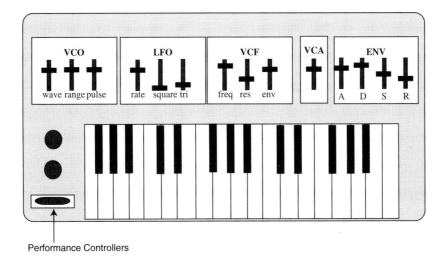

Performance Controllers

VOLTAGE CONTROLLED OSCILLATOR

This is the part of the synth that produces the raw waveforms that are processed to make sounds. Most electronic systems oscillate (vibrate rapidly in a cycle) and produce a 'hum'. Mains hum in Britain is at 50 Hz. The oscillator can be set to produce specific waveforms (square, triangular, and so on) and differing octaves – usually quaintly described by the 'footage' of traditional church organ pipes (2', 4', 8' and 16') Once an octave or range has been selected the pitch, or frequency, will be determined by performance controllers.

VOLTAGE CONTROLLED FILTER

As the name suggests, a filter can be set to allow some frequencies to pass and not others. A tone control on a radio or television is a filter. It does not change the frequency of the sound, but by cutting out higher or lower partials or overtones it alters the timbre or tone of the sound. Resonance creates peaks and can be adjusted to further colour the filtered sound. Altering the filter during a sound will produce a 'wah-wah' effect. In fact, when you say 'wah-wah' your mouth is also acting as a filter and controlling the timbre of your voice!

VOLTAGE CONTROLLED AMPLIFIER

An amplifier alters the amplitude of a sound. In other words it makes it louder or quieter or alters the volume. The word itself means to make larger or expand, and indeed most musicians think this is the more attractive attribute of an amplifier. However, to be strictly accurate, we should call an amplifier by the name 'amplifier/attenuator'.

ENVELOPE GENERATOR

This sets the Attack, Decay, Sustain and Release time of the note and is therefore often referred to as the **ADSR**. As explained previously this is very important in determining the character of a sound.

LOW FREQUENCY OSCILLATOR

This oscillator is not used to produce a waveform that becomes the note, but is used to produce a very low oscillation that cannot be heard but can slowly alter the frequency of a note to produce a vibrato effect (like a violinist gently moving the finger on the soundboard), or the alter the volume of a note to produce tremelo.

PERFORMANCE CONTROLLERS

The most obvious performance control is the keyboard on a synthesizer, but others include the pitch and modulation wheels and any arpeggiators, sequencers or transpose devices.

Summary

If we hark back to the previous pages about the physics of sound we can relate the main elements of all sound to features of the synthesizer.

Element of sound	Controlled by
Pitch	Voltage Controlled Oscillator & keyboard
Volume	Voltage Controlled Amplifier
Timbre	Voltage Controlled Filter
Articulation	Envelope Generator, keyboard & performance controls

Effects can be controlled by the Low Frequency Oscillator (vibrato, tremelo) and the Voltage Controlled Filter (wah wah).

Whether you are trying to create an original sound or recreate an acoustic one the first step is to analyse the sound required with reference to the four main elements.

On choosing a sound, analyse:

- pitch   (oscillator 'footage')
- timbre   (waveform, filter)
- articulation   (envelope shape)
- volume   (amplifier)

These principles apply to digital synthesis but are not as straightforward to achieve.

TASKS

- Create and name an original sound on an Analogue Synthesizer.
- Recreate an orchestral sound on an Analogue Synthesizer.
- Name two disadvantages and two advantages of analogue synthesis.
- Complete the following table :

	Stands for:	*What it does:*
VCA	_____	_____
VCO	_____	_____
VCF	_____	_____
ADSR	_____	_____

- Match the following:

Violin	*Synthesizer*
Strings	ADSR
Fingerboard	Oscillator
Violin body	LFO
Bow	VCF
Tremolo	Keyboard
Tone	VCA

Digital synthesizers

In the early 1980s analogue synthesizers were superseded by digital ones. Whereas most analogue synths would 'lose' their sound when the controls were moved, the new generation could store all the sound parameters as numeric memory, to be recalled at the touch of a button. They were also more powerful in terms of wave generation and could produce more complex and realistic sounds.

They were mostly all **polyphonic** and many were **multi-timbral** (meaning they could play more than one instrument sound at the same time).

Some might argue that the digital sounds are not as 'warm' or 'thick' as analogue ones (usually the same people that argue that CDs do not compare to vinyl records) and undoubtedly they are not as intuitive to program because each manufacturer has their own individual system for building sounds. One of the most obvious visual differences between digital synthesizers and their analogue predecessors was the presence of a **LCD** (liquid crystal display) or **LED** (light emitting diodes) display and an absence of knobs and faders to alter sounds. Programming digital synthesizers is a complicated business as most of the information has to be entered as streams of numbers. The basic parameters of sound are the same but often it is advisable to use pre-programmed sounds or computer editing packages to aid the slog (see Figure 5.6).

Figure 5.6 *The digital synthesizer*

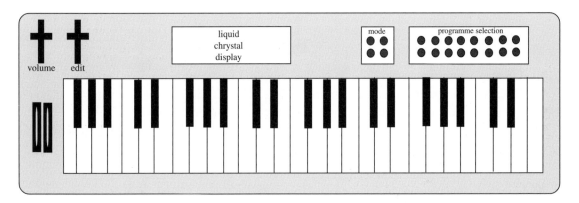

As is often the way with these things, at the time of writing the fashion is tending towards digital synthesizers with knobs and faders on that hark back to the analogue synths and allow you to control filtering, cut-off and resonance to shape the timbre of pre-sampled sounds. Examples are the Yamaha AN1x, the Roland JP8000 and the Korg Z1, which uses a MOSS (multi oscillator synthesis system). The Korg prophecy is an earlier monophonic version of the Z1. These can be grouped under the wonderful term **virtual analogue**!

For this reason it is difficult to discuss the generic digital synth, so we shall group them into broad types (see Figure 5.7):

- Additive synthesizers
- Samplers
- Composite synthesizers
- Workstation synthesizers
- Sound modules
- Mother/master controllers
- Virtual Analogue synthesis

Figure 5.7 *Broad types of synthesizers*

Broad term	Definition	How is sound produced	Examples	
Subtractive synthesis	A rich sound source (noise, pulse wave) is filtered to produce a new sound like analogue synthesis	Oscillators are filtered, resonated, amplified and envelope-shaped by applying a controlled voltage to them	Mini Moog the 60s	The original mono synth from
			Roland SH101	Monophonic – great for bass
			Roland Juno	Polyphonic – great wash sound
			Prophet	The missing link because it was microprocessor based, programmable and polyphonic
Additive synthesis	Two or more signals added together to produce a new sound	FM (frequency modulation) – one oscillator (the modulator) acts upon another oscillator (the carrier) to produce an operator the way these operators are interlinked is called an algorithm.	Yamaha DX range	The DX7 was the first mass-produced digital, polyphonic synth – difficult to programme but a wide range of accurate, pre-programmed sounds were featured on almost every hit during the 80s
		LA (linear arithmetic) – complicated computer techniques used to synthesize sound arithmetically	Roland D50	Roland's challenge to the DX7 – the new sounds were a welcome change
			Korg M1	
Sampling	Digital storage of any sound but usually an acoustic one	Not strictly synthesis, because sounds are recorded as digital information and their output controlled by a synthesizer type device.	Akai S range	Ubiquitous market leaders – various memory sizes in module form 4Mb memory – well recommended
			E-mu e6400	
			Yamaha A3000	2Mb – professional quality
			Roland DJ70	2Mb designed for DJs

Figure 5.7 *Broad types of synthesizers (continued)*

Broad term	Definition	How is sound produced	Examples	
Hybrid synthesizers or composite synthesis	Uses both sampled and synthesized sounds	Sampled sounds plus LA synthesis	Roland D70	Sampled sounds plus LA synthesis
		Sampled sounds plus FM synthesis	Yamaha SY77	
Workstation synthesizers	Digital synthesizers plus sequencers and effects	As normal synths with added 'outboard' controls	Ensoniq RS10	12 multi-timbral, 32 poly 300 sounds, 24 track seq, 74fx
			Korg Trinity	16 multi-timbral, 32 poly 256 sounds & touch screen
			Roland XP50	16 multi-timbral, 64 poly 318 sounds, seq and arpeggiator
			Yamaha QS300	16 multi-timbral, 32 poly and many features
Sound modules	The sound engines of synthesizers without the control devices such as keyboards and often rack mountable		Hammond XM1	Classic organ sounds in a box
			Roland SC range	Sound canvas – very popular
			D110	Synth sounds as module
			U220	Sampled sounds as module
			Yamaha MU range	Full range of GM modules
			EMu Proteus range	Great orchestral sounds
			Korg X5DR	Module version of X5D Keyboard
			Casio GZ50M	Low cost GM module

Figure 5.7 *Broad types of synthesizers (continued)*

Broad term	Definition	How is sound produced	Examples
Mother/master keyboards	A keyboard controller that enters MIDI data into a computer, sampler or sound module	Has no internal sounds of its own	Roland A50/A80 Yamaha KX88 Akai MX76 Casio GZ5 Fatar Studio 900 Cheetah
Virtual Analogue/ Analogue Physical Modelling	The best of all worlds – digital and sampled sounds and analogue typesynthesis control – often with a sequencer or arpeggiator thrown in	Analogue sound wave designs are analysed and a mathematical models created that copy almost every nuance of the sound	Korg Z1 Yamaha AN1X Roland JP8000
Controllers	Used to control synth sound engines or modules using sax-like 'wind controllers', guitars, drum pads or bass pedals	Have no internal sounds of their own	Yamaha WX11 – wind controller Yamaha G50 – guitar to MIDI converter Roland TD5 – drum controller

ADDITIVE SYNTHESIS

Digital technology in the early 1980s enabled complex sounds to be created by adding many sine waves together. The two market leaders were the famous Yamaha DX7 and the Roland D50.

The Yamaha DX7 uses Frequency Modulation (FM) synthesis whereby one oscillator (the modulator) acts upon another oscillator (the carrier) to produce an operator. Up to six op-

erators are linked together to produce an **algorithm**. These algorithms form the basis of complex and realistic instrument voices.

The Roland D50 uses Linear Arithmetic (LA) synthesis whereby sounds are created using complicated computer techniques to arithmetically produce rich and complex instrument voices.

Sampling

Sampling is the digital recording of sound to be triggered (or played back) later by a keyboard or midi controller which uses the 'sample' as its voice or sound source. CDs and DATs use the same idea but are not controlled by a musical device.

The **sample rate** is the speed at which the sampler takes audio 'snapshots' of the sound. This is usually 44.1 Hz which means 44,100 'snapshots' per second.

Accuracy to **16 bit resolution** corresponds to a signal to noise ratio of 96dB and is equivalent to the quality of a CD player.

The **n**umber of samples taken is equal to the **s**ampling rate multiplied by the sample length (in seconds) or **t**ime – the common equation used being $N = s\,t$.

The Nyquist Sampling Theorem (heavily paraphrased!) states:

The bandwidth is slightly less than half the sampling rate.

In practice – given constant memory available in your system – this means you can sample a short high quality sound or a longer, poorer quality sound. In other words sounds that need to be accurate should be kept short with a high sample rate, and sounds that need to be longer should use a lower sample rate and will not be of such a high quality.

At the moment a top quality 24 bit sampler, with a sample rate of 44.1 kHz, needs about 1Meg Byte of memory for each 12 seconds of recorded sound.

TASK

- Describe some sounds that would benefit from a high sample rate and others that would suit a low sample rate. If possible try these out on a sampler to verify your choice.

Sounds are converted to numbers using analogue to digital converters (AtoD or ADC) and converted back from numbers to sound using digital to analogue converters (DtoA or DAC)

Absolutely any sound can be sampled, which has led to many accusations of theft or plagiarism – the more commonly sampled artists being James Brown, Chic and other orchestral hits. Let's not beat around the bush, unauthorised use of other peoples' sounds – however short – is theft. To use a sample commercially, the artist should seek permission from the original composer/musician, their record company and their publishers.

Artists such as Michael Jackson, Led Zeppelin and Anita Baker rarely give permission for their work to be sampled, while most other artists are happy to arrange a fee that will usually consist of a one off 'clearance' payment plus a percentage of royalties.

The first big sampling hit was 'N-N-N-N-N-N-nineteen' (actually titled '19') by Paul

> One number one hit in this country used samples that had not been cleared and the artist ended up paying **over** 100% of his royalties every time the record was played on air or bought. Each playing or sale cost him £19 ! Naturally he did not promote his song and begged radio stations not to play it! It was his first and only hit!

Hardcastle, but the technique really evolved from black street musicians mixing and 'scratching' vinyl singles for riffs and drum beats to create rap and hip hop.

There are four main steps when sampling:

1 Selecting and preparing the sound to be digitally recorded
2 Recording the sample
3 Editing the sample
4 Choosing performance controls

SELECTING AND PREPARING THE SOUND TO BE DIGITALLY RECORDED

This involves setting up the equipment, minimising any background noise, choosing the best section to take a 'snapshot' of, and choosing the optimum pitch to record.

THE RECORDING OF THE SAMPLE

Carefully set the input level so that the recording does not distort or record too quietly, then set the trigger level to capture the beginning of the sound rather than any movement before the sound starts or the sound without its natural 'attack'. Then choose the best sample rate and length and the most convenient record key. Alternatively, most machines now feature auto sampling for the faint-hearted.

EDITING THE SAMPLE

Splicing (joining sounds together), truncating (setting the start and end points of the sample) and looping (joining the end of a sound to the beginning) techniques hark back to the *musique concrète* days of literally splicing and looping tape so that a signal was continuous. This is useful for string washes and choir 'oohs and aahs'. The trick is to select a loop point that blends the beginning of the sound to the end in terms of pitch, volume and timbre, to avoid 'glitches' (these are what they sound like). Most machines now have an 'autoloop' function and these are to be applauded and used!

Visual representation of the sound helps a great deal but as with most other issues featured within this book, at the end of the day you have to rely upon your most useful tool – your ears!

PERFORMANCE CONTROLS

These include all the usual synthesis techniques plus mapping and mixing sounds.

Key mapping is assigning samples to different octaves, or notes of the keyboard, and **velocity mapping** enables samples to change depending on how hard you hit the key. For example you may require a bass guitar to switch to slap-bass or a trumpet to switch to muted or overblown trumpet depending on the way you hit the keys.

Assigning different samples to different midi channels, or channel mapping, allows multitimbral sound production and the mixing of these sounds creatively.

TASK

- Record, store and use a sample or samples to create a new invention of your own. Describe the process from beginning to end explaining why you made the decisions you did at each stage.

COMPOSITE SYNTHESIS

Composite synthesizers use both sampled and digitally synthesized sounds. The advantage of sampled sounds are realism and accuracy. Digitally synthesized sound can then extend the length of note without using up too much memory and afford an element of creativity. As discussed previously, the ear decides what instrument is sounding from the attack rate. If this is sampled the ear is not critical of the sustain and decay of a note which can be produced through digital FM or LA techniques.

WORKSTATION SYNTHESIZERS

With most musicians linking their keyboards to sequencers and effects units it was only a matter of time before manufacturers started to produce all-in-one units. The sound engines are usually exactly the same as synths or sound modules within a company's range.

SOUND MODULES

These are the 'guts' of synthesizers without the performance controls. There are two advantages – they will be smaller and they will be less expensive. Instead of linking up banks of keyboards (see any 1970s supergroups such as Yes, Pink Floyd, Tangerine Dream for example) the keyboard player could use one 'master' keyboard linked to several, rack-mounted sound modules containing the exact 'sound engines' of their favoured keyboards.

Figure 5.8   *The sound module*

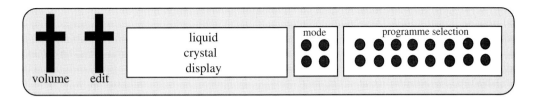

MOTHER/MASTER KEYBOARDS

With rack-mounted sound modules and samplers becoming so popular, musicians often prefer to use one multi-purpose keyboard that has all the control aspects of synthesizers without the sound engines, to control all their various devices.

The player can choose the length of the keyboard and amount of weight in the keys to suit them.

CONTROLLERS

Although the keyboard is the most common tool for controlling digital music input, there is no reason why wind instrumentalists, guitarists and even drummers could not use their own tools to access music technology using wind controllers', midi guitars, drum pads or bass pedals.

VIRTUAL ANALOGUE SYNTHESIS

This is the best of all worlds – digital and sampled sounds and analogue type control, often with a sequencer or arpeggiator thrown in for good measure. This should be the synth for the new millennium.

TASK

●   Design your own 'perfect' equipment set up for

●   studio use and
●   live work

Money is no object, but space and number of hands might be!

MIDI

MIDI was originally an acronym for **M**usical **I**nstrument **D**igital **I**nterface, but is a term so often used that it has been accepted as a word in its own right.

Confusingly mid-size home entertainment units are referred to as 'midi hi fis'. This is a completely different use of the word, that is midi as opposed to mini or maxi!

MIDI for musical instruments is no more than a industrial standard, but what an important one it has become!

In 1983 several musical instrument manufacturers decided to meet in Switzerland and agree on standard modes of communication. Electronic instruments had long been able to 'talk' to other instruments but not to instruments manufactured by different companies. Deciding on a system that would allow different brands of equipment to interface was a bold move. Previously musicians had been encouraged to purchase systems made by the same firm. A drum machine, sequencer and synthesizer would happily synchronise if they all belonged to the same 'family' (for example Roland or Yamaha). Now a musician could choose a Linn drum machine, a Roland synthesizer and a Yamaha sequencer.

MIDI was established as a 16-channel system that worked as a 'telephone exchange' to route digital information.

Keyboards, drum machines or sequencers had three MIDI ports – MIDI In, MIDI Out and MIDI Thru (sic). Vast arrays of keyboards could be daisy-chained and riffs or sequences could be triggered and synchronised by the drum machine tempo.

In 1983 16 channels seemed enough, if not excessive, but today MIDI is too basic to cope with the explosion of uses that musicians have found for it. Every digital device can be linked to, and controlled by, MIDI information: effects, video, lighting programmes, keyboards, guitars, drums, wind controllers, and even by dancers interrupting a light beam!

MIDI works in 128 steps. The information it carries is simple:

- Note on
- Note off
- Note pitch
- Note velocity
- Programme number

Using a computer all this information can be recorded, sequenced, edited, stored and replayed.

MIDI MODES

MIDI modes decide how a device will respond to incoming messages. There are four of them, as follows:

Omni on/poly	Receive on any channel and play polyphonically
Omni on/mono	Receive on any channel and play only one monophonic voice
Omni off/poly	Receive only on the selected channel and play polyphonically
Omni off/mono	Receive only on the selected channel and play monophonically

MIDI MESSAGES

Channel voice messages	Used to carry performance data
Channel mode messages	Used to specify channel and voice assignments
System common messages	Specifies song numbers and beat locations within songs
System real time messages	Convey timing information
System exclusive messages	Carry information for a specific make or model

GENERAL MIDI

General MIDI is a protocol agreed between manufacturers on a set of conventions that are common to all midi set-ups. This means that sequenced data can be outputted using different midi keyboards and/or sound modules and the voices will be similar. Obviously different models produce their own distinctive sounds, but a certain timbre programme number will activate the same instrument sound on all general MIDI machines. For example prog no. 43 will be a cello for all gm sound modules.

The following features will be found on all general MIDI sound modules:

- Velocity/touch sensitive voices
- Middle C will be MIDI key 60
- 24 voice multi-timbrality
- 16 polyphonic MIDI channels with the drums always on channel 10
- 128 pre-set instruments or sounds mapped out as follows:

Prog no.	Instrument family	Prog no.	Instrument family
1–8	Piano	65–72	Reeds
9–16	Chromatic percussion	73–80	Pipes
17–24	Organ	81–88	Synth lead
23–32	Guitar	89–96	Synth pad
33–40	Bass	97–104	Synth effects
41–48	Strings	105–112	Ethnic
49–56	Ensemble	113–120	Percussion
57–64	Brass	121–128	Sound effects

For example:

41–48	Strings	65–72	Reeds
41	Violin	65	Soprano sax
42	Viola	66	Alto sax
43	Cello	67	Tenor sax
44	Double bass	68	Baritone sax
45	Tremelo strings	69	Oboe
46	Pizzicato strings	70	Cor anglais
47	Orchestral strings	71	Bassoon
48	Timpani	72	Clarinet

Drums will be mapped as follows:

MIDI key	Drum sound	MIDI key	Drum sound	MIDI key	Drum sound
35	Bass drum	51	Ride cymbal	67	High agogo
36	Bass drum	52	Chinese cymbal	68	Low agogo
37	Side stick	53	Ride bell	69	Cabasa
38	Snare drum	54	Tambourine	70	Maracas
39	Hand clap	55	Splash cymbal	71	Short whistle
40	Electronic snare	56	Cowbell	72	Long whistle
41	Low floor tom	57	Crash cymbal 2	73	Short guiro
42	Closed hi hat	58	Vibraslap	74	Long guiro
43	High floor tom	59	Ride cymbal 2	75	Claves
44	Pedal hi hat	60	High bongo	76	High wood block
45	Low tom	61	Low bongo	77	Low wood block
46	Open hi hat	62	Mute conga	78	Mute cuica
47	Low mid tom	63	Open conga	79	Open cuica
48	High mid tom	64	Low conga	80	Mute triangle
49	Crash cymbal	65	High timbale	81	Open triangle
50	High tom	66	Low timbale		

Figure 5.9

Note number 60 is always middle C. Yamaha calls this note C3 and most other manufacturers followed suit. Roland and Kurzweil however call this note (middle C) C4! A 61-note keyboard extends from C1 (36) to C6 (96), a 76-note keyboard extends from E0 (28) to G6 (103), and an 88 note keyboard extends from A-1 (21) to C7 (108)

61 note keyboard with standard MIDI configuration

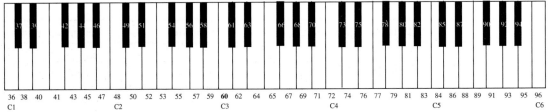

Sequencing

Sequencing is the recording, editing, storing and playing back of musical data. The important difference between sequencing and tape recording is that it is musical data rather than actual sounds that are recorded.

A drum machine is a sequencer that is dedicated to percussion.

Early analogue synthesizers were often equiped with simple step-time sequencers or arpeggiators. These would allow the arpeggios of a chord held down to be sequenced, and the speed would be controlled by a LFO

There are two ways of entering data or notes into a sequencer: **real-time** and **step-time**.

Real-time is where the sequencer acts as a tape recorder and stores the information as it is actually played. **Step-time** is where information is entered, without rhythm, note by note (not unlike a typewriter).

Real-time sequencing demands a higher level

of musical competance, but step-time sequencing requires an understanding of the ratio of different note lengths.

When entering step-time data the trick is to ascertain the shortest note to be sequenced and consider all other notes as multiples of that note. For instance, if the shortest note to be sequenced is a semiquaver a quaver will be two steps, a crotchet 4 steps, a minim 8 steps, a semibreve 16 steps and so on. See the table on page 118.

Quantisation

All sequencers will **quantise** rhythms. This means inaccuracies when playing or entering notes will be corrected and moved to the nearest step determined by the quantisation rate.

A quantisation rate of 16 will move notes to the nearest semiquaver or sixteenth note, a quantisation rate of 8 will move notes to the nearest quaver or eighth note and so on.

An understanding of music theory is essential in deciding the quantisation rate, which is normally the shortest note to be sequenced, and whether triplet rates are needed if the music is in compound time (for example in a 6/8, 9/8 or 12/8 time signature, swing or reggae).

If the music to be sequenced is all of a similar rhythmic pattern one quantise rate such as 16 might work, but often it is necessary to select sections and quantise each one separately. Always check each section by listening carefully after quantisation and if the notes have been moved to the wrong beat, joined together or have lost their correct feel, then undo the quantise and try a different rate.

TASK

- In the boxes under the stave write down the best quantise rate to use for the notes in that section.

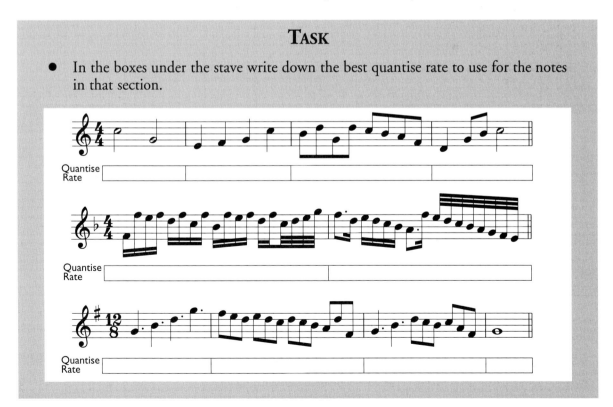

Note duration	American equivalent	Quantise symbol	Notation symbol	Rest symbol	Step table
semi-demi-semiquaver	64th note	64			1
dotted semi-demi-semiquaver		64.			
demi-semiquaver	32nd note	32			2 1
dotted demi-semiquaver		32.			3
semiquaver	16th note	16			4 2 1
dotted semiquaver		16.			6 3
quaver	8th note	8			8 4 2 1
dotted quaver		8.			12 6 3
crotchet	quarter-note	4			16 8 4 2 1
dotted crotchet		4.			24 12 6 3
minim	half-note	2			32 16 8 4 2
dotted minim		2.			48 24 12 6 3
semibreve	whole-note	1			64 32 16 8 4
dotted semibreve		1.			96 48 24 12 6
breve					128 64 32 16 8
triplets are three notes in the time of two					
triplet semiquaver		16T			
triplet quaver		8T			
triplet crotchet		4T			

Computer sequencing software

Dedicated sequencers were generally time-consuming to edit, had small displays and limited memory storage. This led to them being largely superseded by computer sequencing programmes. The computer screen display made the recording, storing, editing then playback of MIDI music extremely user-friendly and brought solo multi-part music composition within the grasp of every musician. The first popular sequencing package was Steinberg's Pro 16 in 1984 and the more comprehensive Pro 24 in 1987. The most popular computer for these sequence programs was the Atari ST, but nowadays music software will happily function on all platforms with almost identical packages for PC and Apple Macintosh.

Choosing the machine and software is a matter of personal taste. Everyone who uses a particular set-up will proclaim them to be by far the best (because they know and are comfortable with them). The truth is that they are all much of a muchness.

Some recommended packages are:

- Cubase series by Steinberg
- Notator Logic series by Emagic
- Finale by Coda
- Sibelius

Individual systems will come with their own instructions and guides to use, so we will limit ourselves to some generic features that are common to all. Nearly all are based on the functions of a multi-track recorder and mixer and share the same terminology.

The number of tracks that can be layered is far greater than analogue multi-track recorders and digital functions such as cut, paste and edit are far simpler to accomplish.

TRANSPORT BOX

This contains icons (a graphic that symbolises a job to be done by the computer) that represent the normal tape transport controls :

- Rewind
- Record
- Play
- Stop
- Pause
- Fast forward

and are activated by clicking the mouse on the icon (see Figure 5.10 below).

Figure 5.10

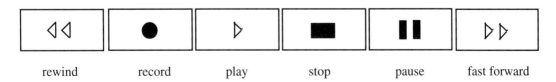

| rewind | record | play | stop | pause | fast forward |

It may also contain:

Click	This provides a metronome for recording.
Left and right locators	These set the bar numbers and/or beat at the start and end of a recording.
Punch in and punch out	This allows you to re-record and correct one section without having to record the whole track again.
Cycle	This allows you to record or playback a section determined by the left and right locators.
Sync	Transport controls are activated by an external synchronisation code such as MIDI clock or SMPTE to 'lock into' another recording or video.
Mastertrack	Transport controls follow a predetermined track containing changes in tempo and/or time signature.
Tempo	This sets the beats per minute that the music will record and playback.
Time signature	This sets the number of, and type of beats in a bar.

EDIT

Sequenced data can be edited in various ways.

Remember the sequencer does not store sounds – every time a note is entered the computer will record:

- which note was played
- how long it was played for
- the velocity of the note
- how fast it was played.

All these parameters are stored as numbers from 0 to 127.

A musician may play a 'forte' (loud) middle C for two beats followed by a 'piano' (quiet) C one octave above middle C for a quaver (half a beat).

Arrow	Normal cursor mode for selection
Pencil	Changing sizes and writing in data
Eraser	Deleting
Scissors	Separating sections to be edited
Magnifying glass	Enlarging or auditioning sections to be edited
Glue tube	Joining sections together
Q	Quantising
Mute	Silencing tracks on playback

THE TOOL BOX

The tool box is a collection of icons that allows you to perform the following functions using the computer cursor and the mouse. See Figure 5.11.

The computer will register this information as:

	i.	ii
Note number	60	72
Velocity	110	20
Note length	384	96

Figure 5.11

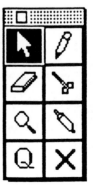

OTHER COMMON FEATURES

Auto quantise	Sets the quantise rate as notes are being played
Grid edit	Edit notes on a table where each note is represented by a block
Key edit	Edit notes represented by their number values
Score edit	Edit notes on a traditional stave
Snap	Sets the shortest value stored in the score
Solo	Silences all tracks except the one selected
Transpose	Move notes or series of notes up or down by steps of a semitone – i.e. an octave up will be +12, an octave down –12

SYNCHRONISATION

Almost all modern recordings will involve some form of synchronisation – sequenced and sampled MIDI sounds need to 'lock onto' live vocals or guitars recorded onto a multi-track machine.

Also music often has to be synchronised to video and film.

The standard digital time code used in professional recording studios, film, TV and video editing suites is SMPTE (Society of Motion Pictures and Television Engineers).

SMPTE features an 80-bit word every video frame. Each word carries a frame count, second count, minute count, hour count and a sync word – in that order.

Another synchronisation standard is MIDI Clock which uses 24 ppq (pulses per quarter note). Some computers have internal SMPTE readers, so MIDI Clock does not have to be used.

DIRECT TO DISC RECORDING

Until recently vocals and live instruments had to be recorded separately and time-coded to synchronise with the MIDI information. Now direct to disc recording has brought this within reach of anyone with enough computer memory.

Dedicated digital multi-track recorders are now widely available and affordable. They combine the editing facility of computer sequencers with the live recording advantages of analogue multi-track recorders. This means a chorus section containing MIDI instruments, live instruments and vocals can be copied and pasted with ease.

TASK

- Compare the advantages of the following three methods of recording sounds:
- analogue multi-track tape recording
- computer sequencing
- direct to disc digital recording

TASK

- Discuss:

Does music technology

- Make you a better musician?
- Replace traditional musical skills?
- Save time?
- Provide easier access?
- Encourage the less able musician?
- Improve access for musicians with disabilities and additional needs?

Is technology the musicians' servant or vice versa?

Landmarks of music technology

1759 La Borde invents a static electricity driven harpsichord

1874 Elisha Page invents the Musical Telegraph

1900 Thaddeus Cahill develops the Telharmonium – the first synthesizer

1919 Leo Thérémin invents the Thérémin – the first expressive and commercially viable electronic instrument

1920 Oskar Vierling develops the electric piano

1925 Amplifiers and speakers developed

1928 Maurice Martenot invents the Ondes Martenot

1930s Growth of composers using electronic music such as Antheil, Cowell, Milhaud and Varèse

1931 Adolph Rickenbacker develops the first commercially viable electric guitar

1935 Laurens Hammond invents the Hammond Organ

1935 The Magnetophone (magnetic tape recorder) invented

1937 Harald Bode invents the Warbo Formant-Orgel, a polyphonic, multitimbral electronic keyboard

1938 Harald Bode invents the Melodium – a monophonic, touch sensitive keyboard

1947 Transistors invented

1948 Vinyl LP records developed

1949 Musique Concrète and Elektronische Musik composed by Eimert, Stockhausen and Varèse

1950 Les Paul and Mary Ford use electric guitar and multi-track techniques for popular music

1964 Robert Moog invents the Moog Synthesizer, the first monophonic, analogue and commercially available synthesizer

1970 Various other monophonic analogue synths appear

Figure 5.12 *An early Moog synthesizer*

1972 Microprocessors developed, and hence first digital synthesizers

1975 Robert Moog and David Luce develop the Polymoog – a polyphonic synthesizer

1976 New England Digital produce the Synclavier – the first commercial digital synthesizer

1977 Sequential produce the Prophet 5 – a fully programmable polyphonic synthesizer using microprocessors

1979 Fairlight produces the Fairlight CMI – the first synthesizer to use sampling and a computer

1983 MIDI developed

1983 Yamaha produce the DX7 – a digital synthesizer utilising FM synthesis

1984 All other companies produce digital synthesizers

TASK

- Compile your own list of landmarks of music technology over the last 15 years. Decide what are passing fashions and what are important technological advances. Examples might include: virtual analogue, music down the internet, digital recording equipment, wireless systems and so on.

Terminology

ADAT Alesis Digital Audio Tape – eight track digital recording on a standard VHS cassette

ADC Analogue to Digital Converter

ADSR Attack, Decay, Sustain, Release – the envelope of a sound

Aftertouch When modulation or vibrato can be introduced to a note played on a keyboard by pressing the key down further or wobbling it

Algorithm A series of operators that make up a sound on a Yamaha digital synth

Ambience The colouration of sound or reverberation in a particular room

Amplitude The height of a waveform or volume

Analogue Literally a copy of something in another form – usually taken to mean non-digital synthesis or recording

Arpeggiator Facility on keyboards that will automatically play notes of a chord (two or more notes) separately

Attenuation The opposite of amplification – a reduction of volume

Auxiliary An extra route or 'bus' a sound can be sent on by mixer – usually to an effects unit and back to add reverb, delay and so on

Balance The relative volumes of two or more sounds

Bandwidth The range of frequencies of a sound or piece of equipment

Binary Number system using 0 and 1

BIT A Binary digIT – a grouping of binary numbers

Breath Controller Device used instead of a piano type keyboard to generate sound on a synthesizer using a woodwind type interface

Buffer Temporary storage of data in a computer

Byte A group of 8 Bits

Cans Headphones

Channel An isolated sound route

Clean A distortion free signal

Clipping A distorted signal

Combo An amplifier and speaker combined into one unit

Compatibility The ability of pieces of equipment to work with others

Compression Squeezing sound into a given dynamic range

CPS Cycles Per Second – also called Hertz

Crossfade One signal increases as another decreases

Crossover Device in a loudspeaker that selects different audio ranges for different speakers' sizes

Cursor Flashing marker on a computer monitor that is manouvered by the mouse

Cue A marker to indicate the start of a recording or performance

CV Control Voltage in analogue synthesizers

DAC Digital to Analogue Converter

DAT Digital Audio Tape

Data Information in a computer

dB Decibel

DBX Noise reduction system

DCA Digitally Controlled Amplifier

DCC Digital Compact Cassette

DCF Digitally Controlled Filter

DCO Digitally Controlled Oscillator

Decibel Unit of measuring sound level

Default The set up of a device when it is first switched on or arrives from the factory

Detune Slight difference in pitch to thicken the sound of a note

Digital Opposite of analogue – where information is stored as numbers

DIN Deutsche Industrie Normal – German standard used most commonly in tape types and lead connections

DI Direct Injection – connecting an instrument to the mixer without using a microphone

Dolby Noise reduction system

Drop In Sometimes called 'punch in' where a particular part of a recording is corrected by dropping in at a mistake then dropping out straight after

Dry A sound without reverberation or other effects

Dual function This allows the use of two instrument sounds at the same time

Dubbing Addition of music and speech onto film or video

EQ Equalisation – boosting or reducing certain frequency ranges

Expandable Device that can be added to

Fade Slowly decreasing volume

Fader Control that allows fading

Feedback The howling produced when a signal is amplified and re-amplified

FM Frequency Modulation – used to produce sound in a Yamaha DX synthesizer

Foldback Used on stage or in a studio so musicians can hear a low level mix of the overall sound

FX Effects

Gain Amount of amplification

GM General MIDI – a standardisation

GS Roland's version of GM standard with a few extra sounds

Glitch Computer talk for a jump or unexpected event

Guide Vocal Vocal track used as a guide for other musicians but will be re-recorded properly later

Handshaking Computer term for transmitting date from one device to another

Hard Copy Computer information printed on paper rather than in the digital domain

Hard Disc Device for long term storage of data

Hertz Unit for measuring frequency

Hz Hertz

Icon Graphic that symbolizes a computer function

Interface Device that joins two or more pieces of equipment

IPS Inches Per Second – tape speed

Keymap Assignment of different sounds to different keys on a keyboard

Layering Building sounds on top of one another

LCD Liquid Crystal Display

LED Light Emitting Diode

LFO Low Frequency Oscillator

Limiter   A compressor that limits volumes

Line Input   Input for high impedance signals, not microphones

Master Keyboard   Controls others

Memory   Data storage

Menu   List of options on a computer

MIDI   Musical Instrument Digital Interface

Mixing Desk   Device for combining and balancing a number of signals

MM   Metronome Mark, or Maelzel's Metronome – beats per minute

Modem   Device that allows computer data to be transfered down a telephone line

Modulation   Change in frequency or volume

Monophonic   One note at a time

Mother Keyboard   Controls others

MTC   MIDI Time Code for synchronisation

Multi-Timbral   More than one sound at a time

Mute   Used to silence a track of recorded or performed music

Noise   Unorganised frequency or unwanted sound

Ohm   Unit for measuring impedance

Omni   All

Oscillator   Device that generates waveforms in an analogue synthesizer

PAM   Pulse Amplitude Modulation

Panning   Position of sound left to right

Patchbay   Used to connect various pieces of equipment via plugs and sockets

PCM   Puls Code Modulation

Phantom Power   Supply voltage from a mixer to a condenser microphone

polyphonic   Several notes at the same time

Portamento   Sliding from one note to another

PPM   Peak Programme Meter – a type of VU meter that lingers at the top of the signal for a while

Preset   Single control that recalls several parameters on a keyboard or synthesizer

PSU   Power Supply Unit

PZM   Pressure Zone Microphone – mounted on a flat surface to pick up all ambient sounds in a room

Quantisation   Correcting rhythms

QWERTY   Computer keyboard – from first 6 letters on the top row

Retrofit   Fitting new bits onto old equipment

Reverberation   Reflections of sound

ROM   Read Only Memory

Sampling   Digital Recording

SCSI   Small Computer Systems Interface

Sequencer   A digital recorder

SMPTE   Society of Motion Picture and Television Engineers – timecode for synchronising audio and vsual devices

Solo   Mutes all tracks but the one selected

Sys Ex   SYStem EXclusive – a message that sends information such as voice settings between synthesizers via midi

Talkback   Microphone system on a mixing desk that allows the producer to talk to the musicians in the studio

Tie Line   Connection between two points in a studio

Timbre   Tone

Touch sensitive   Reacts to different pressures applied to the keys

Transpose   Changes key

SMF   Standard MIDI Files – format that is compatible with most machines

VCA   Voltage Controlled Amplifier

VCF   Voltage Controlled Filter

VCO   Voltage Controlled Oscillator

VDU   Visual Display Unit

Velocity   Speed at which a key is pressed

Vintage   Old and/or classic design

VU Meter   Volume Unit Meter – displays the amplitude of audio signals

Weighted/semi weighted keys   Similar to a real piano action

WIMP   Windows, Icons, Mouse Pointer – as in computers

Workstation   Keyboard with on-board sequencer and drum machine

XLR   Heavy duty lead connections

c h a p t e r   *6*

RECORDING MUSIC

The history of analogue recording

Magnetic material has been used to record sound throughout the twentieth century. The first steel wire recorders gave way to steel ribbon, and then iron particles applied to paper, acetate, plastic and polyester film.

During and immediately after the Second World War magnetic tape recorders using quarter inch-tape were developed and marketed in Germany.

HOW TAPE RECORDS

Magnetic tape is a clear plastic strip coated in Metalic Oxide.

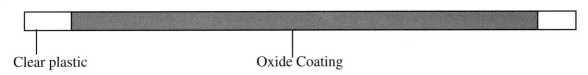

Clear plastic   Oxide Coating

If the oxide coating were magnified it could be considered to be thousands of tiny particles acting as magnets.

There are three 'HEADS' in a tape recorder – the erase head, the record head and the playback head.

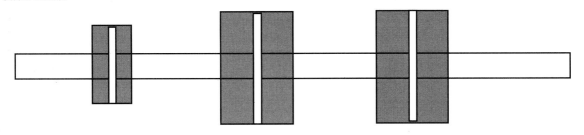

Erase head   Record head   Playback head

The record head arranges these particles into a
pattern that represents the sound.

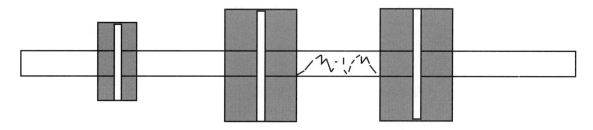

Record head

The playback head reads this pattern.

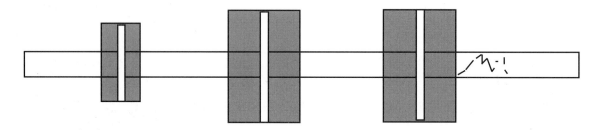

Playback head

The erase head rearranges these particles into a
random pattern again.

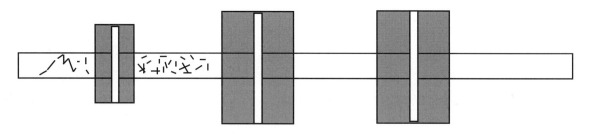

Erase head

TASK

- Undertake some research into the different types of tape coating available. How do
  they vary in cost and why?

TAPE TRANSPORT

The basic transport system of all tape recorders consists of a motor that pulls the tape between the capstan spindle and rubber idler and across the erase, record and playback heads at a constant speed (see Figure 6.1 below).

Figure 6.1   *How a tape deck works*

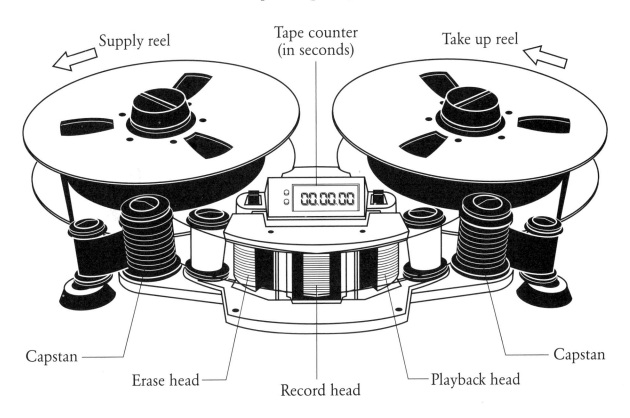

Tape transport system

Supply reel — Tape counter (in seconds) — Take up reel

Capstan
Erase head
Record head
Playback head
Capstan

TASK

- Carefully examine the tape transport of various machines. How do they differ and what are the similarities?

MULTI-TRACK RECORDING

In the early 1940s legendary guitarist Les Paul, not content with designing electric guitars, started experimenting with over-dubbing two or more tracks using existing mono tape recorders by playing a previously recorded track and playing along with it as it recorded onto a separate machine. By the mid 1950s stereo machines were available and Les Paul had built prototype 4 and 8-track machines.

Figure 6.2   *Les Paul and Mary Ford*

TASK

- Listen to early Les Paul and Mary Ford recordings such as 'Lover' and 'How High the Moon'. Does the lack of technology detract from the end product? Are there lessons in economy to be learnt from these classics?

By the mid 1960s most studios were using 4-track multi-track machines. The pinnacle of this was The Beatles album *Sgt. Pepper's Lonely Hearts Club Band*, produced by George Martin using only 4-track machines. Often a large arrangement would require linking up several machines together. This was long before synchronisation equipment was available.

TASK

- Listen carefully to the *Sgt. Pepper's* album. Can you detect any moments where the orchestra is slightly out of sync? Do these detract from such a milestone of modern music?

TASK

- Occasionally chart records are sourced from 4-track home recordings. Musicians such as Bruce Springsteen, k. d. lang and many dance producers return to the format. Why do you think this is? Is it purely for economic reasons or are they making a statement about what is ultimately important about a recording?

Figure 6.3   *George Martin at Abbey Road Studios*

SEL-SYNC

From the diagram below we can see that the main problem encountered with over-dubbing using standard tape recorders is that there is a small gap between the record head and playback head. This means that previously recorded tracks can be heard but over-dubbed parts will not be on the same piece of tape – causing a slight delay.

The solution to this problem is to allow monitoring from the record head. This is called **selective synchronisation** or **sel-sync** for short. When a multi-track machine is in record mode the musician hears what has been previously recorded as it passes the record head.

During the 1960s stereo home recorders became popular, and in the 1970s quadraphonic home systems were launched. Although these did not catch on the redundant 4-track systems were easily modified to make 4-track multi-recorders available and affordable for musicians.

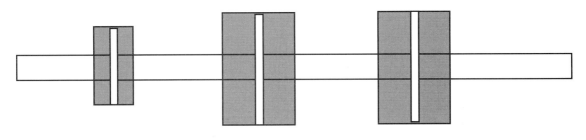

Erase head   Record head   Playback head

THE 4-TRACK MULTI-TRACK RECORDER

Normal cassette tape is divided into two pairs
of tracks – side A left and right and side B left
and right.

A right
A left
B left
B right

This is why cassette tape can be turned over
and recorded on both sides.

A multi-track recorder uses four tracks of tape,
but can only be used on one side.

Track 1
Track 2
Track 3
Track 4

Normal cassette recorders record on left and
right at the same time.

A 4-track recorder can record on each track
separately. This means that a different instrument can be recorded on each track. For
example:

Track 1	Drum machine
Track 2	Bass guitar
Track 3	Piano
Track 4	Vocals

If you wish to use more than four instruments
it is possible to 'bounce' or 'ping-pong' tracks.

Step one	Record the drums or drum machine onto track 1
Step two	Record the bass onto track 2
Step three	Record the guitar onto track 3
Step four	Record the piano onto track 4 and simultaneously 'bounce down tracks 1, 2 & 3 onto track 4

Track 1	1 Drum machine
Track 2	2 Bass guitar
Track 3	3 Guitar
Track 4	4 Drums, Bass, Guitar and Piano

Step five	Record the synth strings onto track 1 (the drums are now on track 4)
Step six	Record the synth brass onto track 2 (the bass is now on track 4)
Step seven	Record the orchestral stabs onto track 3 and simultaneously 'bounce' tracks 1 and 2 onto track 3

Track 1	1 Strings
Track 2	2 Brass
Track 3	3 Strings, Brass and Orch. stabs
Track 4	4 Drums, Bass, Guitar and Piano

Step eight	Record a saxophone solo onto track 1
Step nine	Record a guitar solo onto track 2 and simultaneously 'bounce' track 1 onto track 2

Track 1	1 Saxophone solo
Track 2	2 Saxophone and Guitar solo
Track 3	3 Strings, Brass and Orch. stabs
Track 4	4 Drums, Bass, Guitar and Piano

Step ten	Record the vocal onto track 1

Track 1	1 Vocals
Track 2	2 Saxophone and Guitar solo
Track 3	3 Strings, Brass and Orch. stabs
Track 4	4 Drums, Bass, Guitar and Piano

In this way ten tracks can be recorded on a 4-track machine.

Care has to be taken to plan out how each track should be used. **Remember** – if at this stage you wish to increase the volume of the bass you will also have to increase the volume of the drums, the guitar and the piano.

TASK

- Plan a ten-track recording of your own. Think carefully about the order that instruments and voices should be laid down in. What can you control, volume wise, for the final mix down onto stereo?

Better quality was originally achieved by increasing the amount of magnetic tape used per second. This meant a wider piece of tape – usually one inch per eight tracks rather than the normal ¼ inch tape, or a faster tape speed – 15 inches per second rather than the usual 7.5. Advances in tape quality, tape-head designs and electronic noise-reduction systems have made it possible to achieve better results with more convenient tape widths. Technological advances have resulted in 8 track cassette multi-track recorders producing the same quality as 1 inch 8 tracks from the 1980s.

TASK

- Compile a chart listing the development of analogue tape recording since 1950. List information on tape widths, tape speeds and number of tracks.

	1950s	1960s	1970s	1980s	1990s
Tape width					
Tape speed					
Tracks					

Digital recording

The difference between analogue and digital recorders is comparable to the difference between the traditional typewriter and word processors. Just as vinyl records are all but obsolete, tape machines could be replaced by tapeless systems within the next ten years.

Analogue means that a physical quantity (in this case sound waves) is represented in another manner (in this case magnetic patterns on tape). A tuning fork produces frequency against time.

A microphone converts sound waves into voltages against time.

Tuning fork

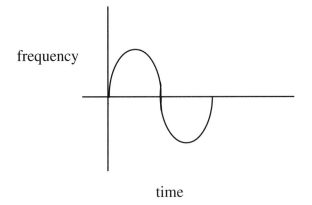

frequency

time

Microphone

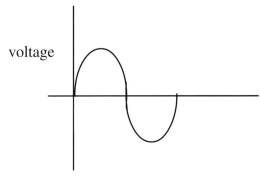

voltage

time

With digital systems **measurements** are made instead of substitutions. These are measurements of absolute values periodically and stored onto computer-like hard disks as binary numbers.

Compact Disc uses a sample rate of 44.1 KHz. This means 44 100 measurements are made per second. Digital Audio Tape uses a sample rate of 48 KHz. (Hard disk recorders can work at either rate.)

Digital Recorder

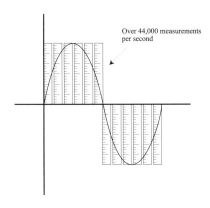

Over 44,000 measurements per second

Stored as binary numbers   i.e. 16 bit =1010 1011 0101 1011, or ...

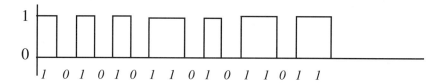

The two most important components of a digital recorder are the **Analogue to Digital converter (A to D)** and the **Digital to Analogue converter (D to A)**.

The A to D can be imagined as a person taking measurements of a sound at a given rate. The D to A can similarly be imagined as another person building a sound using the measurements taken by the A to D.

Most digital recorders retain the protocol of analogue tape systems and there is an easy step from one to another. This applies especially to the use of tracks, bouncing and panning.

TASK

- Compile a list of functions that are similar on both analogue and digital recorders. Which functions are unique to one and not the other?

At the moment the main **disadvantage** of digital systems is the cost due to the enormous amount of data to be stored – between 1 and 2 million bits per second.

The **advantages** of digital recording are:

Accuracy	Binary information stored as either a 'I' or a '0'. This is less prone to distortion or interference and therefore the error rate is very small leading to better reproduction and quality.
Random access	Digital machine will move to a later or earlier part of the recording instantly, whereas a tape recorder will have to rewind or fast forward.
Non-destructive editing	As digital recording uses random access, music can be edited without changing the original recording. To play sections in any desired order the disc head will fly around recorded material and changes of mind or mistakes can be undone easily.
Lack of hiss, wow and flutter	Unused parts of magnetic tape are randomly shaped and therefore produce white noise or hiss. Also, however accurate the tape transport system is, the mechanical nature of it results in slight 'dragging' on starting to move and some amount of 'wobble' giving wow and flutter.

How a song is heard

Intro	Verse 1	Chorus	Verse 2	Chorus	Mid 8	Chorus	Chorus

How it is recorded

Intro	Verse	Chorus	Mid 8

How it is played back

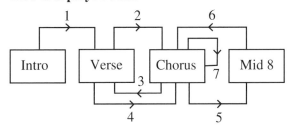

TASK

- Choose a song from the charts and analyse its structure into sections. Ignoring the vocals, try to establish the least number of sections needed if random access is used to record it.

There are various formats using digital recording technology. These include:

ADAM	Akai Digital Audio Multi-track – twelve tracks on a standard video-8 cassette giving 15 minutes digital recording at 44.1 KHz.
ADAT	Alesis Digital Audio Tape – eight tracks on a standard S-VHS cassette at 44.1 KHz.
DAT	Digital Audio Tape – similar to a small video cassette that records two channels of 16 bit audio information on 3mm tape travelling at 50 cm per minute. There are three common sampling rates – 32KHz, 44.1 KHz and 48 KHz.
DCC	Digital Compact Cassette – uses the same tape size and speed as standard audio cassettes. Will probably not survive as a format.
CD	Compact Disc – 5 inch disc that stores digital information to be read by an optical laser. Can now be read only and recordable.
MD	Mini Disc – an erasable optical disc similar to, but half the size of a CD
RDAT	Rotary-head Digital Audio Tape – another name for DAT!

At the moment the more common digital recorders are:

Dedicated Hard Disk Recorders	**Computer based systems**
Roland VS-880	Steinberg Cubase Audio
Fostex DMT8	Emagic Logic Audio
Tascam 564	Pro Tools
Yamaha MD4	Opcode Vision

Synchronisation

Almost all modern recordings will involve some form of synchronisation. Sequenced and sampled MIDI sounds need to 'lock onto' live vocals or guitars recorded onto a multi-track machine and/or synchronised to video and film (See Chapter 5).

FSK	Frequency Shift Keying – digital data recorded onto audio tape as two distinct frequencies representing the '1' and '0' of binary code to give a low cost means of synchronising sequencers and drum machines to tape.
SMPTE	Society of Motion Pictures and Television Engineers – the standard digital time code used in professional recording studios, film, TV and video suites features an 80 bit word every video frame. Each word carries a frame count, second count, minute count, hour count and a sync word – in that order.
MIDI Clock	A system real time message that is a relative time clock using 24 ppq (pulses per quarter note) to synchronise sequencers to drum machines.
MTC	The implementation of SMPTE in MIDI that represents absolute real-time locations as opposed to (and preferable to) MIDI clock's relative time locations.

The recording studio

Whether your studio is a bedroom or a lavish specialised professional suite, the main components should be an acoustically isolated interior designed to allow the recording of the original acoustic sound without colouration or additional unwanted noises. Also a control room which acts as a perfect listening environment where all the equipment that controls the recording process, is situated.

Task

- Design your ideal recording studio and list the basic equipment you would require.
- Now design a studio giving yourself a budget of:
  £500 000
  £50 000
  £5 000

The mixing console

The mixing console is at the centre of the studio and all signals pass through it during all stages of recording.

There are two basic console types – 'split' and 'in-line' and on both types the greater part of the design is taken up with input channels.

Consoles always appear intimidatingly complex on first sight, but careful observation will reveal a great deal of repetition. Whether there are 2 or 96 input channels, the basic layout of each channel will be identical.

Each input channel has 4 distinct sections (see page 141):

- input
- auxiliary
- equalisation
- routing and output

A single channel strip from the mixing console

Input

Input switch — Microphones produce a low signal, instruments produce a higher one – this switch allows selection of each.

mic   line

Phantom Power Switch — Capacitor microphones require electrical voltage – by activating this switch the 48v can be supplied from the mixing desk.

Trim or Gain control — The Trim or Gain controls the input level or volume of the initial signal entering the mixer.

Auxiliary

Aux 1 send

Aux 2 send — Auxiliaries allow the signal to be sent to external effects such as reverb or echo.

Aux 3 send

Equalisation

High EQ — EQ is short for equalisation. This is a tone control that can cut or boost the high, middle or low frequencies. The number of bands can be increased to give extra Mid EQs in more sophisticated desks.

Mid EQ

Low EQ

Pan — Pan is short for panoramic and allows the movement of sound from left to right in the stereo mix.

Routing and output

1
2
3
4
5
6
7
8

Channel Assign or Routing Switches — Channel Assign Switches or Routing buttons allow the signal, or mixes of signals to be groups or 'bussed', and sent to selected channels for recording.

Fader — The fader allows the volume of the signal to be lowered or raised without having to adjust the trim or gain.

Solo and mute buttons — The mute button silences the channel – the solo button silences all the other channels which allows checking of separate parts. This can be done PFL (pre-fade listen) or AFL (after-fade listen).

Extra features of the mixing console

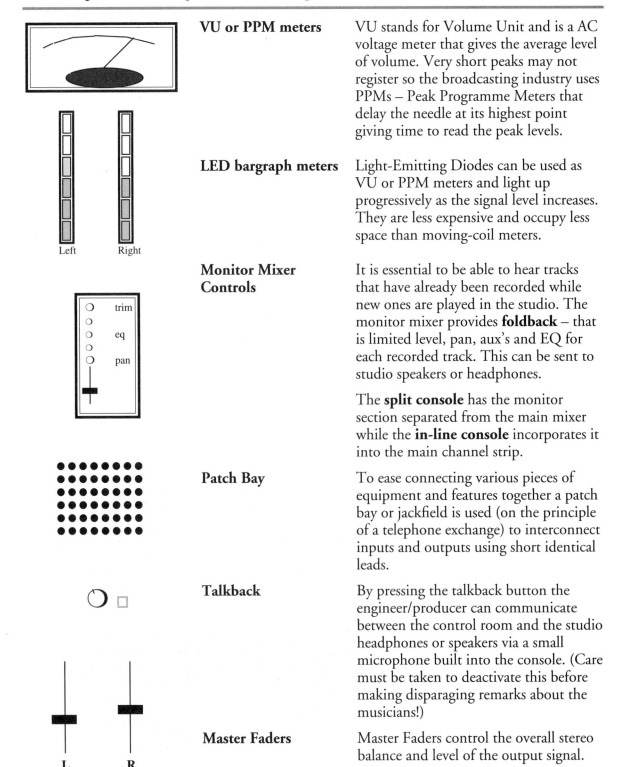

VU or PPM meters

VU stands for Volume Unit and is a AC voltage meter that gives the average level of volume. Very short peaks may not register so the broadcasting industry uses PPMs – Peak Programme Meters that delay the needle at its highest point giving time to read the peak levels.

LED bargraph meters

Light-Emitting Diodes can be used as VU or PPM meters and light up progressively as the signal level increases. They are less expensive and occupy less space than moving-coil meters.

Monitor Mixer Controls

It is essential to be able to hear tracks that have already been recorded while new ones are played in the studio. The monitor mixer provides **foldback** – that is limited level, pan, aux's and EQ for each recorded track. This can be sent to studio speakers or headphones.

The **split console** has the monitor section separated from the main mixer while the **in-line console** incorporates it into the main channel strip.

Patch Bay

To ease connecting various pieces of equipment and features together a patch bay or jackfield is used (on the principle of a telephone exchange) to interconnect inputs and outputs using short identical leads.

Talkback

By pressing the talkback button the engineer/producer can communicate between the control room and the studio headphones or speakers via a small microphone built into the console. (Care must be taken to deactivate this before making disparaging remarks about the musicians!)

Master Faders

Master Faders control the overall stereo balance and level of the output signal.

TASKS

- Look at the following photographs of commercial consoles. Do they all follow the four basic sections mentioned?
- Make line drawings that simplify their layout and indicate which buttons and knobs are within each section.

Figure 6.4   *A 4-track console*

The sound recording process – pre-production, production and post production

PRE-PRODUCTION

Before the record stage it is important to undertake pre-production planning. Take careful note of the following:

Material	Is the material worth recording? This may seem harsh but sometimes it is better to delay recording until your compositions are stronger. No amount of recording technology will improve poor material. Also ensure that you record your strongest numbers. If in doubt canvas advice in the form of home or live recordings.
Quantity	Be realistic about how much material you can afford to record.
Arrangements	Have a clear idea of instruments and players to be used before entering the studio. Never waste valuable studio time deciding 'what happens next'. Have song structures and words written down clearly beforehand – with clear indications of what should be playing when.
Rehearsal	Rehearse your chosen material thoroughly.
Equipment	Ensure all instruments are in good working order beforehand (guitar strings, drum skins and so on).
Information	Ensure the engineer and/or producer have all the information they need before the recording process begins. If possible give them a 'draft recording' of the songs to be worked on.

PRODUCTION

There are three main steps to production:

- record
- over-dub
- mixdown

First we **record** the sounds (acoustic, electrical or digital) that determine the important elements of a piece of music.

Next we **over-dub** (add or subtract sounds to the basic first step recording).

Finally when satisfied we **mix** or balance all the sounds together.

These sounds are then combined, processed, mixed and transferred onto a format that is easily reproduced on domestic systems.

TASK

- Make a comprehensive list of domestic sound systems.

Equipment set-up

This is a time-consuming but essential part of the process.

Planning ahead will save a great deal of time and prevent frustration during the important creative process to follow.

Often it is advisable for the drummer to turn up early to set up and establish a working sound and drum mix.

Other questions that can be answered before wasting valuable studio time are: How many microphones will you need? What order will instruments be recorded in? Will the drummer work to a sequencer or click track? Do you want a 'live' or heavily produced final sound?

There are no strict rules to what should always be a creative process, but a general plan for recording may be similar to the following:

Rhythm track	If this is sequenced it is not a problem. Some producers prefer to use a sequenced track, then add a guide backing and guide vocals and then build all the other instruments around this, eventually dropping the guide tracks out. Some musicians prefer to play live and then use this as a guide.
Guide vocal	The quality of the voice is not important but it helps the other musicians to locate their position in the song.
Backline	Add bass, guitar and keyboards to the rhythm track.
Wash	Add strings or synth washes.
Horns	Brass and woodwind stabs and riffs.
Solos	Guitar or keyboard solos.
Vocals	Usually this is the last part of the process when the guide vocal is dispensed with and the real vocal (and backing vocals) are added. It is important that the singer is relaxed.

TASK

- The list above is very general. Choose a song of your own, or one you admire, and plan the order in which everything is recorded. Next try the same exercise with a totally different style of piece.

Mixing techniques

Mixing down all the recorded tracks, achieving a satisfactory balance and adding effects/sound enhancements is both an art and a science. It is a highly personal process and best not done 'by committee'!

If at all possible allow a day or at least half a day before mixing finished tracks. This should ensure 'fresh ears', maximum concentration and objectivity.

Start by checking each track separately (using the solo function) for any mistakes or extraneous noises.

Build your final mix up systematically, taking care not to make your own instrumental or vocal efforts too dominant in the balance!

Try to mix sounds at the same volume and from the same speakers that the music will be listened to. For example, television background music will be heard at low levels out of a mono speaker, dance music will be heard at a high level from large speakers. In practice most popular music is first heard through small radio or car speakers so it is not surprising to see tiny, cheap speakers at home in the most sophisticated and luxurious studios.

POST-PRODUCTION

After the recording process is completed the post-production stage involves giving approval to test pressings, art work, marketing and promotion.

COST

Studio rates currently start at £15 to £20 per hour or about £150 for a ten hour day.

Professionals can use between 24 to 48 hours per song (even though the early Beatles albums were recorded in a day).

For your first recording you should budget for roughly 1 to 2 hours for setting up and microphone placement, 2–3 hours to put down the backing, 3 or 4 hours for over-dubs and 4 or 5 hours for mix down. This is for each track!

Your first CD of 10 songs may cost:

To the recording cost of £2 150 add:

Artwork	£300
Pressing	£1 500 (per 1 000 copies)

This results in an overall cost of about £3.50 to £4.00 per CD. If you sell 500 at £8.00 you will have the other 500 to send off to companies, agents and venues.

	Studio time per song		
	Best	**Worst**	
Set up	1	2	(hours)
Backing	2	3	
Over-dubs	3	4	
Mix down	4	5	
Total	10	14	
Cost	£150	£280	
× 10	£1 500	£2 800	
Average		£2 150	

TASK

- Investigate the current costs for all the above in your area.
- Calculate the budget you will require to produce a CD (10 tracks) and how many you will need to sell, and at what price, to make a profit.
- How could you minimise costs and maximise profit?

Outboard effects

Reverb

This is by far the most used effect and is featured on most of the sounds in any mix. It is associated with 'ambience' and giving the impression that the sound is 'live' and performed in a large venue. The reverb processor will add hundreds of delays (simulating reflections off walls) to the original dry sound, in a pre-set pattern which will naturally decay over time. The amount of delay, decay and size of the room can be selected at the touch of a button.

Equalisation

Equalisation involves filtering out or boosting low, middle or high frequencies in the manner of a sophisticated tone control. There are three types of equaliser:

- A **graphic** equaliser allows you to boost or cut several frequencies bands simultaneously.
- A **sweep** equaliser can cut/boost only one set frequency at a time.
- A **parametric** equaliser will allow adjustment of all parameters of equalisation.

The compressor/limiter/expander

These are involved in the process that boosts or lowers the gain to ensure the sound stays within a given dynamic range.

A **compressor** will decrease the level of the loud parts and increase the level of the quiet parts. The amount of compression is set by the ratio control. A ratio of 2:1 means a 2dB change on the input will give a 1dB change at the output.

A **limiter** compresses the sound with a ratio of 20:1 and above. This is to such an extent that the output will be at a constant level no matter what the dynamic range of the input.

An **expander** will increase the dynamic range of a sound, making the quiet parts quieter and the loud parts louder.

The noise gate

The noise gate is a switch that cuts off a signal passing though it if it falls below a certain level. It is useful in removing hiss or extraneous noise from acoustically recorded sounds where sniffing, breathing or coughing may ruin a great take.

Delay

Delay is sound stored temporarily then played after the original.

Echo

Echo is separate copies of the entire sound in ever-decreasing volumes.

Chorus/flange/phasing/vibrato

These are special effects that are used to 'liven up' flat sounds:

- **Chorus** will make a single instrument or voice sound like an ensemble by adding short delays with slightly altered pitch
- **Flanging** will thicken the sound by slowly oscillating an echo of the original.
- **Phasing** is a copy of the original sound shifting backwards and forwards in time over the top of the original sound, producing variable cancellation effects.
- **Vibrato** will modulate the pitch of a sound in varying degrees adding expression.

Enhancers

These are processors that alter the sound by distorting the mid/high harmonics of the sound source and combining a small amount of this with the original. This gives increased brightness and is sometimes known as an 'aural exciter'.

Pitch shifter

This is a device that will move a sound up or down in pitch to correct faulty intonation or creating chorus and doubling effects to a vocal.

ADT (Automatic Double Tracking)

To thicken up tracks in the studio producers would ask musicians to record their parts again. There would naturally be slight slowing down and speeding up in the second take as they tried to listen and play simultaneously. An ADT unit will imitate this variable modulation/delay effect creating a realistic doubling.

TASKS

- Listen to a wide selection of recordings and list the effects used on each.
- Which instruments/voices use which effects and which effects are used the most?

Recording studio personnel

The **Producer** has overall responsibility for the recording project. He or she is the overseer and artistic controller of the recording process. They will make sure the final product is as perfect as possible, realise the artists' ideas by acting as an interpreter to the engineer and make important creative decisions in regard to the performance of the artist, the organisation of recording, over-dubbing and final decisions on the mix.

If working for a company the project budget will also fall to the producer, but above all the producer must build empathy with the artist and have the experience and integrity to inspire the confidence of the whole team involved in the recording.

The **Sound Engineer** is the main person responsible for the technical and operational side of the recording process. There are two broad (but not mutually exclusive) types. The more traditional role involves selecting and placing microphones and instruments. The more modern function entails computer programming and digital management. The engineer is

Figure 6.5 *A sound engineer at work*

an important member of the team and he or she often progresses on to producing.

In larger recording studios the **Assistant Sound Engineer** has a role which varies from being the archetypal 'tea person' to performing as many and important tasks as the main engineer. There may be up to three assistants as part of the recording team.

The **Maintenance Engineer** makes sure the recording studio technology is in good working order and carries out necessary repairs.

The **Tape Operator** or **'Tape-op'** is an obsolete role since the advent of digital recording and remote control tape machines. Traditionally it involved starting and stopping the large tape machines that were kept as far away from the mixing console as possible to avoid extraneous noise and heat. It was often the entry occupation into the studio world and is only mentioned because the term has become a euphemism for a young trainee who will serve refreshments and be a poorly paid apprentice in return for a foot up the ladder.

The **Executive Producer** is a largely non-functional role that provides a title for someone who must appear on a credit when a more meaningful designation cannot be found.

With the advent and accessibility of cheap digital recording and sound processing, MIDI networking and computer sequencing, the roles and procedures in small to medium sized recording studios have become blurred at the edges. The engineer operating a computer sequencer and various sound generators on behalf of an artist often becomes part producer and part artist, due to the amount of control this system has on the final product. In the larger and more traditional studios the roles and procedures have become simply more fragmented. The main engineer may delegate the technological aspects to an assistant or dedicated MIDI person. Flexibility is the name of the game nowadays – the more you know the more useful you become.

TASKS

- Consider some of the personal and technical qualities required to be able to perform the roles listed above.
- Analyse which qualities you have or could develop in the near future.

c h a p t e r   7
THE MUSIC BUSINESS AND THE LAW

Contracts

A contract is an agreement between two or more parties on work to be done.

A verbal contract is not worth the paper it is written on, or so they say. Be warned – if it has been made in front of independent witnesses and is reasonable, both sides could be held to it.

Always insist on written agreements wherever possible and if one is not forthcoming presume the worst.

The first rule about any contracts is: ask an **independent lawyer with relevant experience** to advise you as to the content and meaning of any contract before you sign it. Remember, make sure they are an entertainment specialist and completely unconnected to the other party signing the contract.

Musicians on low income may be able to claim legal aid and often lawyers will give one piece of advice free as a 'loss-leader', commonly referred to as 'green form' work. The Musicians' Union also provides a contract vetting service for members.

Occasionally contracts amount to little more than a rip-off. If for example you sign all obligations to one company and receive no returns, your first step would be to send them a 'cure notice'. This gives them 30 days to put matters right or you terminate the contract and demand the return of your masters and copyrights. If you hear nothing from them and start litigation, then find the company has folded and the liquidator has sold your assets to a new company, even if some or all of the directors of the new company are the same as the old one they have no obligation to pay royalties to you. At the moment this form of theft is not illegal and the scenario **has** occurred to several big groups.

TASK

- How many of theses words and phrases, commonly found in contracts do you know the meaning of? Translate each into plain language, if you are unsure – have a guess and then check your answers with the short definitions given on page 167.

1 **Retail price**	9 **Paternity**
2 **Wholesale price**	10 **Cross-collateralisation**
3 **Blanket agreement**	11 **Duration**
4 **Advance payment**	12 **Royalty**
5 **Buy-out**	13 **Material form**
6 **Power of Attorney**	14 **Gross income**
7 **Per diems**	15 **Net income**
8 **Recoupable**	

It is important to understand the difference between **gross** and **net** income. If, for example, you perform a number of gigs that just about cover expenses to promote yourself, the total income maybe £2 500 and costs involved £2 000.

If your manager receives 20% of your **net income** at the end of the tour you should pay him or her £100 leaving yourself £400. If the agreement was 20% of your **gross income**, your manager is owed £500 – leaving you nothing!

Contracts range from simple agreements on a scrap of paper to 100 page documents that few can understand. Here are some of the more common forms:

Venue contract	A simple agreement to perform at a certain place, date and time in exchange for an agreed fee. Negotiable extras may include free food and drink, a guest list of friends who get free admission and bonuses for a full house or large audience.
Management contract	An agreement for a person or company to develop and enhance your career in exchange for a percentage of your earnings over an agreed term.
Agency contract	An agreement for an individual or company to find 'live' work for you in return for a percentage of the fee.
Publishing contract	An agreement to collect royalties for your compositions for printed and recorded music in return for a percentage.
Recording contract	Exclusive rights for a company to record and sell your songs over an agreed term.
Production deal	Studio time and help is offered in exchange for royalties and payback if you are taken up by a larger company.
Band agreement	This can range from setting up limited companies to very informal friendships with little or no agreement about how bills and profits are shared, decisions are made and members are appointed and dismissed. A simple agreement made early on can formalise these issues and avoid conflict at a later date.

See also the Contracts checklist at the end of this chapter.

Royalties

MANAGER'S COMMISSION

Manager's commission is usually 15 to 20% of earnings from publishers, record deals and live performances.

Avoid signing up with a manager for too long and make sure you specify exactly what he or she gets a share of. Try to limit this if you have several sources of income (for example teaching, acting, and so on).

Be very careful to specify the term that the manager can claim on your earnings after ceasing to be your manager. At best none at all, but at most two or three years.

Be careful about the amount of money your manager can spend on your behalf or any rights that he/she can sign away to other companies. Also make sure you appoint an independent accountant to check the figures on a regular basis.

AGENT'S COMMISSION

Agent's commission is usually 10 to 15% of earnings from work found by the agent. Sometimes an agency contract is tantamount to a manager's contract. Make sure you know what you are signing and apply the information above.

PUBLISHING ROYALTIES

You should expect between 10 to 15% of earnings on sheet music sales and 60 to 85% of record royalties, performing royalties and any other uses of your music (for example film, video, television and commercials).

Reputable publishers never charge composers to print or record their songs.

Publishing contracts usually last between one and five years. Do not sign up for longer.

If the publishers do not use your songs make sure you can 'have them back' after one or two years. If they do use them you should **not** expect them back for ten to fifteen years.

RECORD COMPANY COMMISSION

You should expect between 6 to 10% of the retail price of the recording as an unknown artist. Foreign sales will bring you about half this amount. Costs for recording, videos, production and other musicians will be paid **by you** out of this.

Do not be fooled into thinking a ten album deal is better than a one album deal. If the first album does not make money for the company they have the option to not record the subsequent nine. If the first album does make the company money but the second and third don't, they will hold onto profit from the first until they have covered their costs on the other two.

If you wish to change companies they may expect you to produce the remaining seven albums before they release you from your contract. Many think this is tantamount to slavery – ask the artist formally known as Prince or George Michael or many, many other top artists.

If you sign to a record company they will often encourage you to sign over your publishing and merchandising rights to their own or subsidiary companies. This is not necessarily your best option because losses on one can be taken from your profits on the other before you ever see the money.

Options

Recording contracts are often offered for one year plus options. These give the company 'first refusal' on a further five to ten years' worth of recordings. It is important for the artist to negotiate a reasonable advance and royalty percentage for these options, that increases to take account of inflation and the presumption that the act has been successful.

ADVANCES

Record companies and managers sometimes offer an advance. This is a one-off payment to encourage you to sign with them. It should be non-returnable – that means you do not have to give it back, **but** it will be repaid direct to the company or manager when you start making money. This will be recovered before you see any profit so don't expect a massive cheque as soon as you hear your song on the radio!

A large advance may indicate how much faith the company put in you, but always think about the long term and negotiate the best deal over ten years of success rather than a wad of notes to flash on signing and poor returns for your work over the long term. Typical advances range from £50 000 to £250 000 usually paid in two instalments – on signing an agreement and completing recording – but don't be blinded by the advance alone. Always go for the best deal like Oasis, who settled for £35 000 from Creation Records.

PRODUCTION DEALS

Production deals may help you get started, but do beware. If you are successful you will be charged top hourly rates although most of it may have been hanging around while the pay-ing bands used the most convenient times. Always keep a record of exact times and expenses and be careful not to sign away any copyrights.

AND FINALLY . . .

If you are unsure over who eventually pays for anything – promotional videos, hotels, back-stage drinks, chauffeur driven limousines, hotel breakages – presume that **you do!**

Do not forget taxes: one day you will have to pay them. Not your manager, your agent, your publishers or your record company – **you**.

Tony Iommi (of Black Sabbath) gives the following advice: 'Learn how to play two chords and then get yourself a lawyer before learning the third'.

Remember the adage which is as old as popular music itself: 'where there's a hit, there's a writ'!

TASK

- Draw up your own management contracts for other musicians. Complete one that favours yourself over the long term, one that favours the musician over the long term and one that is fair to both (if such a contract exists!). After reading through see which they will 'sign'. At the same time they should do the same. Anyone with a surfeit of enterprise may like to fashion a boardgame along these lines!

Some advice
A ten album deal always sounds impressive, especially when accompanied by a large advance. The trick is to secure long term royalties that will recoup all your original costs.

Figure 7.1   *A typical music industry contract can look daunting*

Percentages of sales

It is impossible to predict exactly how much profit an artist can expect to make on record sales. Each record deal is negotiated differently and there are many changing factors such as tax legislation to take into account.

Smaller independent companies sometimes offer a 50/50 split of profits after all costs have been recovered, but most larger companies work on an intricate percentage system.

A new artist may start with a royalty of 12% of the wholesale price or PPD or PDP – published price to dealers. This is roughly equivalent to 8% of the retail price.

A successful artist with a proven track record may negotiate up to 20% of the PDP, which is about 14% of retail.

The artist's percentage on single sales is far less,

possibly half of the album percentage, the single being thought of as a tool of promotion and possibly even a 'loss leader'. Also within this half-royalty category are: foreign sales, compilation albums, soundtrack albums, and all other 'budget albums'.

A fair deal would be 15% of PDP or 10.5% of retail. For a CD retailing at £14.99 this might equate to roughly £1 after various deductions. This pound would then be divided by the number of people in the group or musicians who contributed.

Unfortunately this is far from the end of the story. Suppose your album 'goes gold' and sells 100 000 copies. The band will not receive £100 000. You will only be paid on 90% of sales to cover 'returns' – a shady hangover from the days of 78 rpm records on delicate shellac and vinyl, to cover returns, breakages and faulty copies! The record company can then start to recoup its costs from your royalties. These may include the advance, recording costs, advertising, photo sessions, half the costs of video shoots, travelling expenses and hotel bills.

A debut album by a new signing to a major label may cost the label £250 000 in advance, recording and marketing costs. Presume the band are on a royalty of 15% of PPD. For every CD sold at £15, 17.5% will be taken by the VAT straight away leaving £12.37. Then the shop will deduct their 30% leaving £8.66, and marketing costs of 30% will leave you with 15% of £6.06 – which is the princely sum of £0.91 per CD sold. You will now have to sell 274 726 CDs before the original £250 000 is recouped.

On the brighter side, these royalties are payable for the 50 year copyright life span of the recording. Bearing this in mind, never agree to have your royalty as a fixed sum in pounds and pence rather than a percentage. Inflation over the 50 years will reduce the figure to negligible amounts.

Royalties should be paid to the artist or artist's manager at least twice a year, maybe on 31 March and 30 October. Make sure any contract you sign states this clearly and gives you recourse to legal action if it is not paid within either 30 or 60 days. If you move to a different recording company ensure that the original company maintains these payments for the full 50 year copyright of the record while they are selling it. This may seem obvious but has not always been the case. Yet another detail to check in the small print!

The size of your advance from the record company gives an indication of their commitment to promoting you. The larger the sum, the harder they have to work to get it back from your royalties. Although you should bargain for a publishing deal that releases your songs back to you as soon as possible (preferably after three years), a large advance will usually tie them to the company for longer. For a £150 000 advance most companies would require at least 15 years' copyright to enable them to take advantage of their financial speculation, but **never** sign over ownership of your songs 'in perpetuity' (that is, for ever).

Cross-collateralisation

Cross-collateralisation is where all the money spent by the record company on a band or artist's behalf will be added up and deducted from their royalties. The only cost that shouldn't be deducted is the payment of mechanical royalties which the record company has to pay to the publisher – unless the record company and publishing company is one and the same and your publishing royalties have been cross-collateralised. This means that all the earnings from a massive selling album can be withheld from the artist if the next or previous one did not make a profit.

Where the money goes

There follows a diagram showing the percentage that can be expected by various beneficiaries from the sale of a standard priced compact disc, and the same diagram showing these percentages in money terms.

Where the money goes

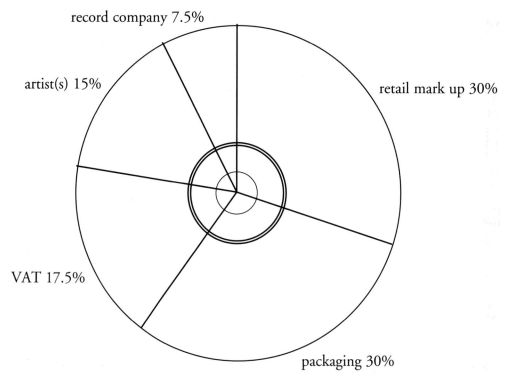

record company 7.5%

artist(s) 15%

retail mark up 30%

VAT 17.5%

packaging 30%

... of the artist(s) 15%

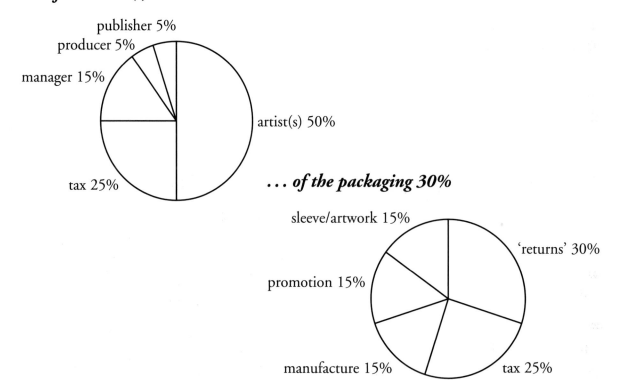

publisher 5%

producer 5%

manager 15%

artist(s) 50%

tax 25%

... of the packaging 30%

sleeve/artwork 15%

'returns' 30%

promotion 15%

manufacture 15%

tax 25%

for a £14.99 CD – where the money goes

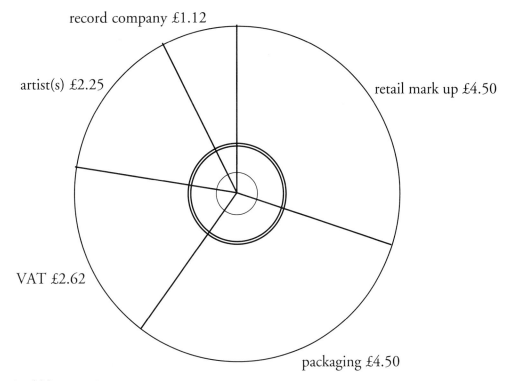

record company £1.12

artist(s) £2.25

retail mark up £4.50

VAT £2.62

packaging £4.50

... of the artist(s)' £2.25

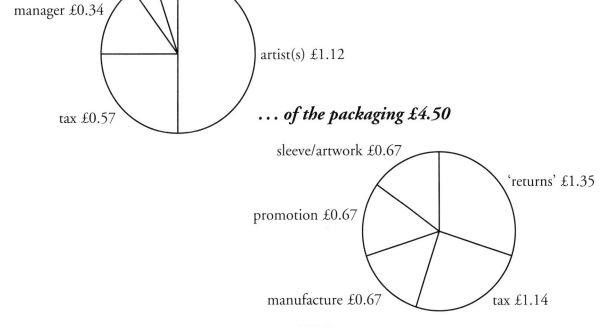

publisher £0.11

producer £0.11

manager £0.34

artist(s) £1.12

tax £0.57

... of the packaging £4.50

sleeve/artwork £0.67

'returns' £1.35

promotion £0.67

manufacture £0.67

tax £1.14

TASKS

- Select a CD from the charts. It will help if you own or have access to a copy to check details from the sleeve.
- Find out roughly how many copies have been sold, multiply the cost of the CD by this amount and calculate how much all the beneficiaries listed below may have earned from UK sales.
- Hazard an educated guess as to how much they have earned from world-wide sales. (presume 15% of total sales are in Britain).

To help calculation presume:

- most albums in the top ten go silver after 3 weeks
- most albums that reach number one go gold
- an album in the charts for three months will go platinum
- silver = 60 000 sales
- gold = 100 000 sales
- platinum = 300 000 sales

Beneficiaries:

	UK	World
Retailers	£	
Manufacturers	£	
Government (tax)	£	
Record Company	£	
Management	£	
Publishers	£	
Producer	£	
Musicians (each)	£	
Artist(s) (each)	£	

Copyright

Copyright protects the creator of a work against others copying it without permission. The work must be original and involve some skill and labour. Nowadays this includes the exclusive right to perform a work in public, to broadcast it and to publish it. It is therefore possible to assign different rights to different people.

Copyright exists as soon as a work is put into material form – that is, written down or recorded. It is commonplace to put the symbol (c) with the name of the copyright owner beside it.

If a composer assigns the copyright to a publisher in return for a share of the royalties on sales of music, performances and recordings, the publisher then owns the copyright. However, if the composer belongs to the PRS (Performing Right Society) they have already assigned certain rights to the PRS to collect monies on their behalf and this is not affected by the publishing deal.

In Britain copyright lasts for 50 years after the death of a composer, but even when out of copyright a publisher will own the rights of the layout of the printed version for 25 years from its publication date.

The key elements of copyright are:

> 1 Performing the work in public
> 2 Broadcasting the work
> 3 Reproduction of the work in any form
> 4 Publishing the work
> 5 Adapting the work

1 and **2** make up the performing right which is controlled by the PRS,

3, **4** and **5** make up the publishing right which is usually controlled by the publishing company and/or the record company.

TASK

- List ten well known songs (such as 'Happy Birthday', the National Anthem, 'Jingle Bells' and so on) and find out who owns their copyright.

There is a growing trend for top performers to insist on a composition credit on songs they record but did not write. This is because artists have realised that the writers of songs are still earning decent royalties long after the current 'stars' are forgotten. The composers often relinquish half of their royalty in the knowledge that the song will only be a hit if covered by a popular act and 100% of nothing is nothing!

At the risk of serious litigation we will not suggest artists who we suspected of this practice – but you could hazard a guess at ten that *you* suspect. A starting point may be singers who originally covered other peoples' songs or who were management-created bands who suddenly developed highly-skilled compositional talents when they became top acts, artists who produce albums containing highly polished hit songs that do not stay in one particular style or genre, and bands with song credits that read like a football team sheet – with all members of the group mentioned.

Try to include at least one suggestion from the 1950s, 1960s, 1970s and 1980s.

PHOTOCOPYING

Photocopying is illegal unless permission has been granted by all the copyright owners (usually the publisher) or the copy is solely used for private research and study.

TASK

- All institutions (schools, colleges, libraries and so on) should have a guide to what is and is not permitted to be photocopied on their machines. Find out how much you would legally be allowed to copy, and what you have photocopied illegally in the past.

RECORD COMPANIES

Despite the existence of thousands of record labels there are only five major international record companies – BMG, CBS, EMI, Polygram and Warner Bros. They each have a stable of smaller labels, and independent labels under licence, that cater for market niches to engender brand loyalty and 'street credibility'. Occasionally artists struggle through long, bitter law suits to release themselves from a company only to find that the major company has bought the label that they moved to!

TASK

- Using the five 'majors' as headings on a page, underneath each list as many subsidiary labels as you can that are controlled by them.

The structure of a record company can be divided into four main areas:

Artists & Repertoire

A & R departments receive hundreds of demos, read scores of reviews, watch dozens of bands live, and are contacted by several managers, agents and lawyers each week. Their job is to check out all of the above and predict the most successful candidates to fill gaps in the company's roster of artists. After the discovery they sign and develop this talent for the company.

Manufacturing & Distribution

The factories that make CDs, cassettes and records are often owned by a record company but will undertake work for others. They deliver the product to distribution centres to be transported to warehouses and shops. Care must be taken to produce the optimum amount needed as calculated by liaising with the company's sales, marketing and retail teams.

Marketing, Promotion & Press

The record company marketing team will plan a campaign to dovetail release dates with television, radio, newspaper and advertising coverage of a new product.

Legal & International

Although British acts have been responsible for up to a third of world recording business, Britain only brings in 8% of total sales – well behind the USA (33%), Japan (15%) and Germany (9%). Given that British talent accounts for up to half of all American sales, companies put a great deal of time and effort into international liaison and promotion. This also entails an expert understanding of the different overseas legal systems.

INDEPENDENT RECORDING AND PUBLISHING COMPANIES

Many independent record companies have emerged during the last decade. They offer an alternative to the 'majors' (although they are often funded by, and ultimately controlled by, the 'big five' companies) and operate on the principal that 'small is beautiful'. They will not have as many artists on their roster and will usually provide a more focused and personal approach, thus giving the artist more creative control.

The downside of this is that they rarely offer large advances and do not have the marketing clout and publicity contacts the high spending organisations command.

TASKS

- List ten independent record companies with at least one artist they handle.
- List at least five advantages and five disadvantages of signing to an independent company rather than a major.
- Name two artists or groups that you think would benefit from each and explain why.
- Which would suit *your* talents best?

RECORDING MECHANICALS

When a recording is made of a work it requires another control known as the mechanical right, which administered in Britain by the MCPS (Mechanical Copyright Protection Society).

The right to perform or broadcast recordings is controlled by the PPL (Phonographic Performance Limited).

- To perform a work in public PRS permission or licence is required.
- To record a work MCPS permission or licence is required.

To play a recorded work in public two permissions or licenses are required – one from the PRS for the performance of the music and one from the PPL for the use of the recording of the work.

The creator or composer of a work should expect to receive between £5 to £20 per three minute broadcast on local radio, between £30 to £50 on network radio, and between £150 to £300 for television broadcast.

TASK

- Choose a well known advertising jingle and calculate how much the composer may expect to earn from it in a week from local, national and television coverage.

Touring

At the beginning of an artist's career touring will usually result in a loss rather than a profit. Hopefully their record company will finance the tour as a loss-leading promotional exercise, but yet again, these losses are recoupable from the artist's future royalties. There is a tendency to imagine everything is provided 'on the house' but all food, drink and creature comforts will be paid for by the band at a later date!

Often the amount of financial dealings involved will require setting up a separate limited company with its own accountant and tour manager to arrange day-to-day details – leaving the musicians to concentrate on what they do best. This however does require extra expenditure and care must be taken that the tour costs to promote an album do not eat up all the profit made from it.

MERCHANDISING

T-shirts, hats, caps, badges and any other merchandising (or 'swag' as it is sometimes known) can be a tidy earner on tour. Companies who manufacture and organise selling the goods usually estimate between £3 to £5 per person will be spent on items at each gig. For a 500-seat venue this may bring in £2000. The artist can expect up to 25% of retail price in Britain and up to 40% in the USA. Advances of up to £50000 are sometimes paid for big tours, but artists may wish to approve any merchandising before it is offered to their fans.

INSURANCE

Musicians can insure their voices, fingers and instruments but the premiums are always high due to their 'rock'n'roll' reputation. If it is in a record company's interest to guard against the worst happening they will undertake the expense, especially if a large advance has been paid out. Third party or public liability insurance is essential if touring and this is offered free of charge by the Musicians Union and Incorporated Society of Musicians to their members. The MU and ISM also offer competitive rates for instrument insurance. You may be led to believe that your instruments are covered by non-specialist companies on home insurance policies but be wary of clauses that exclude professional use, theft from vehicles and damage caused in pubs, clubs or any other gigs.

Tax for the self employed

Tax laws are complex and perplexing, hence the number of accountants earning more money than musicians.

The two main tax codes for musicians are Schedule D and Schedule E.

Schedule E is where tax is deducted at source or Pay as You Earn (PAYE). Under this classification your employer sends the money to the Inland Revenue before you get your share of what is left.

Schedule D is where the Inland Revenue's share of your earnings is paid to you direct.

At the end of each financial year you submit an account of earnings and deductions and pay the Inland Revenue what is owed to them. It is essential therefore to put aside a reasonable proportion of your earnings for when the tax bill arrives. This could be up to two years later. Many musicians earn good money and spend it all and then are landed with a bill much later when they are not earning as much and find great difficulty paying it.

DEDUCTIONS

Allowances are the amounts you are allowed to earn before being taxed and are set by the government each budget.

Expenses can be deducted from your overall profits before tax is calculated. These are items or services paid for (and receipts kept) without which you would not be able to carry out your work. Working out which of these is **necess-**

arily incurred is both an art and a science. Some of the more obvious ones might be: travelling expenses, instrument maintenance (strings, reeds and so on), hotel costs when on tour, telephone charges incurred when arranging work, advertising and hire charges.

Instrument or equipment purchases are classed as 'capital allowances' that can be carried over and used partially over several years if you wish.

National Insurance contributions should be made for when you need to claim Social Security benefits. You are advised to pay your maximum contribution allowed as soon as possible. If the price of the 'stamp' is increased you will have to pay the new rate rather than the old one.

TASKS

- Make a list of deductible allowances you could have claimed over the past month.
- Discuss these with others and decide if they are necessary, possibly necessary or dodgy!

RECORD KEEPING

All of the above relies on one main ingredient – accurate record keeping. This is unfortunate because musicians are historically very bad at this.

Record keeping can be as simple as a small book with amounts received on the left hand side of a page and expenditures on the right hand side, together with an envelope or box containing payslips, bills and receipts filed by date.

Many musicians utilise the 'shoe box' technique for accounting. They put all their receipts into a box or bag and forget about them until the tax demand arrives. At this point their lives become miserable for a period where they either hand the shoe box to an accountant who can perform miracles (at a cost), or start trying to organise all their receipts into a logical order. The expensive romantic meal out with a partner becomes the essential wining and dining of a prospective client or agent, the new

outfit for a friend's wedding metamorphoses into fancy stage wear, holiday travel reconstructs as a mini-tour abroad, phone calls all relate to the musicians livelihood, gas bills are solely for the purpose of keeping hands warm while practising the latest riff, electric bills are exclusively clocked up to allow you to read music into the early hours, and so on and so forth. Remember, revenue officials are not stupid and have dealt with more accounts similar to yours than you have had blisters on your fingers.

By all means use an experienced accountant, but make life easier for them and less expensive for yourself by systematically storing receipts in chronological order (an old-fashioned spike on your desk works as well as anything) and making a note in a receipt book of why this expense was legitimately incurred.

EXAMPLE OF SIMPLE RECORD KEEPING

Monies In April 1999			Monies Out April 1999		
1/4/99	Bert's Bar gig	£90.00	2/4/99	Strings	£9.59
				Plectra (3)	£1.38
4/4/99	Lesson	£19.00	4/4/99	Petrol	£28.00
				Laundry	£15.50
8/4/99	Bert's Bar gig	£90.00			
			10/4/99	Phone Bill	£84.00
				Flyers	£124.00
12/4/99	Royalty cheque	£545.00	12/12/99	Stage jacket	£545.00

TASKS

- Calculate the profit or loss in the above example.
- How much tax will the musician have to pay?
- Investigate the current tax and allowance rates.
- List your own profits and losses over the past 3 months. If you have neither – invent some!

Organisations

There are several professional organisations you may wish to join such as the Musicians' Union, The Incorporated Society of Musicians and Equity.

They cannot guarantee your success in the music business but they offer indispensable support in areas such as insurance for instruments, personal liability, legal advice and support in the unfortunate circumstance of you needing it. These aspects alone can justify the annual subscriptions.

COLLECTING SOCIETIES

The **Performing Right Society** (**PRS**) is an indispensable members' organisation that collects monies from the public performance and broadcast of musical works. This includes royalties from radio and television stations, concert halls, theatres, shops, restaurants, hotels, bars, clubs and cinemas.

The PRS has links with their international counterparts – ASCAP and BMI in the USA, GEMA, SACEM, BUMA, JARSAC and SCAE in Europe, SOCAN in Canada, JASRAC in Japan and APRA in Australia.

The **Mechanical Copyright Protection Society** (**MCPS**) handles mechanical, that is recorded, royalties and after increasing collaboration between the PRS and MCPS the two have 'merged' in the interests of efficiency.

The **PPL** collects royalties for record companies when recordings are performed or broadcast and the **VPL** does the same for videos.

TASK

- Your group has been invited to support an established act on a tour of Britain.

In practice if this is a major act you will have to pay them for the privilege of the exposure to their fan base and the possible profits of future record sales and merchandising.

If it is not an established act you may get a share of the profits – or losses.

For our example let us presume that the headline act will pay you to support them.

Can you afford to miss this opportunity, or can you afford it? The figures look as follows:

Guaranteed income from concerts:	£1 200 per gig on a 12 gig tour
Possible income from merchandise:	25% of T-shirts, photos, caps amounting to anything between £500 and £1 000 per gig.
Cost of backing musicians:	£120 per gig for 4 other backing musicians
Cost of equipment hire:	£220 per gig
Accommodation and sustenance:	£63.33 per night each
Agent's gross percentage:	15%
Manager's net percentage:	20%
Income tax at 25%	

Calculation

12 gigs @ £1,200 per gig =	12 × 1 200	£14 400
4 musicians @ £120 per gig =	4 × 120 × 12	£5 760
Equipment hire @ £220 per gig =	12 × £185	£2 220
Accommodation and subsistence =	5 × £64 × 18	£5 760

(NB although there are 12 gigs they are spread out over 18 days)

Agents fee =	15% of £14 400	£2 160

so far: income =   £14,400

costs   =   £5 760 + £2 220 + £5 760 + £2 160 = £15 900

At this point you have lost £1 500 … but let's not forget the merchandising!!!

At **worst** it will net you 25% of £500 × 12 = 125 × 12 = £1 500

That is, no profit and no need to pay your manager.

If you have kept and recorded all your essential receipts (accommodation, equipment hire and so on), and employ a good accountant, you should not have too much tax to pay.

At **best** the merchandising will net you 25% of £1 000 = 250 × 12 = £3 000.

This earns you the princely sum of £1 500. Your manager will now require his 20% which is £300, leaving £1 200. The inland revenue will now demand 25% of this which is also £300 – leaving you with £900.

At this point you usually realise that the drinks and sandwiches you eagerly consumed backstage while the main act was playing has been billed to you.

Each band member ate and drank £15 worth per gig.

This totals as £15 × 5 × 12 = £900.

Thank heavens you sold so many T-shirts. Next time get out and sign posters and baseball caps instead of lounging around backstage pretending to be superstars!

Contract checklist

Having read this chapter, hopefully all musicians will realise the necessity of always taking expert legal advice before signing any contract.

The following checklist may help prepare for questions you will want to ask.

Venue contract
- **Where is the gig?** — Make sure you have clear directions.
- **When is the gig?** — Check 'get in time' and finishing time.
- **What is the fee?** — Is this guaranteed or dependant on take?
- **What extras are included?** — Who pays for the 'rider'.
- **How many guests are allowed?** — Check before inviting friends and family.

Management contract
- **What commission is being agreed?** — 15 to 20% is usual.
- **How long is the agreement for?** — Shorter the better, maximum 5 years.
- **How long after termination of agreement can the manager claim commission?** — This requires delicate negotiation.
- **Are monies paid to the artist or manager?** — Usually the manager but preferably an appointed accountant.
- **What expenses are met by the manager?** — Office overheads and own travel and accommodation seem reasonable.
- **What is the limit on the amount a manager can spend on the artist's behalf?** — As little as deemed necessary.
- **Can the artist audit the manager?** — Essential.
- **How is the agreement terminated?** — If he/she has not acted in good faith or in the artists' best interests.

Agency contract
- **What commission is being agreed?** — 10 to 15% is usual.
- **How long is the agreement for?** — Shorter the better, maximum 3 years.
- **Are monies paid to the artist or agent?** — The artist preferably.

Publishing contract
- **What commission is being agreed?** — Expect 10 to 15% on music and 60 to 80% of recording royalties.
- **How long is the agreement for?** — Shorter the better, usually 3 to 5 years.
- **How long before copyright is returned?** — Shorter the better.

Recording contract
- **What commission is being agreed?** — 10 to 14% is usual.
- **How long is the agreement for?** — Check options carefully.
- **Does the royalty increase with each option?** — At least 1% per year with added bonuses for large sales.
- **What expenses are met by the company?** — Videos, support bands, promotion.

Band agreement
- **Who owns the band name?** — Agree beforehand in the event of a split.
- **Who is financially responsible?** — Agree equal liability.
- **How are profits shared?** — Again equally.
- **How are new members appointed?** — By majority or unanimous agreement.
- **How are band members dismissed?** — By majority or unanimous agreement.
- **Writing royalties?** — Do non-composing members of the band receive a royalty or part of it?

TASK

- Using your personal experience write a checklist for other musicians to prevent them making the same mistakes you or your friends may have encountered.

TASK: ANSWERS TO PAGE 150

1	**Retail price**	The price that goods are sold to the public.
2	**Wholesale price**	The price that goods are sold to the retailer.
3	**Blanket agreement**	Exclusive rights to all an artist's work over a fixed period of time.
4	**Advance payment**	Non-returnable monies paid to an artist which will be recovered from later profits.
5	**Buy-out**	Gives the company permission to use a song or performance at will, without having to pay royalties to the artist.
6	**Power of Attorney**	The right of a company or individual to act on behalf of an artist.
7	**Per diems**	Day-to-day living expenses paid to artists on tour or when working.
8	**Recoupable**	Financial losses that can be recovered at a later stage.
9	**Paternity**	The right to be identified as the composer of a song.
10	**Cross-collateralisation**	The right of a company to calculate all the money they have spent on you (including advances) and not pay you a penny until your royalties exceed the whole of it. If, for example, one record has sold well you will not reap the rewards of it until the three that did not do well are paid for.
11	**Duration**	The length of an agreement or contract.
12	**Royalty**	Percentage of profit paid to an artist for each unit sold or performance of their work.
13	**Material form**	Creative work that is written down or recorded.
14	**Gross income**	Total income before any deductions are made.
15	**Net income**	Profit after deductions have been made.

chapter 8

MUSIC AND THE MEDIA

What are the media?

Music and the media are inextricably linked as each needs the other to survive. Music is communicated through more ways than sound heard on CD, vinyl or cassette. Television, radio, the print media and the internet enable music and performers to be heard, seen and, most importantly, promoted. Likewise music aids other media by reinforcing brand identity in radio advertising jingles, injecting tension into television drama with sound effects, or attracting readers to newspapers with rock'n'roll stories.

In this chapter we will explore what the music media are and how they work to enable effective promotion of your own music. We will also examine current media issues concerning the music business such as press intrusion and representation and the portrayal of individuals, ideas and social groupings across the mass media.

So what are the media? The word is the plural of medium, a means of communication, which we use routinely and indifferently. Every day we make contact with people: we may phone someone, send a letter, fax or e-mail, or meet to discuss a project face to face. These are all basic, but vital, forms of communication.

Consider these common forms in a musical situation. A student pianist performs for her teacher and two cats. So impressive is this performance, the teacher decides to phone a few colleagues and invite them along to listen. Now there is a small audience. So stunned are these colleagues, they suggest a short concert at the college. The teacher pins up a simple poster on the noticeboard, phones or writes to everyone she knows and more than one hundred people attend the concert. Talking and listening, writing, reading and viewing are the everyday forms of communication, which if employed carefully and intelligently effect positive change.

On a larger scale, these common forms of communication are known as the media. Writing, reading and viewing translate into print media pieces, photographs and designs. Talking and listening become radio. Add moving visuals and you have the essence of television, film and video. Newspapers, magazines, books, radio, television, video, film, the internet and music are the major forms of mass media which all exist in our lives, sometimes without our knowing.

TASK

● How much do the media affect your life?

Calculate the level of media saturation in your life each week by taking a typical day's activities and multiplying by seven. Yesterday is a good day on which to base your study.

Firstly consider the primary level of media saturation in your life. This means concentrating wholly on a media form to the exclusion of everything, for example reading *NME* and doing nothing else. Calculate the number of hours spent this way for all the major forms of media during one day.

Now consider the secondary level of media saturation. This means listening to the radio, for example, as a secondary activity while you eat breakfast, cook a meal, chat to friends, read a newspaper or write an essay. Calculate the time spent this way recently during one day.

Now work out the tertiary uses of the media. This is when a form of media is the third most important activity at any given moment. For example, you are doing the washing up, chatting to a friend, but have Top of the Pops on in the background in order to catch the new number one! Calculate the time spent in this way during one day.

Now multiply each level by seven and add together. Create a new table, similar to the one illustrated below, and compare the results with your fellow musicians. Enter the information in a new portfolio for music and the media.

MEDIA DIET	TV	Music	Print media	Radio	Video	Internet	Film	Total
Primary								
Secondary								
Tertiary								
Grand Total								
Brief comments on results								

LOCAL VERSUS NATIONAL

The media are becoming increasingly market segmented, which means targeting their own particular section, but all can roughly be divided into three broad categories: local (or regional), national and international.

Local media are targeted at specific regional areas and are not usually broadcast, promoted or sold outside these locations. Normally there will be one major newspaper per city, for example the *Evening Standard* in London and the *Evening News* in Edinburgh. Freesheets, mostly comprising advertising, cultural magazines such as *Time Out* and gig guides may also be on offer. Independent local radio stations often attract larger audiences than their national counterparts in regional areas, and with the advent of cable, local TV is an expanding business.

National media are those forms which are broadcast or sold throughout an entire country, for example *The Times*, Channel Four and Radio 1. Television channels and newspapers, however, will have special regional aspects, for example editionised news and features which give a local flavour.

International media are broadcast or sold throughout the world. Examples of these forms are satellite and cable television, worldwide current affairs titles such as *Time, US Today*, the women's magazine *Cosmopolitan* and BBC World Service Radio. Certain national and local publications, books, films, television and radio programmes are sold and broadcast across the world.

Music falls into all of these categories, with the extent of media coverage reflecting the success of the artist. A broad understanding of the workings of the media at large is crucial to your success in the music business.

TASKS

- Research the broad divisions of local, national and international media.
  On an A3 sheet of paper, create column headings of all the major media forms, as in the list above. Underneath each heading, list the local media of which you are aware. Research this further by consulting newsagents for more local print media, newspapers for local TV and radio stations, and the internet.
- Do the same for national and international media, this time consulting large newsagents, national press and a publication called *The Writers' and Artists' Yearbook*, available in the library, and a highly-recommended purchase if you are serious about getting into the music business.

Keep these charts in your music and media portfolio for reference. Leave plenty of space to add contact names and addresses later, as you delve deeper into the subject. You should now have an accurate picture of your own local, national and international media.

SPECIALIST MUSIC MEDIA

Some forms of media target readers with specific interests, such as football fans, budding chefs, the medical profession and, of course, music lovers. Music magazines are big business both in the popular and serious genres. Some of these publications are spin-offs from radio or television programmes such as *Top of the Pops* magazine or *Classic FM*. Each is there for a purpose, offering something different to the others in the broad area of specialist music magazines.

Music magazines and newspapers, therefore, generally divide into popular and classical styles then break down into several specialist categories. *Top of the Pops*, *Mixmag*, *Rolling Stone*, *Q*, *NME* and *Smash Hits* are strictly popular music publications, while *Classic FM*, *The Strad* and *Music Teacher* are aimed only at those with classical music interests.

Similarly radio and television stations divide generally into classical and serious music and popular genres. Radio 1 and 2 broadcast popular music, while Radio 3 and Classic FM broadcast mainly serious music. Likewise MTV, VH1 and CMTV transmit popular music, while Performance concentrates on airing classical music.

However, this general division skates on the surface of understanding the specialist music media. Radio 1 listeners probably would not listen to Radio 2, even though both are under the banner of popular music radio stations. Likewise Radio 3 listeners may actively disapprove of Classic FM.

TASK

● Before examining markets more closely, you should be aware of the music media at large. With two or three of your fellow musicians, investigate all music titles in the major media forms. Assign one person to radio, another to TV, cable and satellite, and another to print media.

For radio Refer to your original list on local, national and international media. Consult *Radio Times* or another publication of your choice, and jot down all the stations which offer music as a main element in their schedules. Next divide these up into popular and classical genres. Can you break down these divisions further? In your own words, try to identify the differences in the musical contents of each station and the audiences targeted. Write up the information in a coherent way.

For television Buy a newspaper and jot down every programme (noting the channel) on music, and every satellite and cable television music channel. Next divide these up into popular and classical music genres. In your own words, try to identify the differences in musical content and target audience.

For print media Again referring to your original list on local, national and international media, visit your nearest big newsagent and jot down every single music publication in the shop. Next divide them into popular and serious music categories. Try to identify the further differences between them. Consult a music library or *The Writers' and Artists' Yearbook* for more titles. Write up your findings, carefully.

For all researchers Photocopy this valuable information so that each member of your team has a general guide to the music media in their portfolios.

UNDERSTANDING TARGET MARKETS

Understanding people and their interests is the key to success in any aspect of life. Magnified several times over, this communication skill could earn you success in the music business, if you aim at the right market.

A target market is the intended audience for your product.

So far we have divided the media into local, national, international and specialist interest. However, socio-economic factors are also crucial to analysing markets more accurately. In advertising terms there are three main divisions of the mass market (the general population)

Up-market or AB

A upper middle class
B middle class

Mid-market or C1C2

C1 lower middle class
C2 skilled working class

Down-market or DE

D unskilled working class
E lowest level of subsistance

These socio-economic strata were created in 1945, when divisions and attitudes to wealth and class were rigid. They are now increasingly irrelevant, even offensive, to present-day society. For example, a lorry driver who in 1945 would have been classified as a down-market D type, may have 50 people working for him or her on freelance contracts. Likewise a highly-educated but impoverished 'resting' actor would fit into the E category on purely financial terms.

Nevertheless, the groupings continue to exist in advertising as a blunt tool to form further divisions of the mass market. To create a more personalised, accurate and rounded profile of a target audience the following are also taken into consideration nowadays:

Gender
Age
Interests
Lifestyle

Increasingly, the media reflect our buying habits, aspirations and who we think we are.

TASKS

- In order to increase awareness of the vast variety of markets and their respective media, you are going to create a character, possibly even a stereotype. With your fellow musicians dream up an individual and apply all the market criteria listed above. For example:

Jo James is 23. He is well educated and has just been appointed manager of a new London indie record company specialising in acid jazz. Earning around £25 000 to £30 000 per annum, he fits into the upmarket B category. He enjoys clubbing, driving his new shiny second-hand Mercedes, wearing trendy designer labels, reading about the latest developments in music (including technology) and generally having a good laugh with his mates. Jo is not in a serious relationship at the moment. He probably

Watches MTV, VH1, The Fast Show, Top of the Pops (although he does not broadcast this to his friends), TFI Friday, The Simpsons, Friends, Never Mind the Buzzcocks and Later With Jools Holland

Reads *Q, NME, Music Weekly, loaded, Uncut, The Mix, Future Music, Time Out*, the *Evening Standard* and *The Sun*. Occasionally reads the *Guardian* to prove to himself and others that he does have an intellectual side and vague left-wing tendencies

Listens to Radio 1, Capital Radio and Radio 2 when no-one's around.

By knowing brief but key details about a person, you can make an educated guess about the media they consume. Certain characteristics of Jo James are common to many in his age group, such as lifestyle and interests. If you had just written some acid-jazz songs or wanted to attract an audience to one of your gigs, Jo James and his counterparts would be a target certainty.

Compare your invented characters with other groups, discussing in depth other media possibilities.

Now select a person you know fairly well, preferably with a sense of humour, and choose appropriate media for them. Write down your description and media, show it to your friend and wait for their reaction!

Final task on target markets

● Reread all the information on target markets. These points are crucial to understanding all the media which could be relevant to you as musicians. For every aspect of music you want to promote, you need to know precisely who, where, when and how to contact people to achieve success. Uppermost in your mind at all times should be **who exactly are we aiming this at?**

Print media

Read all about it! The first mass communication form to be created still wields a mighty influence over society. New technology, television and radio have never ousted the power of the printed word. As musicians, this is the most useful and important form for getting started in the business.

So what are the print media exactly? Broadly speaking, newspapers, magazines and books are the main types, but electronic media and publications such as chronicles, guides, pamphlets, newsletters and comics can also be classified as print media. In this section we will concentrate on the two major types essential to the music industry: newspapers and magazines.

Newspapers

The press continues to be powerful because it is so user-friendly. Newspapers can be read at leisure anywhere and at any time, stored for reference and re-read if necessary. Press stories contain more information than those broadcast on television and radio, and pictures have more meaning when dramatically laid out on a page. Births, marriages, deaths, public notices and specific types of advertising and local stories are only to be found in newspapers, which are essential and established communication links in our society today.

Apart from local, national and international press, newspapers can be divided further by size into broadsheets and tabloids.

Broadsheets, as the name suggests, are large newspapers. Titles such as the *The Times*, *The Daily Telegraph*, *The Herald*, *The Scotsman*, *The Irish Times* and the *Guardian* fall into this category.

Tabloids are half the size of broadsheets, for example, *The Sun*, the *Daily Mail*, *The Mirror*, the *Evening Standard*, the *Glasgow Evening Times* or the *Newcastle Evening Chronicle*.

In addition to size newspapers may be divided into popular and quality types.

Popular newspapers are mass market national newspapers with a concentrated readership in the C1C2 DE market. Newspapers such as *The Sun*, *The Star*, *The Mirror*, the *Daily Record* and the *News of the World* are examples of the popular press which are also all tabloids. With their large dramatic pictures and headlines, sense of fun displayed through witty headlines, captions and famous personality

columnists such as Gary Bushell of *The Sun*, they make an entertaining, snappy and informative read. *The Sun*, in particular, has attracted much publicity with its no-holds-barred stories and continues to be the biggest-selling newspaper in Britain, with a circulation of around 4 million copies a day and 12 million readership. Swords are still drawn, however, in the circulation wars as each title tries to outdo the other by special issues in the shock-horror stakes, dramatic exclusive revelations about the rich and famous, big-money competitions, the £1million Bingo Bonanzas of the 1980s and flexible cover pricing in the 1990s.

Quality newspapers are national newspapers aimed largely at the ABC1C2 markets and include *The Times*, *The Independent*, the *Guardian*, *The Scotsman*, *The Herald*, *The Daily Telegraph* and *The European*. Quality newspapers have smaller headlines, more formal language and more in-depth and background reportage, specialist sections on subjects such as the arts, literature, business and reviews of theatre, music, films and books.

Certain newspapers are breaking away from the quality/popular stereotypes. The *Daily Mail* and *The Express*, for example, are tabloids which attract an AB C1C2 readership, and are increasingly heading up market, at the same time as trying to attract the top end of the down-market press.

Thereafter newspapers are divided into daily, evening, weekly, Sunday or freesheet categories.

Newspaper and magazine personnel

All newspapers and magazines have certain aspects in common which are the keys to understanding the forms. The personnel involved

have roughly the same job remits across the two genres. Every large newspaper or magazine staff can be divided roughly into editorial, advertising, marketing, promotion, production and distribution departments. The aspects you need to understand for the music business are editorial, advertising and promotion.

The editorial section comprises all the news and sports stories, pictures, headlines and page designs which appear in the paper. The Editor is in charge of the editorial aspect of a newspaper or magazine and is responsible in law for the publication's content. The Editor will normally have a Deputy and, depending on the size of the paper, possibly an Assistant Editor. Next in line to the senior editorial management team, are the section editors. These are Chief Sub-Editor (in charge of headlines, captions and editing the copy), Features Editor, News Editor, Picture Editor, Sports Editor, Arts Editor, Music Editor, Health Editor, and so on. The number and variety of sections will depend upon the size and type of publication.

The other content of a newspaper or magazine is largely **advertising**, both **display** and **classified**. On a newspaper there will normally be an Advertising Director, Advertising Manager and then other Senior Advertising Executives with specialist responsibilities, for example Field Sales Manager, Classified Advertising Manager, Car Sales Manager, and so on. Newspapers and magazines are shop windows and offer a service to those who want to buy space to sell their goods or recruit staff. All sales executives help to advise their clients on how best to use the space they purchase, and at the same time earn revenue for their paper or magazine. Advertising teams are set targets, which when achieved, can earn them a bonus.

All this information on advertising and editorial will help to produce accurate target marketing for your career in the music business. Music is important in both sections whether on local or national newspapers. Your local press are the most valuable, however, even when you are a world-famous superstar!

Getting to know the names of journalists who write about music is essential, particularly on your local paper, and it helps to know one of the news reporting staff who you can turn to for advice when you feel you have something worthy of publication like a story or picture idea.

TASKS

- With three or four of your fellow musicians, select a tabloid popular or quality broadsheet each (ensuring you have variety within the group) and find the address of the publication. Write a letter to the Promotions Manager requesting a current media pack giving you target readership breakdowns, advertising rate cards and company information. Media packs are commonly issued to potential advertisers. If in a couple of days you have not received one, ring the Promotions Manager, again politely requesting your media pack. When you receive it, read it thoroughly and compare it to the others in your group. Keep these invaluable documents for reference in your portfolios.
- While you are waiting for your media packs to arrive, buy the newspapers of your choice and study them carefully. Make notes on the music stories published in your chosen newspapers, and why you consider they made publication. Try to identify the type of story your newspaper's readers like to see. Discuss the musical contents of your papers with your fellow musicians.

MAGAZINES

In contrast to newspapers, magazines are printed mostly on glossy paper and usually in full colour. They concentrate on features (as opposed to news), cost more and are published less frequently. The marketing is more segmented than in newspapers, dividing more into gender, class, age and specialist interests.

For example, *Cosmopolitan*, *Elle*, *Vogue* and *Marie-Claire* are generally aimed at up-market young executive women, contain in-depth features pieces (articles) and advertisements for expensive products.

In contrast, *Sugar* and *Bliss* are aimed at teenage girls, and contain short but informative pieces on fashion, music, relationships, teenage health issues, and so on.

In teenage magazines, music is an important factor which helps to sell the publications. Once you have gained significant success in the music business, these magazines could be extremely important to you, depending, of course, on the type of music and image you wish to project to the public. Large glamorous photographs of rock stars are popular with teenagers who prefer a highly visual content.

In women's magazines, and publications aimed primarily at men such as *GQ* and *loaded*, music tends to be reviewed on specialist music or arts pages. Nonetheless, a few positive lines in a big-selling glossy magazine could reap tremendous benefits. Several new up-market pop culture magazines, however, promote music in a big way such as *Uncut*, and *Dazed and Confused*. As musicians you need to start taking notes of who is who in music journalism.

Specialist music magazines in focus

Essential to the music business are the music magazines, which break down into many highly specialised categories both in the serious and popular genres. There are magazines aimed at the general music market, the older music reader, the teenage music reader, the guitarist, the violinist, the percussionist and so on. If there is an interest, there is a magazine.

Music print media function in the same way as other newspapers and magazines, in terms of editorial and advertising. The only difference is that every aspect involves music. Every feature, news story, photograph and advert promotes music – either positively or negatively.

Music journalists have their finger on the pulse of the music industry, and you need to know the different categories, readerships and personnel thoroughly. As the music business and the media change so rapidly, it is best to do as much research as you can on current publications yourselves.

TASKS

- Firstly in groups send off for media packs of a variety of music magazines, requesting the same information as before. When you receive the media packs, study the contents in detail and keep them for reference. While waiting for the packs to arrive, buy the respective publications and discuss with your fellow musicians the following aspects

  Language: is it formal, chatty, simple or complex? Does it use musical terms?

Features: are they long, short, informative, funny, scandalous, savagely critical or fawning?

Pictures: are they mostly big, small, sexy, serious?

Design and layout: is it attention-grabbing, modern, old-fashioned, simple or complex?

Colour: is it used copiously or sparingly?

Final verdict: is it worth the money?

● Try setting up an interview with a music journalist either on a local newspaper, national or music magazine to find out more about their working day, and how and why music stories are selected for publication. You could arrange to meet them for an interview, shadow them for a day, conduct a telephone conversation or send a questionnaire. Most journalists prefer to work by phone as they are so busy. A questionnaire takes time, but excellent results have been known!

More on advertising

When you receive the media pack, you will be able to view the rate cards. Rate cards are lists of prices for advertising space which are devised on the cost and circulation of the publication.

For all newspapers and magazines the front page or cover is very important and normally reserved for the top stories of the day in newspapers or in magazines, for promoting the key content.

For newspaper advertisers the front, back and early right-hand pages are preferred, while in magazines the back, inside-front and inside-back pages are regarded as prime positions. Remember, as you open a newspaper from the front, right-hand pages are seen first and are therefore viewed by advertisers as important selling locations.

Advertisements can be sold in many shapes, types and sizes from full colour, to mono to a single line. They can be further divided into two main categories of advertising: classified and display.

Classified advertising is labelled advertising, mostly consisting of a few lines, although sometimes small designed semi-display advertisements appear, for example personal or holiday ads, and so on. Classified advertisements can be surprisingly cheap and useful when starting out in the music business when money is tight.

Display advertising is bigger, often intricately designed, and can be in the form of anything from a single or double column up to a two-page spread in full colour.

Prices for advertisements can be pretty shocking when you first read them. Hold onto your hearts when you receive the media packs! So remember local rates are much cheaper than in national publications, and there are deals to be done with discounting.

TASKS

- Examine the rate cards for your chosen music magazines and compare them thoroughly with those of other publications.
- Imagine you are in a new easy-listening band with an important gig coming up in three weeks' time. You want to attract a good crowd and possibly a few people in the business. With the help of band members, friends and relatives, you have scraped together £500 for advertising in the print media. Select the publications suitable for your target audience and decide on the best sizes and types of advertisements to take out. You will discover that many possibilities are on offer, for example certain days for two or three weeks or a major one for a specific day. Again, never forget the local press for these events.

Later we will be looking at how to write a press release which, if successful in achieving its objective, will get you free editorial coverage and possibly a picture.

Radio

An Italian scientist named Marconi achieved wireless communication for more than a mile just over one hundred years ago. By the turn of the twentieth century, Marconi had transmitted his first radio signals across the Atlantic.

Radio has both progressed and declined in popularity since those early days, fighting a hard battle with other media rivals – in particular, television. It remains, however, an important and accessible form of media for several reasons: it is cheap, can be run on batteries or electricity, is portable and offers a huge range of stations and variety of programming at local, national and international level. At the turn of a dial listeners can tune into intellectual philosophical discussions, whole concerts of pop or classical music, political debate, and programmes in different languages broadcast from other countries across the globe.

The world of radio is as diverse and complex as any other media form, yet it is made up of only two essential ingredients: talking and music.

Like other media forms radio divides initially into local, national and international radio stations.

Local radio stations are those only broadcast in specific areas, for example Forth FM (Edinburgh areas) Capital Radio (London) or Radio Clyde (Glasgow).

National radio stations are broadcast across the country and include BBC Radio 1, 2, 3, 4 and 5 Live, Classic FM, Virgin FM, Talk Radio and Jazz FM.

International radio stations broadcasting across the globe include the BBC World Service.

Thereafter radio stations divide into state-owned and independent.

State-owned radio stations are also referred to as public service radio broadcasting. The state owns all the BBC titles and services which are paid for by licence fee.

Independent radio stations are also known as commercial radio stations, which are often local and paid for through advertising. National stations, however, such as Classic FM and Virgin FM are independent.

National radio stations mostly broadcast both music and speech in their programmes. Local stations are somewhat different, however. Independent stations tend to be music based whereas BBC stations are commonly speech based. For example, Forth FM, broadcasting to the Edinburgh area, concentrates on music, whereas BBC Scotland, while also serving a music-minded audience, has broadened its appeal to include at appropriate times of the day political debate, travel programmes, and much talking generally!

For music-based stations such as Radio 1, playlists are almost entirely based on chart positions. If a song doesn't get into the Top 100, then it is unlikely to obtain airtime. At the opposite end of the scale, a hit song declining in popularity will cease to be played. Other ways playlists work are by requests and audience research.

As musicians you require an understanding of the music-based national and local stations. Your local independent radio station is the most valuable in the early days of your music business career. Local stations are interested in home-grown talent. An interview and chance to play on air could attract several new fans in just a few minutes.

TASKS

- Ring your local radio station. Ask to be connected to the promotions or advertising departments and request a media pack for the station. Do the same for a national music-based station such as Radio 1 or Classic FM.
- While waiting for your media packs to arrive, cut out the radio schedules from a newspaper and examine the different types of programmes for your chosen stations thoroughly. Compare and contrast the essential ingredients through discussion. Listen to each station for around ten minutes, then discuss the differences.
- When your media packs arrive you can build up a profile for each music station. You will notice that radio advertising is sold in time spots. Complete the following, referring closely to the media packs:

Radio profile for...................

Tuning frequency

Target market breakdown

1 Age range

2 Age of most listeners

3 **Interests of listeners**

4 **Lifestyles of listeners**

5 **Socio-economic grade**

Main geographical area of target market

Costs of radio advertising spots

Typical costs of short (cheap) advertisements

Your personal views on this station

Advertising on radio

The best times to advertise on commercial radio are during the peak periods – the points in the day when most listeners will be tuning in. Peak times for radio are weekday breakfast times, up until approximately 9pm when the population is travelling to work, 'drive time' from 4 to 7pm Monday to Fridays, and 8am to 1pm at the weekend. Peak time advertising is more expensive; but again local advertising rates are considerably cheaper than the national equivalents.

The adverts, commonly sold in spots of 10, 20, 30, 40, 50 or 60 seconds, may contain music. This may be composed by in-house jingle writers, in which case the advert will cost more, or by the company's own advertising team.

TASKS

- Study three or four advertising jingles on a commercial station. Jot down the products and try to identify why the music reinforces the identities of the products and why the music adds to the advertisements. Is it the rhythm, melody, or instrumentation? Discuss this in detail with your fellow musicians.

End of radio assignment

- Arrange a trip to your local radio station and write a page on the day out.

Tips for success

Large national station programmes are often produced and edited by people other than the DJ or presenter. Therefore, these are the decision makers to contact if you are seeking an interview or performance on air. To find out the names of producers simply ring the station. This situation, of course, is more applicable when fame has descended upon you. But your local radio station is the one to target initially as many of your potential fans are likely to be avid listeners. Armed with the knowledge of individual shows and DJs, you should know which DJ to target. Local radio presenters have more control over their own shows, although they too are subject to the control of a programme editor or producer.

Writing an effective press release is a key to success, which we will discover after studying all the media possibilities.

Television

The world of moving images changes and develops every decade, and the music business continues to reflect these advances using every new opportunity to communicate to increasingly wider audiences. The established twentieth-century form of television broadcasting, including cable and satellite, has been joined by video, the internet and CD Rom in the showing of moving visuals. Music plays a significant part in this key media area. In this chapter we will be concentrating on television music programme content on both general and specialist music channels, and studying how music is used in other genres.

Television is a highly accessible form if viewed for pure entertainment, news information or research, but for musicians seeking promotion, however, it is the least accessible media form of all in the early stages of your career. By studying what exists at present on television, however, you can increase your knowledge of the music media at large, your awareness generally of how music is used in various types of programmes, and most importantly advance your critical powers of discerning high-quality programmes from low-grade productions.

Television channels, like radio stations, divide into state-owned and independent channels.

The state-owned channels in Britain are BBC1 and BBC2 and, as for radio, are paid for by the licence fee. However, independent television companies, or producers may create programmes for the BBC.

The independent channels in Britain are ITV, Channel 4 and Channel 5, and all accept advertising commercially. As for BBC channels, their own programme-makers or independent production companies provide the content. Cable and satellite television channels are independent and both take advertising.

The various channels offer a considerable variety of programme genres, which can be divided initially into fiction and non-fiction viewing.

Fiction viewing includes the musical, western, science fiction, period drama, situation comedy, police/law, crime, and so on.

Non-fiction viewing includes documentary, travel, sport, wildlife, music, quiz/game shows, comedy/entertainment and current affairs programmes.

There are overlaps between the two, for example crime dramas based on real-life events, goodie and baddie characters, tension, laughter, sadness, and the audience may also use both types for entertainment.

In contrast to radio, which is based on only the two elements of speech and music, television deals in many more aspects including the soundtrack, camera shots, captions, *mise-en-scene* (the props, costumes and sets), lighting and narrative.

Television operates in two types of codes: those through which meaning is conveyed, for example performance, speech, song and *mise-en-scene* and those by which meaning is interpreted, for example, lighting, camera angles, editing suites, and so on.

MUSIC CONTENT IN MAINSTREAM TELEVISION CHANNELS

Music plays a key role in the world of television. A glance at any mainstream channel such as BBC1 or ITV any day of the week will tell you that music is used in five main ways:

1 It provides the main content of the programme, eg Top of The Pops, Later With Jools Holland or Never Mind the Buzzcocks
2 Music provides the identifiable and promotional theme tune for a programme
3 It provides background music for dramas, documentaries, comedies, etc, to amplify meaning
4 It reinforces brand identity in advertising through jingles
5 It acts as light relief in talk-based shows such as The Clive James Show.

Some of these areas overlap. For example, the theme tune for Top of The Pops is used as well as other music (some live, some not). Similarly drama documentaries may include both a theme tune and background music. We will study the types one by one.

MUSIC-BASED PROGRAMMES

Every moment of programmes like Top of The Pops on BBC1 or Soul Vibration on VH1 is concerned with music. From the opening theme tune to the final screen credits, the presenters attract their viewers' attention constantly to music, interspersed only by speech which serves to inform, entertain and keep the programme swiftly moving along. These elements instill in the audience a sense of compulsive viewing – they feel they need to watch.

Presenting styles depend upon the target audience. The presenters on Top of The Pops, for example, will normally be young celebrities working in the media either on radio or television, with an informal, amusing and fast, chatty style. The language will be simple and cheery, with every word stated in an exclamatory style almost like spoken tabloid headlines. In contrast, classical-music based programmes, such as The Young Musician of The Year, deal in more complex and formal language. The presenters often use musical terms which would be meaningless to certain markets, and generally have a more reserved, polite and erudite style. Both types have quite different target audiences, and like all the other media you have studied, each has tailored its contents to suit those audiences. As musicians you should be aware of all the music-based programme contents and presenting styles both on mainstream channels, satellite and cable.

TASK

With your fellow musicians, choose at least three music-based programmes of quite different categories, for example Top of The Pops on BBC1, Mills'n'Tunes from VH1, and a classical-music based programme on either BBC1 or 2 or an independent channel. Delegating the workload equally, each programme analyst should complete the following profile, which should be retained in your music and media portfolios for reference.

Profile for ....

Channel

Time of broadcast

Length of broadcast

Target audience

General description of content

Style of presentation

Length of musical extracts

Unique selling features

Your views

THEME TUNES

Atmosphere, tension, familiarity and comfort are just some of the sensations which can be injected into an audience within a few seconds by a single theme tune.

The theme tune represents a message which is communicated to the audience without words. A theme tune speaks to the audience directly, in an abstract yet universal language, conveying a meaning which is clear, identifiable, attractive, informative and meaningful in a style suitable both to the target audience and the programme.

The writing of theme tunes can be a lucrative business, especially if the programme is highly successful and broadcast week after week. Getting that message across in only a few seconds, however, is not easy. Summarising and crystallising meaning into its most essential, attractive, informative yet sellable form, is a difficult art to refine, comparable to writing a page-one headline or creating a 20 second television or radio advertisement.

Theme tunes rejoice in variety, each having their own identity through instrumentation, rhythm, melody or harmony. Analysing television theme tunes increases awareness of musical language, target audiences and how music is used to such positive effect within the genre.

TASKS

- Take a break from lectures and watch telly all day. Yes! We're not joking. Keep on mainstream TV (BBC1, 2, ITV, Channels 4 and 5) and select your viewing for a day. Ensure you have plenty of variety, for example: a good morning's diet of breakfast news, cookery and topical discussions; a lunch of cartoons, soap operas and more news; an afternoon tea of politics, documentaries and an old film; and an evening of Eastenders, Brookside, Coronation Street, crime drama and debate. It is more fun, and also more practical, to do this in very small groups. For each programme complete:

  Time

  Channel

  Programme title

  Length of theme tune

  Style of theme tune

  Instrumentation

  Musical features

  Target audience of programme

  How does the theme tune reinforce the programme's identity?

- Compare your day's viewing with your fellow musicians. Discuss the theme music in particular of news programmes, and in contrast, comedy programmes.

BACKGROUND MUSIC

Every emotion imaginable can be enhanced through background music, but the golden rule for writing this type of music is that it should not be the dominating element. In other words, music is part of the total programme, assisting in reinforcing a meaning to an audience but not subtracting from the whole.

Strong melody, therefore, does not dominate in background music, as it could distract the viewer's attention from the main messages of the programme. Harmony, instrumentation and motifs are employed subtly, atmospherically and minimally.

TASK

- Choose two contrasting films, for example a crime thriller and romance, comedy or science fiction and assess how music enhances the meaning of the film. Note how and at what moments music is heard, after about half an hour's viewing of each. Compare your notes and discuss thoroughly with your fellow musicians.

MUSIC IN ADVERTISING

Serious money can be made from writing television advertising jingles, especially if one becomes a hit song. Advertising increasingly uses music to sell products, and in these cases the music empowers the products while maintaining a certain amount of its own identity. Some brand advertising is known and watched because of the music, for example for jeans and cars, which have created new hits, utilised current releases, resurrected old hits and increased their sales in the process. Classic come-back songs include 'I Heard it Through the Grapevine' and 'Should I Stay or Should I Go?'

Successful companies seeking to advertise on television can afford celebrity actors, established composers or hit songs, and more time on air. In contrast, companies with smaller budgets may not be able to afford music at all, only the minimum time on air with unknown actors.

Peak times in television advertising are similar to radio in the morning, but from 7.30pm to 10pm in the evening. Certain types of advertising are promoted at specific times of the day. For example, at breakfast time, cereals, youth culture and family-type products are promoted, whereas between 3.30 and 5.30pm, products aimed at children and teenagers are advertised.

The variety of products on offer is infinite, and the music reflects the diversity. Some advertisements in television are known as hard sell ads in which the brand name is repeated over and over, by speech, by visual images or words on the screen or by song. Soft sell advertising may only reveal the identity of the product in the final split second, using music and action to build up intrigue and the need to know.

TASK

- With your fellow musicians, choose a peak time of viewing, and record two or three advertisements. Complete the following, grading likely cost of advertisements as either expensive, moderately expensive or low budget

Product

Time of broadcast

Length of broadcast

Target market

Music

Original or known music

How it empowers brand identity

Target market suitability

Likely cost

- Discuss with your friends which advert you feel speaks to the target market most effectively.

MUSIC IN TALK-BASED SHOWS

A prime-time talk show can seriously boost a musician's career, and spots on programmes such as The Des O'Connor Show are highly sought after. Music is perceived by the audience as a highlight of the programme, providing a full-scale production of contrast, escapism and glamour in only three or four minutes. As there might be only one or two musical slots available, artists are often anticipated eagerly and remembered by a huge mass market audience.

Music spots are placed strategically in the programme to increase the viewer's excitement, to reinforce positive feelings towards the show and to sustain interest throughout.

TASKS

- Choose any prime-time talk show and discuss the importance of the musical slots with your fellow musicians. Consider how the music slots entice the audience to continue watching and how they enhance the show generally.
- Arrange your media and music portfolio into a coherent order. This is invaluable reference material for your music career.

The press release

Accurate target marketing of a press release can earn you significant success. Press releases, containing information about clubs, bands, societies, political parties, companies, and so on are sent to all the major media forms every day, but in this section we will concentrate on targeting local newspapers and radio stations.

Journalists realise that most press releases aim to use the media for free publicity. Well-constructed press releases, however, are welcomed, and this is where you can win through. Busy journalists who can quickly pick up key points to a story with an unusual angle, will use your press release willingly over others, and even suggest a picture and an interview.

Getting an angle is an important starting point. It is not enough to say that your band will be playing at a certain venue on Saturday night, for example. To catch a News Editor's eye you must consider unique-selling features about the story. What makes the band different? What aspects will the readers or listeners be interested in? Having researched your local media thoroughly, you are in a strong position to know the right answers to these questions.

The professional press release should contain:

- a strong highly-readable introduction containing the main-selling angle of the story
- a professional summary of the facts
- substantiation
- a picture opportunity
- an easily-obtainable contact name and number

These essential ingredients, preferably contained within a single page, must be type-written, coherently and fluently communicated in language appropriate to the newspaper or radio station, with key points highlighted.

The introduction is the most important section of all. The first sentence, in particular, must hook the News Editor's interest immediately with the angle of the story which should be delivered in a bright, snappy style. The rest of the paragraph should seek to maintain interest with a 'read on' quality.

Often one sentence will also be a whole paragraph, particularly if you wish to make a point dramatically in tabloid style. So, your total introductory paragraph may consist of only one sensational sentence.

The professional summary of the facts should begin in the next paragraph. The telling of events should be written in clear, simple language, preferably in short sentences. Do not be frightened to take a new paragraph for each new fact. Again, keep asking yourself – is this interesting and directly relevant to the target market and to the story? If not, leave things out. There is nothing worse than a press release bogged down by irrelevant, dull or inappropriate facts.

Substantiation means amplification and evidence of the facts. You can expand on certain details, if you have something extra and newsworthy to say, for example quoting a well-known local person who supports your band, or by talking about other gigs or record deals to give your story credibility. For any story the journalist writes, s/he will be asking: What is happening? Where, how and when is it happening? Are there any other sellable features

here? Your press release should convey this information.

This section is important to build up trust with the journalist, but watch you don't become boring. Remember, your aim is to sustain interest so effectively that your telephone rings.

The picture opportunity is simply a suggestion from you as to what might make a good picture. Be creative! Pictures speak volumes, so don't miss out on this chance to impress.

The contact name and number should be available at the first telephone call. Journalists work to tight schedules, so be there, waiting. If they don't call you in a couple of days, ring and ask persuasively, cheerily and politely if they are considering using your story.

Certain words are wise to put in bold, so that the journalist can see important details such as the contact number at a glance. Space the page out well, write in 10 or 11 point with a simple font (like Palatino, Helvetica or Times) and get someone to read it over for grammatical or spelling mistakes. Do not rely on your computer spell check!

Press releases should be sent either to the News Desk, News Editor or a music journalist who you know at local newspapers or radio stations. Take time to work on the words, and good luck!

Current media issues

This brief section intends to promote and increase your awareness of two current media issues which concern musicians in the media:

representation and media intrusion. Both are interlinked, but we will deal with them separately and simply.

REPRESENTATION

The portrayal of groups, ideas and individuals in the media is known as representation. This can be easily understood by using the verb to represent, in a musical situation. For example,

a few students complain to each other about the lack of facilities to practise for gigs. They discover that most music students at the college feel the same way. The students decide to allocate someone to represent their views at the next student council meeting. One person, therefore, communicates the views of a section of society to an audience. However this person acts, dresses or speaks, s/he represents the whole group of musicians. Magnified several times over in the media, you can see how stereotypes of individuals and groups are created.

The stereotyping of rock musicians is legendary. You are hard-drinking, sex-mad, foul-mouthed, guitar-smashing individuals, who have no time for the older generation or washing. Is this true? Of course not! While we can smile at this scenario, stereotyping is a dangerous and negative aspect of the media. Representations and stereotypes of gender, race, age, youth and politics concern you most in the music business.

TASKS

- With your fellow musicans, select two pop videos, two music magazines and two newspapers. Discuss each one in terms of representation of music and musicians. Consider each of the following elements:

  1 Extent of music coverage (for print media)
  2 How women and men are portrayed visually
  3 How men and women are portrayed through song lyrics or print media pieces
  4 How age, race and politics are communicated to the target market
  5 Evidence of stereotyping

- Discuss the positive and negative aspects of representation.

MEDIA INTRUSION

This is a huge topic, but we will focus on the key aspect concerning musicans: media intrusion into private lives. The following task should provoke much thought and fiery debate!

TASK

- Discuss this statement with your fellow musicians:

'Media intrusion into a musican's life is the inevitable price to pay for fame and fortune'.

YOUR FUTURE

Good luck with your career, and remember to target those markets effectively. Clear focused thinking in everything that you do will ensure success. Always keep that important question uppermost in your mind – who exactly am I aiming this at?

chapter 9

EMPLOYMENT IN THE MUSIC INDUSTRY

Introduction

A career within the world of music is an attractive goal for many with the talent and enthusiasm to make it worthwhile, challenging and glamorous. Unfortunately, competition is acute and remuneration often poor for all but the fortunate and/or incredibly talented few.

There are many different roles and as many different training routes that lead to employment. Qualifications are important but will not automatically secure work. Important attributes are: expertise, reputation, contacts, perseverance and good fortune. Remember the old adage – the harder you work the luckier you get!

Below is a list of some areas of employment within the music business, an industry that is worth two and a half billion pounds to the British economy. This includes performance, management, administration, front of house, sales, promotion, technical and ancillary support.

They are not by any means mutually exclusive. Most musicians overlap jobs, examples being performing and teaching, songwriting and retail, or maybe a bit of all of them at some time or another!

Often the key to survival in the entertainment industry is flexibility, the ability to consistently find gainful employment while awaiting the 'big break'. Never underestimate education and training, but above all a job well done will produce recommendations and a favourable reputation brings opportunities.

Alphabetical list of occupations

A & R Originally 'artist and repertoire'. Before the current trend for artists to write their own material A & R would match composer to performer. Nowadays the A & R person is responsible for spotting talent, signing it to their company and then developing the talent and representing the artist's interests within the organisation. It is a cut-throat business where you are only as secure as your recent successes. Imagination and an eye for talent is essential, a decent musical knowledge an advantage, and scruples almost unheard of! There is often criticism that A & R departments only function in the capital and larger cities, but as talent is not limited by area the readiness to scour the country and recognise a 'buzz' beginning to form around an act is required. This however is always tempered by the current needs of the company and often amounts to filling a specific gap in their catalogue at any given time.

Accompanist Usually a pianist who plays the accompaniment for singers, instrumentalists, dancers and examination candidates. Excellent sight reading skills and a wide musical knowledge are essential, the ability to put performers at ease, inspire confidence and react quickly to surprises are advantages. Adept accompanists are held in high regard and are always busy, but experience can be acquired by offering your services to fellow musicians, local amateur choral, dramatic and dance companies.

(See also **repetiteur**)

Administration Probably the largest area of employment in the business, this covers a massive array of jobs – secretary, telephonist, receptionist, personal assistant, accountant, librarian, diary service, brochure compilation, design assistant, computer operator, and all other office work. When starting out an ability to perform several of these tasks is advantageous and the usual office management and information communication technology skills are essential. There are an abundance of courses aimed at this sector and a popular entry point is work experience placements from school or college. Once in situ your personality, communication skills and enthusiasm for efficient time management will help secure a permanent position.

Agent An agent finds work for artists and arranges tours in return for a percentage of the profits. The most important attributes are a wide range of contacts throughout the business, a good head for figures and faith in the people they represent. Any opportunist with a telephone-directory and a convincing phone manner can try their luck in finding engagements for friends or a local band, but the number of refusals will disappoint all but the most tenacious and thick-skinned. College and university social secretaries and/or entertainment officers book bands on a regular basis and this contact with agents and experience within the music industry is invaluable.

(See also **ents. officer**)

Armed Services The Armed Services provide both training and employment in return for an agreed number of years' commitment. Each branch of the services and the metropol-

itan police have their own music schools accepting students at 16 or over. Demand is mostly for brass, wind and percussion but other instruments are recruited in lesser amounts.

Arranger An arranger is a musician who makes arrangements or adaptations of other peoples' songs. Knowledge of ranges, characteristics and scoring for all instruments together with a high level of musical training and/or education is required. The role of the arranger is growing as musicians who previously used sampled and sequenced strings and horns for recorded and live work start to demand the 'real thing' as they become more successful. Unfortunately a small number of arrangers seem to monopolise all the well-paid work at the moment, simply because they are well known and can be relied on. At some point they will not be able to cope with the demand which should create healthy opportunities for new practitioners.

(See also **orchestrator**)

Backing vocalist This role requires a good voice, an excellent 'ear' and a certain amount of charisma or ability to move. Singing harmonies is a skill that demands that you support and enhance the main vocal without detracting from or outshining it. The ability to read music is an advantage. Many acclaimed frontmen and women started their professional careers as backing vocalists, which helped to hone their technique and stage presence. Vocal training is essential as many promising voices have been ruined by poor technique and irreparable strain on the sensitive vocal chords. Also known as backing vox, b-vox or BVs.

Backing music It is becoming increasingly common for vocalists to perform with a pre-recorded backing on cassette, mini disc, midi disc or DAT. There are a number of companies supplying these, but a musician with arranging and programming skills might

Figure 9.1   *Backing vocalists*

suggest producing bespoke recordings that suit a singer's set list, range and tempo.

Busking   Performing live in the street for coins thrown into your hat or an open instrument case can be surprisingly profitable if you select a good location and time to play. Gimmicks, a popular repertoire, eye contact and a winning smile are important assets to adopt. Different authorities and private owners all have their own policies, which should be checked before starting to perform. The more popular venues are often booked on a rota system between teams of buskers – check with the local busking fraternity or risk their wrath.

Cabaret band   Bands like these play mostly covers for the cabaret and social club circuit. Work is usually sourced through an agency. The main requirement is to play numbers the audience will appreciate rather than material

that satisfies your own artistic aspirations. Image and professionalism are also important. Variations of the cabaret band include the cruise ship band, tribute band and wedding and function band.

Catering   All major artists insist on quality sustenance for themselves and their crew. Catering companies tour with the crew, buy fresh produce and prepare food backstage to demand. Normal catering qualifications, organisational skills and a head for figures are required together with the right personality and a calm demeanour.

(See also **wardrobe**)

Chorus (backing)   See **backing vocals**

Commercials (jingles)   This is a lucrative business that relies heavily on having good contacts and being professional and efficient when work comes your way. Library music companies may finance your recordings. They then send CD albums to all the major TV and radio companies and if your music is used you split the royalties 50/50 with the company. On the surface writing jingles may seem an easy way to make large amounts of money, but making a 10, 17 or 29 second tune make structural and musical sense requires technique and experience. On the other hand agencies are always on the look-out for fresh, different and fashionable sounds to attract younger consumers. Above all, deadlines are tight and must be adhered to if repeat work is hoped for.

Composer This is maybe the most difficult but most rewarding area of musical endeavour. There are very few musicians who survive purely on the profits of their compositions, and fewer still who make millions, but songs can earn healthily throughout their copyright long after fashionable artists are redundant 'has-beens'. The only rule to composition is that there are no rules. It is worth considering various annual and one-off competitions that take place as well as commissions from artists, ensembles and art councils, when starting off.

(See also **songwriter**, **commercials** and **lyricist**)

Computer Programmer These people create new sounds and sequences for musicians in the studio, along the lines of the traditional roles held by the engineer and producer. A good technical knowledge of arranging and MIDI applications is essential and reasonable interpersonal skills an advantage.

Conductor/concert master/musical director/MD All these roles relate to the leader of the band who co-ordinates all the instrumentalists and singers. Requires excellent all-round knowledge and experience and often results from previous accomplishments in lesser roles. Good communication skills, impressive qualifications and a calm disposition are an advantage!

Copyist When composers cannot produce suitably legible scores a copyist is used to write the music out clearly. A copyist is also used if there is not enough time between composition, arrangement and performance for typesetting parts. Command of musical knowledge and a neat clear writing style is required.

Choirmaster This is the musical director/conductor of all the vocalists.

Chaperone Young performers require responsible adults to accompany them while they are working. This is mostly for theatre and musical work.

Concert promoter A concert promoter matches an act to a venue or series of venues on a tour. Choosing the correct size of auditorium that corresponds to the pulling power of the artist and then ensuring transport, sound system, lighting, crew, support, catering, marketing, merchandising, advertising and ticket price are all selected in order to provide profit and enjoyment for all concerned is no small task. This requires excellent interpersonal and accountancy skills and is not a job for the ill-organised or faint-hearted!

Consultancy Consultants offer advice on all aspects of music, particularly education, technology, fund-raising, marketing and resources.

Dealer (record) Record shops and outlets always require enthusiastic sales assistants with a knowledge of popular culture and current trends. There are more specialist stores opening catering for specific needs and the line between retail, DJing and independent record companies is becoming increasingly blurred. Although hardly the most glamorous aspect of the music business, it has been the entry level occupation of many prominent music industry workers.

Dealer (instrument) Musical instrument shops are always looking for personable staff who have a good all-round musical knowledge and can demonstrate equipment convincingly.

Figure 9.2 *Choirmaster and choir*

Enthusiasm, trustworthiness and good communication skills are essential.

Advantages of the job include hands-on familiarity with new equipment and the opportunity to meet local musicians on a daily basis.

Demonstrator All large instrument manufacturers employ skilful musicians to demonstrate the worth of their goods. Charisma, patter and technical virtuosity are required in equal measures.

DJ/disc jockey A DJ chooses and plays records for dancing or radio. The creative use of double turntables led to scratching, hip-hop, house, jungle, drum 'n' bass and so on. Today top DJs are almost on a par with the record producer and musician. Local pubs may be interested in employing a DJ for a fee and when confidence grows try promoting your own 'night' in a club or bar. The secret to success is to give the customers what they want rather than what you think they *should* enjoy.

Distributor (record) A distributor supplies CDs, cassettes and records to the retail outlets from the pressing factories. It is important to

judge the demand and ensure supplies do not sell out, thus depriving the company of valuable chart places, or conversely overstock shops and waste resources. Distribution is an important element of all record companies and entails a large team of factory staff, drivers, stock keepers, administrators and ancillary workers.

Dresser See **wardrobe**

Driver Band, crew and equipment all require transport and although anyone in possession of a HGV or PSV licence is eligible to undertake these roles, specialist drivers tend to be used. Some of the more colourful coach drivers have become legendary and are always in demand. They must be able to lay down the law on smoking, pit stops, non use of the onboard toilets and general issues of behaviour as well as maintaining the patience of a kindergarten teacher and drive like a champion to make tight deadlines.

(See also **road crew**)

Drum roadie This is an on-stage technician who sets up the drum kit, changes drum skins and maintains and repairs all the percussion in-

Figure 9.3   *DJ and studio*

struments. There is no formal training available, to get started offer your services as general roadie and be in the right place at the right time and 'in' with the right people.

(See also **roadie**, **road crew** and **on-stage technician**)

Education   Good communication skills, patience and a sense of humour are essential, enthusiasm and qualifications are an advantage in this role. There are many levels and locations to choose from and this can be a most rewarding way to work within the music world. Music education falls into three main categories – the state system, the independent sector and private teaching. Instrumental and voice teachers can work at home, from private premises, shops, and as a peripatetic or 'peri' teacher which means travelling around local state and independent establishments in primary, secondary, further and higher education.

It is an honourable occupation for musicians who wish to supplement their performing and composing ambitions and workshops that feature professional performers, composers and management are becoming more common. It has always been the case that esteemed musicians have adopted pupils and it still behoves people who have mastered their art to pass on their experience and knowledge to the younger generation. This should be equally true for all styles of music.

Engineer   See **sound engineer**

Ents Officer/Social sec.   College and university entertainment officers are selected by their peers to book and promote acts for fellow students. This is a growth industry that has seen its exponents develop from enthusiastic amateurs to highly paid professionals over the past few decades. It is considered a fine apprenticeship for many roles within the business and the starting point for a large number of very successful entrepreneurs.

Film music This is a difficult field to break into as directors tend to use composers they know and can rely on to deliver the goods to a deadline. One way in is to work with directors who are in the same situation as yourself – try film schools or media and art colleges. Alternatively study with, or offer help to, a practising composer as an apprenticeship. Alternatively send examples of your work to a library music agency who may put your track onto a CD that is sent to TV and film companies and take 50% of your fee in return if it is used.

Fixer See **session fixer**

Foldback engineer While the main sound engineer stands in the middle of the auditorium mixing the levels for the crowd, another will be to the side of the stage controlling the levels fed back to the band. Usually leading on to the more senior post, the same skills are required.

Function band A function band plays covers for party guests, usually in smart stage gear. A large repertoire and high level of professionalism are required.

(See also **wedding band** and **tribute band**)

Ghost musician A session player that plays in the studio or behind stage to cover the errors of less-experienced musicians.

Guitar roadie An on-stage technician who sets up guitarists' equipment, tunes instrument(s), fixes broken strings and assists instrument changes mid-set. There is no formal training available – to get started offer your services as general roadie and be in the right place at the right time and 'in' with the right people.

(See also **roadie** and **on-stage technician**)

Image consultant See **marketing** and **PR**

Independent label Many experienced musicians prefer to retain artistic and financial control over their work by setting up an independent label. There are many pitfalls and demands, both financially and time wise, but obvious advantages to be enjoyed (not least the ability to work from home rather than moving to the capital). Musicians signed to an independent label can expect a more personal treatment than they would with a major and closer contact with the senior managers of the company. Workers within the independent company will probably be required to cover a larger area of responsibility and have less job security.

Instrument repair Musicians with a talent for craft and technology may undertake a course (usually 2 years) in instrument building, repair and maintenance. Entrance is by qualification but more importantly practical aptitude has to be demonstrated. The nature of the work often appeals to mature students but admission can be from 16. After qualifying work is usually situated in larger instrument shops or with instrument manufacturers, but can be undertaken from home if equipment is available. Instrument maintenance is sometimes associated with piano-tuning courses and companies.

Investor People with money to speculate and a love of the arts sometimes invest in new shows or artists. In return they are known as 'angels', made a fuss of on opening nights and may end up considerably richer if their venture is a success. The majority of new ventures do not make a profit, however.

Jingle writer See **commercials**

Journalist There is a plethora of music magazines on the market and in general the best writers have musical knowledge and experience themselves. If you enjoy attending gigs and talking to musicians, start young and amass a portfolio of work for school, college and local publications. Journalist courses and writers workshops can be found in most cities and most free news-sheets would welcome well-written reviews of concerts and recordings submitted to them.

Karaoke jock These are usually singers with a good line in patter and bags of personality who encourage punters to embarrass themselves to the amusement of others. Initial equipment purchase is expensive but there are companies who take on operatives, mostly by audition.

Keyboard roadie In this job you need specific knowledge about how a keyboard player sets equipment up, samples sounds, organises presets and MIDI routing. In the early days of sampling, unreliable machines usually necessitated taking two of each piece of equipment on the road in case one failed to load or became 'temperamental'. Usually the keyboard roadie is an accomplished keyboard player with previous experience of live work.

(See also **roadie** and **on-stage technician**)

Lawyer This role is becoming more important all the time as specialist music lawyers are necessary for artists, management, agents, record companies and promoters. Qualifying is extremely demanding, but work and financial reward plentiful thereafter.

Librarian (music) Orchestras and large bands often employ a librarian to look after all the scores/band parts. Good organisational skills and a traditional music education are preferred.

Lighting designer/engineer This skill is important to the overall effect of large scale concerts. The lighting designer and/or engineer work closely with the production manager and set designer to enhance the effect of the band/artist. Electrifying special effects are common at larger gigs and it is important that lighting engineers are fully conversant with safety regulations and guidelines. Training is usually aimed at theatre work but the skills required are the same for the music industry.

Lyricist The lyricist collaborates with a songwriter and is responsible for the words to songs. A love of words, a thesaurus and a rhyming dictionary are essential and most successful lyricists have some musical ability. There is a subtle difference between lyrics and poetry: often song lyrics mean very little without the music, and poetry does not always fit easily with music. The chemistry between tunesmith and wordsmith is all important and the key to success.

(See also **songwriter**)

Maintenance engineer (See **sound engineer (recording)**)

Manager The manager represents all an artist's interests in return for a share of the profits made. The manager co-ordinates the financial, legal and logistical aspects of their clients' careers. Experience, contacts but above all a belief in, and commitment to, their protégés are essential. Thick skin and self-confidence are advantages. Most bands starting out on their career would welcome managerial support but care must be taken to ensure that all parties understand the full implications of any agreement either formal or informal. Managers would be expected to make a sizeable contribution to the act in terms of finance and/or effort if they are to receive a share of the artist's wages at a later date.

Marketing See **public relations**

Merchandising This area involves the selling of non-musical goods associated with a group or musician – T-shirts, hats, posters and so on. It can be very lucrative (especially for heavy rock and teeny bands) but artists now realise this and negotiate a hefty percentage up front. A handful of firms cover most of the larger venues but bands starting off can earn extra cash by selling their own swag at gigs. A well-designed T-shirt will often make more money than cassettes and CDs after the performance, and has the advantage of advertising the act for free until the novelty (or logo) wears off.

MIDI programmer Many solo or duo acts

Figure 9.4 *A music therapist at work*

perform to backing tracks or midifiles and there is a growing market for musicians to sequence popular songs.

(See also **synthesizer programmer**)

Mixer   See **sound engineer (live)**

Monitor mixer   See **foldback mixer**

Multi-media   CD-Roms store information as audio, graphics, text and video. Authoring software enables computer conversant musicians to create their own packages. These are used in education, marketing and games and is very much a growth area. Many companies are eager to trade and advertise using the internet and there is quite a market for authoring web sites and pages. This has become a useful part-time vocation for musicians because the work can be done from home and is not time specific, thus enabling performing, composing and recording work to continue.

Music therapist   A music therapist uses music to alleviate serious medical and physical conditions. A worthwhile and rewarding occupation, but places are restricted to those with qualifications and experience in both music and therapy. Study is usually at post-graduate level but can be undertaken at several universities and therapy centres throughout Britain.

On-stage technician   This is a generic term for guitar, drum and keyboard roadies and other technicians who assist musicians on stage.

Orchestral manager   See **session fixer/fixer**

Orchestrator   An orchestrator arranges popular songs for orchestra, brass band, school band and other ensembles. He or she works for, or by license through, the publishers of the song. Good theoretical knowledge of music and instruments and usually a formal musical education are required. Orchestrators need to know the ranges of all instruments, different clefs and notation systems, how instrument timbres combine with each other and how certain groupings of notes fall under the fingers on each instrument to avoid unmanageable or problematic part writing.

Piano tuner   A tuner requires specialist skills aquired through intensive training on a 2 or 3-year full-time course. A good ear is essential and the ability to play the piano a definite advantage. A good 'day-job' for pianists who welcome a steady income without the commitment of a 9 to 5 occupation.

Plugger   Hyping or exaggerating the merits of a song or artist to shops and radio stations to push a recording up the charts is common. Legally it is a murky area and most record companies deny their existence, so the job will certainly not be advertised in public!

(See also **PR**)

Press agent   Someone who drums up publicity for a band through various obvious and ingenious means from standard press releases and information to gossip columns (often totally ridiculous), bogus 'news' stories and interview offers.

Producer   The producer has overall responsibility for a recording project, including budget, creative decisions, technical aspects, organisation, artist rapport, session musicians and final mix. Often producers are themselves accomplished musicians with recording experience or they have a technical engineering background and often both. They not only organise everything but, if applicable, add a great deal to the creative process.

Production manager   Similar to the tour manager, but responsible for the technical crew on tour who will arrive at a venue before the artists to set up sound, lighting, staging and catering. A good working knowledge of all technical and transport aspects are required and a healthy rapport with the tour manager a definite advantage.

(See also **tour manager**)

Promoter   See **concert promoter**

Public relations (PR)   PR people promote the interests of their customers by sending out press releases and pictures to local and national newspapers, creating a 'buzz' within the media world and supplying them with 'sound bytes' and stories to publicise and hype acts or individuals. In the past bribery and corruption were *de rigeur* but apart from the odd meal or extravagant Christmas present, originality and gimmick are the tools of the trade today. Often new releases are launched with attention-grabbing packaging, competitions and excessive stunts and ploys. PR operatives often rely on personal contacts built up with radio programmers, producers and journalists. Also known as press agents, pluggers and promo men and women.

Publishing   Publishing is a big business that requires administration, accountancy, and A&R expertise in a similar way to record companies. The publishing company represents, exploits and collects royalties on a composer's work. Independent publishers are often closely linked to an independent label and tend to be much smaller operations with fewer people performing more roles. Experience, credibility, nous and entrepreneurial skills are required in spades to venture into this business.

Record companies   A multitude of employment opportunities exist, but countless candidates for each post. See Chapter 5 for more details.

Rehearsal studio   When neighbours complain of the noise or the garage loses its glamour, bands look for a purpose-built space to rehearse in. Studios require sound insulation and back-line equipment (usually drum kit, PA and amplifiers) and a booking system. Can be surprisingly lucrative if run in a professional manner.

Repetiteur   These are accompanists who rehearse and coach singers in a theatre or opera house. Excellent sight reading skills and a working vocal knowledge are essential. Many musical directors and conductors started out this way.

(See also **accompanist**)

Retail See **dealer** (**instrument** and **record**)

Road crew This is the team of on-stage and back-stage technicians, drivers, managers, lighting team, sound engineers, caterers, wardrobe and roadies that ensure an artist or group can perform on tour.

Roadie This work consists of the essential manual loading and unloading of equipment at venues. Often the bigger venues employ their own regular team of 'luggers' to transfer instruments, PA, amps, monitors, lights and set from van to stage and back again after the gig. Either befriend an up-and-coming local band or contact your nearest major venue direct and offer your services.

Session musician A musician hired to play for other performers' recordings and concerts. The ability to read music is an advantage but 'quick ears', versatility and professionalism are more important. Work is usually found through contacts and by reputation.

Session fixer/fixer A session fixer puts together an orchestra, band or section of session musicians and manages the financial arrangements that result. The job requires a wide knowledge of music and musicians, organisational skills and a large thirst to cope with all the drinks bought for you by musos hoping for gainful employment!

Singer-songwriter See **solo performer** and **songwriter**

Social sec. See **Ents officer**

Software programmer New music programmes, games and multi-media applications are entering the market daily. Companies require young, innovative and dynamic staff to cater for the increasing demand. A background in computing, programming and music is required.

Solo performer This requires good accompaniment skills or sequenced backing. A solo performer needs stage presence, charisma and the drive to work without camaraderie and the support of other musicians. The advantage is of course when the fee does not require dividing!

Songwriter With the trend firmly towards singer/songwriters and producer/songwriters there are very few artists in the tradition of Berlin, Gershwin, Porter and Bacharach making a living outside of Los Angeles and Nashville these days. Some artists do not write their own material so publishers employ teams of songwriters to come up with their next hit. This will usually be in a specified style and invariably the artist will require part of the composition credit. The ability to work quickly in several genres and record your own high quality demos is useful together with perseverance, a knack for a 'hook' and good fortune.

(See also **composer** and **lyricist**)

Stage designer/producer A specialist designer who takes ideas and concepts from an artist or their management and creates the staging for a tour. Tasks include initial sketches, scale models, engineering and logistical considerations. Design training or experience in Art and Design are required.

Studio work So many musicians aspire to studio work that contacts, hard work and expertise are essential. There are many colleges and universities offering courses in this area but the reality is that you will probably have to start at the bottom – making tea, tidying up and answering the telephone.

Sound engineer (recording) This is the main person responsible for the technical and operational side of the recording process. There are two broad (but not mutually exclusive) types. The more traditional role involves selecting and placing microphones and instruments. The more modern function entails computer programming and digital management. The engineer is an important member of the team and he or she often progresses on to producing. In larger recording studios an assistant sound engineer's role varies from being the archetypal 'tea person' to performing as many and important tasks as the main engineer. There may be up to three assistants as part of the recording team. The maintenance engineer makes sure the recording studio technology is in good working order and carries out necessary repairs. Electrical knowledge and a full awareness of safety in the workplace are essential for all three roles.

Sound engineer (live)   The sound engineer controls the live mix that the audience hears from within the auditorium. As home systems become more sophisticated fans demand a hi-fidelity live sound to match. Good sound engineers are in great demand. They need to be familiar with the artists' repertoire and have a confident all-round technical proficiency. Knowledge of acoustics acquired through training or experience are required, but above all 'big ears' are essential.

Synthesizer programmer   As keyboards become more significant and intricate dedicated programmer engineers are employed to programme new sounds for live and recording work. Good technical and arranging skills are required together with the ability to sequence tracks to replace or augment drummers, horn and string sections. Instrument manufacturers employ experienced synth programmers to create new pre-set sounds for keyboards and sound modules at the factory.

Talent scout   Often part of the A&R job responsibility, but the busier ones will appoint scouts to tip them off about acts creating a 'buzz' around the country. If you enjoy going to gigs and have an eye for flair and marketability, offer your services to the A & R departments of the major labels. Contacts within the business or previous involvement in the industry are usually the pre-requisites of the job however.

Tape operator   This has become an obsolete role since the advent of digital recording and remote control tape machines involving starting and stopping tape machines. Often the entry occupation into the studio world, the term 'tape op' has become a euphemism for a young studio trainee.

Theatre musician   Often known as 'pit musician' from their location in the pit of the theatre when working. A lucrative career that requires excellent sight-reading skills and a high level of all-round musicianship. Work is usually arranged through a 'fixer' who will be reluctant to take risks with an inconsistent performer. West End positions are highly sought after but less than first-rate players are not asked back!

Tour manager   The tour manager is responsible for the buses, trains, boats and planes that transport an artist from gig to gig on tour and the travel, accommodation and living expenses incurred on the road. A calm demeanour or explosive bellow as appropriate, tight hold on the purse strings, good organisational skills and the ability to command the respect of the irresponsible are some of the job specifications. Although the music industry is highly structured and involved, on tour the tour manager is considered to outrank everyone and tends to call all the shots.

(See also **production manager**)

Transcriber   Listening to a recording of a song and writing it down for sheet music sales, magazines, bands and solo club musicians is the work of a transcriber. A good ear and knowledge of musical theory is essential as well as a working knowledge of the instruments involved.

(See also **copyist** and **typesetter**)

Tribute band   This is a fast-growing market where bands imitate (fondly) a supergroup that people love but cannot see live such as The Beatles, ABBA, Pink Floyd, Queen and T-Rex. Audiences will expect a high standard of musicianship and showmanship but in return successful tribute bands work constantly and lucratively to large appreciative audiences.

Typesetter   Music publishers require specialist printers who can understand and typeset sheet music and albums. Good IT skills are required along with a comprehensive knowledge about the language of music. Employees are usually music graduates, but a good typesetter who is willing to enter the profession straight from school will receive training and have the advantages of youth, a genuine love of the music being worked on and a three or four-year headstart on the others. Interviews will usually involve being played a track and asked to notate it and evidence of previous work notated.

(See also **copyist** and **transcriber**)

Usher   This involves theatre or concert work directing the audience to their seats, collecting tickets and selling programmes and refreshments. Not terribly well paid but you are close to the action and get to see lots of acts for free. Simply approach your local venues and offer your services. The most important attribute required here is reliability.

Video production   Since the growth of TV music shows (especially MTV) video production has become an increasingly important aspect of the music business. As equipment has become more affordable the main requirement is imagination and a track record. Most bands starting off will welcome the chance to make a demo video to accompany their pitch to a company and this might be a good way to start with low budget, high imagination examples of your work that can be grouped together on a show reel to attract more lucrative commissions.

Voice-over   This work is done by an unseen artist who narrates or sings to accompany a film, video or commercial. An interesting/distinctive voice and the ability to 'get it right' first time is an advantage.

Wardrobe   You don't really think that the big star on stage washed and ironed his/her stage outfit before the show do you? Wardrobe staff ensure stage outfits are ready backstage and act as 'dressers' (helping the performers into their clothes) especially when in-between songs quick changes take place.

Wedding band   A wedding band performs covers at wedding receptions. Smart appearance and the ability to play, or learn quickly, the happy couple's favourite song is essential. Tribute bands such as the Blues Brothers, Glam-Rock or ABBA are popular. Bookings are usually made through personal contacts or by booking a stand at local wedding fairs, entertaining the happy couples and negotiating a deal.

(See also **function band**)

TASKS

- Match the following attributes to at least five jobs in the music industry requiring them.

    1 Excellent sight reading ability
    2 Good interpersonal skills
    3 Degree level qualification
    4 All round technical knowledge
    5 Wide musical facility
    6 Good head for figures
    7 High level organisational competence
    8 Readiness to gamble and take risks
    9 Creative talents
    10 Lack of scruples

- List ten different personal qualities and repeat the previous question.
- List three of your own attributes and explain how they qualify you for any particular function within the music industry.
- List three of your failings and then describe the least suitable career you should pursue and why.

TASK

- Taking the most recent major concert you attended make a list of all the people who contributed to staging the event for your enjoyment. Points to consider are:

How did you know about the concert?
How did you buy your ticket?
Who collected the ticket?
What were the security arrangements?
What equipment was used?
Who might have been backstage working?
Did you purchase merchandise?
How were the band/artist supported on stage?
How many musicians were on stage?
Who promoted the concert?

Education and training

A ROUGH GUIDE TO QUALIFICATIONS

The arts presently account for 100 000 full-time and 250 000 part-time students studying for up to 400 different awards. It is difficult to make a table of award equivalency but there are three main strands: Academic, Vocational and Skill Training.

Academic	Vocational		Skill training
PhD/DMus MA/MMus	GNVQ 5 GSVQ 5	NVQ 5 SVQ 5	
BA/BMus	GNVQ 4 GSVQ 4	NVQ 4 SVQ 4	Conservatoire Graduate
			Conservatoire Licentiate
			Conservatoire Diploma
2 A Levels	National Diploma HND		
A Level SYS	Advanced GNVQ GSVQ	NVQ 3 SVQ 3	Grade VIII
			Access / Foundation
AS Level Higher			Grade VI
4 GCSEs	First Diploma National Certificate HNC		
GCSE (A–C) Standard Grade (old O Level)	Intermediate GNVQ GSVQ	NVQ 2 SVQ 2	Grade V
GCSE (D–G) (old CSE)	Foundation GNVQ GSVQ	NVQ 1 SVQ 1	Grade III
Key Stage 4 National Curriculum			Grade I

Qualification:	Stands for:	Means/Definition
A Level	Advanced Level	Studied in schools and tertiary colleges age 16–19. 2 year course.
AS Level	Advanced Supplementary /Advanced Subsidiary	Half an A Level 1 year course
BA	Bachelor of Arts	University degree 3 or 4 years
Bmus	Bachelor of Music	Music equivalent of BA
Dmus	Doctor of Music	Music equivalent of PhD
GCSE	General Certificate of Secondary Education	Studied in schools age 14–16
GNVQ	General National Vocational Qualification	Studied in schools and colleges age 16–19
GSVQ	General Scottish Vocational Qualification	Scottish equivalent of GNVQ
Higher	Higher Grade	Scottish post 16 award equivalent to AS
Advanced Higher		Scottish unified post 16 equivalent of GNVQ
HNC	Higher National Certificate	Pre HND 1 year course
HND	Higher National Diploma	Post HNC 2 year course
MA	Master of Arts	Post BA academic study and research
Mmus	Master of Music	Music equivalent of MA
NVQ	National Vocational Qualification	Studied in the work place any age
PhD	Doctor of Philosophy	Highest academic award post MA study and research
Standard	Standard Grade	Scottish equivalent of GCSE
SVQ	Scottish Vocational Qualification	Scottish equivalent of NVQ
SYS	Certificate of Sixth Year Studies	Scottish post Higher 1 year study

WHERE YOU CAN STUDY FOR THE QUALIFICATIONS . . .

Grades I–VIII	Private instrumental teacher – any age
GCSE	Schools in England and Wales – usually 14 to 16
Standard Grade	Schools in Scotland – usually 14 to 16
AS Level	Schools in England and Wales – usually 16 to 19
A Level	Schools in England and Wales – usually 16 to 19
Higher	Schools in Scotland – usually 16 to 19
GNVQ	Schools and further education colleges in England and Wales – usually 16 to 19
GSVQ	Schools and further education colleges in Scotland – usually 16 to 19
NVQ	Workplace in England and Wales – any age
SVQ	Workplace in Scotland – any age
HNC	Further/higher education colleges – any age
HND	Further/higher education colleges – any age
Diploma	Music college/conservatoire – usually post-18
Licentiate	Music college/conservatoire – usually post-18
BA/BMus	University – usually post-18
MA/MMus	University – usually post-20
PhD/DMus	University – usually post-21

ENTRY REQUIREMENTS . . .

Most music courses will select students by suitability, musical attainment and enthusiasm judged by audition and interview. The following list is a guide to the usual entry requirements to various courses. There are always exceptions and creditation of prior experience. This enables keen musicians who did not pass any exams but worked in the industry to bypass some of the normal preconditions set.

Award	Usual entry requirements
Grade I	None
Grade VI–VIII	Grade V theory of Music
GCSE	None
Standard Grade	None
AS Level	GCSE Music
A Level	GCSE Music
Higher	Standard Grade Music
GNVQ	GCSE Music + 3 others
GSVQ	Standard Grade Music + 3 others
NVQ	Work related experience
SVQ	Work related experience
HNC	2 GCSEs/Standard Grades or work related experience
HND	4 GCSEs/Standard Grades or work related experience
Diploma	Grade VIII practical or equivalent
Licentiate	Grade VIII/Advanced diploma practical or equivalent
BA/BMus	2/3 A Levels or 5 Highers or Advanced GNVQ or National Diploma or mixture of all
MA/MMus	BA or BMus at honours level
PhD/DMus	MA or MMus

chapter 10
ESSENTIAL GUIDE TO NOTATION AND COMPOSITION

Whether you are a performer or composer, understanding the essential language of music empowers you with more confidence, ideas and awareness. This is true for both classical and popular genres.

Notation seems mysterious when viewed initially, but in reality the signs and symbols are clear, simple and unchanging. So let's have a go at deciphering this exciting language.

Firstly musical notes appear on a **stave** (or **staff**) comprising five lines. Staves always have a **clef** at the far left hand side, which tells you how high or how low the notes are to be played.

A stave with a **treble clef**, used for high notes, looks like this:

A stave with a **bass clef**, used for low notes, looks like this:

The treble clef is used for instruments like the flute, oboe or violin. The bass clef is used for instruments such as the bass guitar, double bass and cello. Other clefs appear for different instruments, for example the viola, but we will concentrate on the treble and bass clefs as they are by far the most common. The piano uses both.

The notes on the treble clef are:

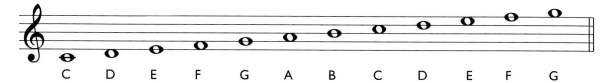

These may be remembered by dividing the notes into **lines** and **spaces**, for example:

lines

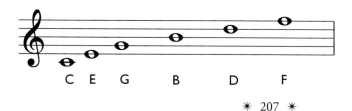

spaces

Notes such as Middle C, which appear above or below, the stave, are written on leger lines, for example:

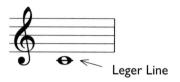

The notes on the bass clef are:

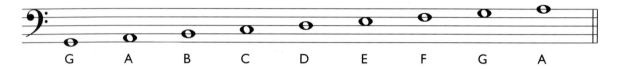

Time

The musical notes and staves are divided into units of time, called **bars**. These bars are indicated and separated by **barlines**. Here is an example of a plain treble clef stave, divided up into bars:

At the beginning of this example there are two numbers. The top one is the most important as this tells you how many beats each bar is worth, in this case 4. Therefore, for each new bar you count 1, 2, 3, 4.

The bottom note tells you the type of beat, but this is not essential to know about at this stage.

Most pop music has four beats to the bar. Waltz time, which has three beats to the bar, and two-beat music are also common.

TIME VALUES

All the notes on the staves you have viewed so far are **semibreves**. These are long notes which last four beats each. You play one note, and hold on for four. This is the longest note you are likely to see initially in any music, so we will start with the semibreve. Learn this simple table thoroughly:

Number of beats	Musical symbol	UK name	USA name
4	𝅝	semibreve	whole-note
3	𝅗𝅥.	dotted minim	dotted half-note
2	𝅗𝅥	minim	half-note
I	𝅘𝅥	crotchet	quarter-note
I/2	𝅘𝅥𝅮	quaver	eighth-note
I/4	𝅘𝅥𝅯	semiquaver	sixteenth note

A dot, written close to the right of a note, increases the time value by half again, for example a minim with a dot beside it lasts three beats as 2 + 1 = 3.

This note, played once, lasts eight beats.

Sometimes it is easier to see the symbols illustrated in a hierarchy of time value (excluding the dotted minim). The top note is the longest, and each individual line below, adds up to make a semibreve.

Notes can also be 'tied' across barlines, to create even longer values. Tied notes look like this:

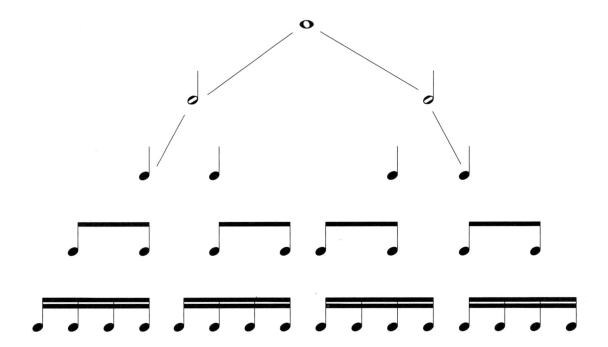

Scales and keys

An understanding of keys and scales increases musical language for both performers and composers. A scale is a series of eight notes, which rises or falls. The scale of C, for example, can be played on the white notes of a piano or keyboard, by starting on the note C and ascending.

The notes you play – C D E F G A B C – are all adjacent. Play them over and over so that you hear the sound of what we call a **major scale**. The music sounds bright and cheerful.

Now play the first five notes of a scale on the white notes of a keyboard, starting on A. These notes sound sadder. This is the sound of the **minor scale** for the first five notes. Thereafter the scale will continue as a melodic or harmonic minor scale.

These eight-note scales make up the key system. In music we describe a piece of music containing mostly notes of the C major scale, as 'in the key of C.'

The simplest keys in music are C, F and G as they contain few **accidentals**. An accidental is an extra note added to a scale to make up the normal major or minor sound. Accidental notes are called either sharps or flats, with symbols ♯ sharp, and ♭ flat. They appear as black notes on the piano or keyboard.

The key is indicated immediately after the clef on a stave, by the key signature. C major does not contain any flats or sharps, so there is no key signature, but the most common ones are:

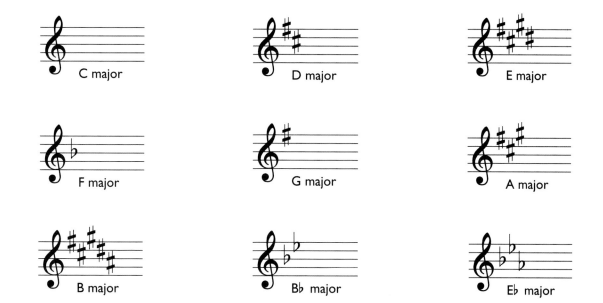

Chords

If two or more notes are sounded together, they form a chord.

Chords are essential tools for composition, accompanying and understanding harmony. A chord can be built from any note of the scale, but the most common in any type of music are chords I, IV, V and VI. The numbers derive from the position on the scale, for example in C major:

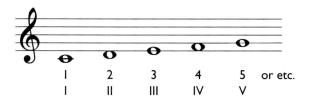

- Chord I, in the key of C is made up of C, E and G.
- Chord IV is made up of F, A and C.
- Chord V is made up of G, B and D.

Every chord is built up of intervals of a third, but the notes themselves can be played in any position.

A typical 12-bar blues format, which is also a standard pop song structure, can be played using the chords above. Counting four beats to the bar play:

```
C – – – / C – – – / C – – – /C – – –
F – – – / F – – – / C – – – / C – – –
G – – – / F – – – / C – – – / C or G7 – – –
```

Use G7 if you intend to repeat the music.

In all types of music, other notes can be added to the chords. G7 means that you play the ordinary notes of G major and add the flattened seventh, in this case F.

GROOVY CHORDS

By adding extra intervals to your chords you can colour the music significantly. At the moment keep in the key of C, and experiment. Consider the root (or name) of the chord as note number 1 of its own scale.

Sometimes it is easier to write the notes out with numbers and letters, for example:

Chord C

1 2 3 4 5 6 7 8

C D E F G A B C

Chord F

1 2 3 4 5 6 7 8

F G A B C D E F

Chord G

1 2 3 4 5 6 7 8

G A B C D E F G

Then write down the chord notes. The ones in bold being the most common.

C = C,E,G
Dm = D,F A
Em = E,G, B
F = F, A, C
G = G, B, D
Am = A, C, E
B = B, D, F

Then add new intervals. For example, chords C or F, with added note 7, create soul sounds. Spend some serious time on chords. Create chord patterns. Try adding note 6 or note 2 to chords for a jazz feel. Experiment next with rhythms to create grooves.

Essential guide to score directions

A tempo   in time

Accelerando   get gradually faster

Adagio   slowly

Allegro   lively, quite fast

Andante   at a moderate pace

Cantabile   in a singing style

Con   with

Crescendo   get louder gradually

Da Capo   from the top, start

Dal Segno   from the sign

Decrescendo   get softer gradually

Diminuendo   get softer gradually

Dolce   sweetly

Espressivo   with expression

Fine   the end

Forte or f loud

Fortissimo or $f\!f$ very loud

Grave   very slow

Largo   slow and stately, broadly

Legato smoothly

Leggiero   lightly

Lento   slowly

Maestoso   majestically

Marcato   accented, marked

Meno less

Meno mosso   less movement

Mezzo forte or *mf* moderately loud

Mezzo piano or *mf* moderately soft

Molto   much

Ped   pedal

Perdendosi   dying away

pesante   heavily

Pianissimo or *pp* very soft

Piano or *p* softly

Pizzicato or PIZZ   plucked

Piu   more

Poco   a little

Poco a poco   little by little, gradually

Presto   very quick

Rallentando or Ral   get gradually slower

Risoluto   boldly

Ritardando or ritard   get gradually slower

Ritenuto or Rit   hold back

Rubato   literally robbed time, music which quickens must then slow up, and vice versa

Scherzo   a joke

Scherzando   playfully

Segno   sign

Sempre   always

Senza   without

Sforzando or *sf*, *sfz* with a sudden accent

Simile   in a similar manner

Sordini   mutes

Staccato   short, detached

Stringendo   get gradually faster

Subito   suddenly

Tempo   the speed of the music

Tempo primo   resume the original tempo

Tenuto   held

Troppo   too much

Vivace   lively and quickly

MUSICAL SIGNS

get louder

get softer

pause

double bar (this passage should be repeated)

Other useful words

Atonal   music with no key

Chromatic   music including 'accidental' notes not normally associated with the key

Discord   notes which would not normally be sounded together in traditional harmony

Dynamics   signs and symbols which indicate how music is to be played, eg softly

Diatonic   tonal music, the established western key system

Instrumentation   instruments present in the music

Modulation   moving from one key to another

Timbre   quality of tone

INDEX

-7. JUL 1999 25170/4